THE PROTEST MAKERS

The British Nuclear Disarmament
Movement of 1958-1965, Twenty Years On

Other Titles of Interest

BOTKIN, J. *et al.*
No Limits to Learning: Bridging the Human Gap

DAMMANN, E.
The Future in Our Hands

FELD, B.
A Voice Crying in the Wilderness

FITZGERALD, R.
Human Needs and Politics

FITZGERALD, R.
The Sources of Hope

JOLLY, R.
Disarmament and World Development

KING, A.
The State of the Planet

NOEL-BAKER, P.
The First World Disarmament Conference 1932-33

PECCEI, A.
The Human Quality

A Pergamon Journal of Related Interest

TECHNOLOGY IN SOCIETY

An International Journal

Editors: DR. GEORGE BUGLIARELLO and DR. A. GEORGE SCHILLINGER,
Polytechnic Institute of New York, USA

This interdisciplinary journal creates a single forum for the discussion of the political, economic, and cultural roles of technology in society, social forces that shape technological decisions, and choices open to society in the use of technology. Subjects include, among others: technology assessment; science, technology, and society; management of technology; technology transfer; appropriate technology and economic development; ethical and value implications of science and technology; science and public policy; and technology forecasting.

THE PROTEST MAKERS

The British Nuclear Disarmament Movement of 1958-1965, Twenty Years On

BY

Richard Taylor and Colin Pritchard

PERGAMON PRESS
OXFORD · NEW YORK · TORONTO · SYDNEY · PARIS · FRANKFURT

U.K.	Pergamon Press Ltd., Headington Hill Hall, Oxford OX3 0BW, England
U.S.A.	Pergamon Press Inc., Maxwell House, Fairview Park, Elmsford, New York 10523, U.S.A.
CANADA	Pergamon of Canada, Suite 104, 150 Consumers Road, Willowdale, Ontario M2J 1P9, Canada
AUSTRALIA	Pergamon Press (Aust.) Pty. Ltd., P.O. Box 544, Potts Point, N.S.W. 2011, Australia
FRANCE	Pergamon Press SARL, 24 rue des Ecoles, 75240 Paris, Cedex 05, France
FEDERAL REPUBLIC OF GERMANY	Pergamon Press GmbH, 6242 Kronberg-Taunus, Hammerweg 6, Federal Republic of Germany

First edition 1980

British Library Cataloguing in Publication Data
Taylor, Richard, *b. 1945*
The protest makers
1. Great Britain - Politics and government - 1945 - 1964
2. Great Britain - Military policy
3. Atomic weapons and disarmament
I. Title II. Pritchard, Colin
327'.174'0941   DA592   80-40269

ISBN 0-08-025211-7

Printed and bound in Great Britain by
William Clowes (Beccles) Limited, Beccles and London

For
Jenny and Beryl

Preface

It should be clearly stated at the outset that this study is not intended as a *history* of the British nuclear disarmament movement. Our aim is two-fold: to explore the political and ideological dimensions of the Movement and the problems which its experience has posed for achieving radical change in modern Britain, and to analyse the current attitudes and activities of Movement supporters some 20 years later. On the basis of a questionnaire completed by over 400 'core activists', and in-depth interviews with leading figures in the Movement, we try to analyse and discuss these themes and draw some conclusions about the nature, purpose and significance of the Movement. The focus is thus political and sociological rather than historical. Despite Christopher Driver's valuable book *The Disarmers* the Movement still awaits its historian and it is to be hoped that this important task will be undertaken in the near future.

This book could not have been written without the considerable help of a large number of people. We would like to express our sincere thanks to all those who completed the lengthy and complicated questionnaire on which a large part of this study is based. Not only did we receive full, detailed, and thoughtful responses to the questions, we were also sent a large amount of useful and interesting material giving information about local, and individual, involvement in the Movement. Moreover, we received a number of critical but constructive suggestions about the questionnaire — and about the study in general. For all these — too numerous to cite individually here — many thanks.

An equal debt of gratitude is owing to all those very busy and eminent people who agreed to be interviewed: Frank Allaun, MP, Pat Arrowsmith, Hugh Brock, April Carter, George Clark, Canon L. John Collins, Diana Collins, Peggy Duff, Michael Foot, MP, Olive Gibbs, Arthur Goss, Stuart Hall, Jacquetta Hawkes, Lord Home (formerly Sir Alec Douglas-Home), Msgr. Bruce Kent, Alan Lovell, George Matthews, Ian Mikardo, MP, Dick Nettleton, J. B. Priestley, Michael Randle, Duncan Rees, Professor J. Rotblat, Lord Soper (formerly the Rev Dr Donald Soper), A. J. P. Taylor, Arnold Wesker, and Sir Harold Wilson. In every case we were given the utmost cooperation and helpful assistance. The degree of interest, and the willingness to discuss the issues at length, testified not only to the lasting impact of the Movement upon all these leading figures, but also to their (various) commitments and integrity.

We were also very fortunate in having the help and advice of a number of friends and colleagues. In particular, we are very grateful to Andrew Duff without whose assistance the statistical information, which forms the basis of Part II, could not have been brought together and analysed, and to Alan Lewis who gave patient consideration to all our statistical queries.

Hugh Brock, April Carter and Arthur Goss were kind enough to let us have access to the papers of the Direct Action Committee and the National Council against Nuclear Weapons Tests.

Leeds University granted a year's study leave to Richard Taylor in 1977/8 during which time the bulk of the research for the book was undertaken, and thanks are due both to the University and to Professor Norman Jepson for making this possible.

We would also like to thank those who struggled, successfully, with the typing and checking of the drafts of this study at various stages: Margaret Aykroyd, Janet Day, Gill Fieldhouse, and especially Carol Jones who bore the brunt of our deadlines.

The photographs are reproduced by courtesy of Roger Mayne of Lyme Regis, Dorset.

We must also make it clear that although a large part of this study is based upon the *post facto* analysis and sentiments of both 'leaders' and 'rank and file' in the Movement, we alone are responsible for the interpretations made, and for the conclusions drawn.

Finally, we would like to thank our families for their forbearance in living with this project for the past two and a half years. We hope that the outcome will make some small contribution to the creation of a society in which they can develop free from the fear of nuclear destruction.

July 1979   RICHARD TAYLOR
                                                         COLIN PRITCHARD

Contents

"Something Ought to be Done": the Rise and Decline of the Nuclear Disarmament Movement

Britain in the 1950s

The 1950s is too recent a decade for a comprehensive and authoritative 'history' to have yet been written. However, despite its nearness in time, the pace of change in modern society — at all levels — is such that it is very difficult to recapture and evoke the ethos of the period. In social, political, economic, and cultural terms the society of the 1950s belongs to a different age from our own. At the most obvious and superficial level, the only head of state of a major nation spanning the decade is Queen Elizabeth II!

At the outset of the decade Britain was only just beginning to emerge from the period of austerity and post-war reconstruction, and the war leader, Sir Winston Churchill, headed the new Conservative administration.[1] Perhaps most significant of all, in terms of mass political psychology, Britain still retained an extensive Empire: only India, of the Third World countries, had attained full independence[2] — and no sovereign black African state yet existed.[3]

On the international scene the frenetic wheeling and dealing between the two 'Super Powers' — and the other nations involved in the war — had been concluded and the world divided into Eastern and Western 'spheres of influence'. The Cold War stalemate between East and West was becoming an accepted and permanent feature of the international scene, embodied in the West by the formation of NATO and in the East by the Warsaw Pact. The Korean War marked the first full-blooded test of ideological and economic will between the two 'Super Powers' and was a grim portent of the pattern of international conflict which was to ensue in the coming decades.[4]

Britain, although fast fading as a major world power, kept in touch with the two 'Super Powers' by virtue of her central role in the War and hence the post-war settlements. An indication of Britain's self-image and of her determination to keep in the 'top league' was her development of nuclear weapons. For the political leaders of the UK — Labour as well as Conservative — the Bomb was demonstrable proof of her status as a world power and guaranteed her a 'seat at the top table'. In both political and psychological terms the British Independent Nuclear Deterrent was always more important as a virility symbol than as a serious strategic arm of the West's 'defensive system'.[5]

Socially, the 1950s was a watershed in a number of ways. The prolonged economic growth, which characterised all the industrialised economies of the capitalist world from 1945 to the early 1970s, was less marked in Britain than elsewhere[6] but was nevertheless the major underlying determinant of social change. A new, ordered and systematic economic system appeared to have replaced the chaotic and harsh 'bad old days' of 1920s and 1930s capitalism where everything had seemed subject to the vagaries of 'boom and slump'.[7] Keynesian techniques of economic management appeared to have secured permanent full employment, economic growth and slow but sure expansion through a centrally managed economy.[8] The material affluence which resulted from this economic success had profound consequences for the social and political structure, and the attitudes, of all classes in all Western societies.[9] Not least amongst these consequences, and particularly important in our context, was the growth of a new and unique youth culture: for the first time in industrial society the young wage-earners had the economic basis for independence which enabled them to reach out and build their own cultural autonomy. Coupled with the rapid technological development of the media[10] this produced, from the mid-1950s onwards, the now familiar institutions of pop culture — pop music, teenage fashion, and a general move towards debunking 'high culture'.[11]

Politically, the early 1950s was a period of confusion, retrenchment and disillusion on the Left, and of quiet but fundamental adjustment on the Right.[12] The 1945-51 Labour governments, arguably the greatest reforming administrations in twentieth-century Britain, had seemingly ushered in a new 'mixed economy' structure in which the State, acting, it was argued, on behalf of the people, was to take a far greater role in the rational planning and control of the economy. Of equal if not of more importance, the foundations of the 'Welfare State' were laid and there was, in the late 1940s, the feeling in the Labour Movement that a new, socialist system based on different structures and different ideological criteria to the old capitalist society, was in the process of construction.[13] The lack of advance through 1948 to 1951 and the subsequent electoral defeat was a rude shock to Labour activists,[14] and paved the way for years of internal division in the Party and the Movement between the 'Bevanite' Left and the 'Gaitskellite' Right.[15] By the mid-1950s the heady optimism of the late 1940s amongst socialist activists within the Labour Movement had evaporated: there was a realisation that the undoubtedly great achievements of the Labour government had *not* brought about a socialist society, that the new mixed economy was *not* the first stage on the road to a socialist transformation, and, perhaps most important of all in our context, the new material affluence and economic security had *not* induced an ideological commitment to socialist principles amongst the mass of the people.[16] By 1956 the time was indeed ripe for 'a new kind of politics' to rekindle the idealism and commitment of the radical strata in British society.

On the Right, on the other hand, the 1950s was a time of both acclimatisation and consolidation. The Conservative Party had to come to terms with a changed domestic structure — principally the mixed economy and the Welfare State,[17] and, internationally, with the even more fundamental process of rapidly dismantling the British Empire in Africa and Asia. With an ease and expertise acquired through numerous *volte faces* over the centuries, the Conservative Party achieved this remarkable ideological (and psychological) adjustment with relatively little effective dissension.[18] The Right also consolidated its ideological hold through the period of economic growth and affluence — and of course maintained its directly political hold through three successive General Election victories (in 1951, 1955, and 1959).

The placid progress of Conservative rule was, however, rudely interrupted by two events of major importance in 1956: the Suez invasion and the suppression of the Hungarian uprising.[19] Both, in their very different ways, were key events in the process leading to the formation of the Nuclear Disarmament Movement. Suez was the last convulsive fling of the old imperial 'gunboat' style of diplomacy — and the degrading failure of the whole preposterous episode demonstrated once and for all that Britain could no longer act alone as a world power. Psychologically, this was a devastating message for a population nurtured on the imperialist propaganda of a predominantly jingoistic press and still resting on the assumption that Britain, as the victor of World War II, was a 'Super Power'. Equally important, the reaction against the Suez invasion not only united the Labour Movement but created a new mood of idealistic purpose on the Left. A crusading spirit was born, and this commitment — more moral in inspiration than political — carried over into the Nuclear Disarmament Movement. The impact of the brutal Russian repression of the Hungarian uprising had no less profound an effect. Most immediately, of course, it brought home to everyone in the starkest possible way the new realities of the 'Super Power' stalemate: as the West stood helplessly by whilst the Russians imposed their rule by undisguised military force, it became apparent that within the implicitly understood respective 'spheres of influence' the 'Super Powers' could operate as they wished. The only effective form of Western intervention — certainly in the European context — would rapidly have escalated to nuclear war. The effect on those who had supported, or had at least had sympathy for, the USSR as a genuinely Communist society was dramatic. There was, at that time, little firm and detailed information about the Stalinist repression of the 1930s and 1940s, but Hungary provided irrefutable evidence of the totalitarian, authoritarian, and brutally repressive nature of the Russian régime.[20] The result was a mass exodus from the Communist Party (in Britain as elsewhere in the West) of intellectuals and workers who were committed to humanistic socialism,[21] and thus an upsurge of discussion and activity on the Left.

The combined result of these two crises was to produce a heightened political atmosphere but, simultaneously, an increased scepticism and mistrust of the old ideologies and the old institutions. After 1956 a new idealism was in the air but, as with Osborne's 'Jimmy Porter', it seemed that there were 'no good, brave causes left':[22] there was political interest, political will and political and moral commitment, but no political issue (and certainly no political party or movement) around which this newly created political mood could crystallize. The new drama of the mid-1950s expressed this mood succinctly: passionate but cynical, idealistic but negative, it gave vent to the feelings and frustrations of a generation which realised that the old ways were false and/or inadequate, but was not yet positively committed to any alternative. It was into this vacuum that the Nuclear Disarmament Movement erupted: what better symbol of the insane, corrupt, crassly materialistic yet technologically sophisticated, society could there be than the H-bomb? Here was a cause indeed, and the new generation — or a substantial proportion of it — flocked to its banners.

Before we begin our detailed analysis of this Movement, its supporters and their political and social attitudes and development, a brief account must be given of the origins and development of the CND, the DAC and the Committee of 100.

The Mass Movement in Britain for Nuclear Disarmament 1958 to 1965
Without an appreciation of the complex cross currents it is impossible to evaluate

the orientations of the core activists and the leadership which forms the major part of our study in Parts II and III. What follows here, then, is not intended as an exhaustive historical analysis of the Movement's growth but a brief account of some of the major component organisations and the more important events in the Movement between 1958 and 1965.[23]

The atomic bomb was exploded by the USA over Hiroshima on the morning of 8 August 1945. But, as Christopher Driver has noted, the first public protest in Britain against the manufacture and use of nuclear weapons took place more than 2 years earlier when Bob Edwards drew attention to the dangers of nuclear weapons at an ILP meeting in January 1943 in St. Helens.[24] This, however, was an isolated incident and little attention was paid to the 'nuclear issue' until considerably later: indeed, the British decision to make the A-bomb was taken with virtually no discussion, let alone protest, by Attlee's government in 1948. Virtually the only warnings of nuclear dangers came in fact from ecclesiastical and scientific circles.[25] The first signs of public anxiety were seen in the establishment by the Peace Pledge Union[26] of a non-violence commission "to study and discuss the possibility of direct action to seek withdrawal of American forces, stoppage of the manufacture of atomic weapons in Britain, withdrawal of Britain from NATO, and disbandment of the British Armed Forces".[27] With the American decision, in 1950, to develop the H-bomb, protests began to mount, and, in 1951, the non-violence commission founded 'Operation Gandhi', a programme for direct action to put the objectives into practice.

A small sit-down demonstration took place outside the War Office on 11 January 1952: it was as a result of this that Michael Randle, subsequently Chairman of the Emergency Committee for Direct Action Against Nuclear War (DAC) and secretary of the Committee of 100, became involved in the Movement.[28] Following the announcement that Britain was to test her own A-bomb, Hugh Brock organised a small demonstration at an Atomic Weapons Research Establishment which he had discovered at the small Berkshire village of Aldermaston. These demonstrations, however, were very small scale and drew little public attention: consequently none of the activists of 'Operation Gandhi' could have had any idea of the huge movement they were about to spawn.

On the Parliamentary front too moves were afoot in the early 1950s to mount an anti-nuclear campaign. Following a debate in the House of Commons on 5 April 1954, the Hydrogen Bomb National Campaign was founded, with the Rev. Dr. Donald Soper as Chairman and Canon L. John Collins amongst the prominent members. The Campaign — composed of Church, peace and labour organisations — was not, however, a success: it lacked a clear, unifying policy demand and could only agree on a lowest common denominator support for Mr. Attlee's Parliamentary motion which asked for a disarmament conference to be convened and for the UN to be strengthened. Although the campaign never got off the ground the debate in the Labour Party over nuclear weapons began to gain momentum after the announcement, in the 1955 Defence White Paper, that Britain intended to manufacture her own H-Bomb. Aneurin Bevan took a firm stand against his own Party leadership on the issue of whether Britain should ever use the H-bomb first and was threatened with expulsion from the PLP, and Sir Richard Acland resigned his seat in order to fight a by-election on the unilateralist platform (the declaration of the General Election deprived him of this opportunity, however, and he was defeated by the Conservative candidate, Peter Kirk).

Bertrand Russell secured the support of an international group of scientists for the formation of an investigative pressure group of scientific experts to work for nuclear disarmament. Thus began the long-standing work of the Pugwash Conferences[29] and the involvement of many scientists in the international movement for nuclear peace.

These then were the first signs of the growing groundswell of public concern in Britain over nuclear weapons. 'Operation Gandhi' led directly to the formation of the DAC, but how, organisationally, did CND come into being? The immediate precursor of CND was the National Council for the Abolition of Nuclear Weapons Tests (NCANWT) which in turn arose from a number of local initiatives of protest against nuclear weapons testing. The formative influence for this whole movement lay with the Golders Green Committee for the Abolition of Nuclear Weapons whose moving spirit, Miss Gertrude Fishwick, should, in Driver's view, be credited with triggering off "the chain reaction which ended in CND".[30] Similar groups grew up spontaneously in other areas of the country—in itself typical of the 'unofficial' nature of the whole Movement, as Peggy Duff has observed.[31] Arthur Goss[32] became chairman of the Hampstead Committee Against Nuclear Weapons Tests and, later, of the NCANWT which was formed in February 1957 (with Dr. Sheila Jones and Mrs. Ianthe Carswell as joint secretaries).

As we have argued above, the key catalysts for changing these isolated, sporadic and minority protests into a mass movement were the momentous political upheavals of the Suez invasion and the Hungarian uprising in 1956. There were, however, additional and specific events which provided the immediate reasons for the eruption of the mass movement—encompassing the DAC as well as CND. In April 1957 the annual Defence White Paper was published by Duncan Sandys, the Minister of Defence in the Conservative government. This marked a radical change in defence policy, promising an end to National Service and reducing Defence estimates from £1600 million for 1956/7 to £1483 million for 1957/8, and stating clearly that Britain would in future rely heavily on nuclear weapons for defence. Moreover, the Sandys White Paper affirmed vigorously the need for an *independent* British nuclear deterrent, and acknowledged "that there is at present no means of providing adequate protection for the people of this country against the consequences of an attack with nuclear weapons".[33] Such a clear and obviously hazardous commitment to nuclear policies raised public awareness of the very real dangers and, as neither the Labour Party nor the Pacifist organisations were prepared to mount a full-scale attack on the new Sandys doctrine, a political vacuum was created: a vacuum which CND was shortly to fill. Also in April 1957 the Emergency Committee for Direct Action Against Nuclear War (DAC)[34] was set up, in the immediate context to raise funds for Harold and Sheila Steele to travel to the Pacific to protest against the British nuclear test at Christmas Island.[35] Its sponsors included several Quakers and a number of prominent public figures.[36] The DAC was very much under the sway of Hugh Brock and it was Brock who, taking up a suggestion made to him earlier by Laurence Brown, suggested that the DAC should organise a March to Aldermaston. The DAC subsequently established a small sub-committee to organise the first March and Pat Arrowsmith, as organising secretary of DAC, was largely responsible for its success.[37] Just before this first March took place, Sir Stephen King-Hall published an influential and widely discussed book on the theme of unarmed resistance as the only feasible policy in the nuclear age.[38]

This is to anticipate somewhat, however. There were four specific events in the autumn of 1957 which acted as the final precipitants of CND. On the international scene, October saw the launching of the Russian sputnik, an undeniable challenge to American missile supremacy and a further tightening of the screw in the nuclear arms race. In November, Professor George F. Kennan, the former US Ambassador in Moscow, delivered the Reith Lectures on the theme of 'Russia, the Atom and the West'[39] in which he argued forcefully against the hard-line Cold War orientation of Dulles' American foreign policy, and outlined the real dangers of nuclear confrontation between East and West. Meanwhile, in the world of Labour politics, Aneurin Bevan had profoundly shocked the Left of the Party by his powerful and unequivocal denunciation of the unilateralist position at the Party's annual Conference in 1957. This was of immense importance, in a number of ways, for the future of the Movement — as we argue at length later.[40] All that we need to record here, however, is the fact that this apparent desertion by Bevan shocked many unilateralists inside and outside the Labour Party into action. One immediate and highly significant result was J. B. Priestley's seminal *New Statesman* article in November 1957 which marked, in effect, the beginning of CND.[41]

The massive response to Priestley's article prompted Kingsley Martin, the editor of the *New Statesman,* to call together at an informal gathering a number of prominent people interested in nuclear disarmament. Among those attending were Bertrand Russell, J. B. Priestley, Jacquetta Hawkes (Mrs. Priestley), George Kennan, Professor P. M. S. Blackett, and, somewhat incongruously, Denis Healey. From this there developed close contact with the NCANWT and, as a result, Peggy Duff and Canon Collins (and his wife, Diana) also became involved. The Executive Committee of CND was elected at a meeting, held in Canon Collins' home at Amen Court (St. Paul's Cathedral) on 16 January 1958. In Driver's view there was "little doubt that the composition of the new Executive had been effectively decided beforehand among the Martin/Priestley group".[42] Be this as it may the officers elected at this meeting — Canon Collins as Chairman,* Bertrand Russell as President and Peggy Duff as organising secretary — dominated the Movement in their different ways through the early years. There is no doubt that the CND leadership constituted a glittering array of the nation's progressive intelligentsia. Elitist and unrepresentative of the Movement's rank and file it may have been, but nobody could deny its immense and charismatic impact.[43]

The NCANWT merged itself, and its finances, into the new organisation, although only two of its representatives were included on the CND Executive (Arthur Goss and Dr. Sheila Jones). The initial policy statement of the new campaign was, as Peggy Duff has noted, "ambiguous. It was not entirely unilateralist."[44] However, the inaugural meeting of CND held at the Central Hall on 17 February 1958 (a booking the CND took over from the NCANWT) was such a massive success — several overflow halls were filled — that all caution and inhibitions were thrown to the winds and the following day the Executive, under some pressure, decided upon a much tougher policy statement: in part it stated that

*According to Peggy Duff, the NCANWT representatives were not altogether happy with Canon Collins as Chairman and would have preferred Ritchie Calder. However, as Ritchie Calder was unwilling, Collins' appointment was confirmed at the second meeting of the CND Executive Committee on 28 January (Source: Peggy Duff, *Left, Left, Left,* p. 122.)

The purpose of the Campaign is to press for a British initiative to reduce the nuclear peril and to stop the armaments race. We shall seek to persuade the British people that Britain must:

(a) renounce unconditionally the use or production of nuclear weapons and refuse to allow their use by others in her defence;

(b) use her utmost endeavour to bring about negotiations at all levels for agreement to end the armaments race and to lead to a general disarmament convention;

(c) invite the cooperation of other nations, particularly non-nuclear powers, in her renunciation of nuclear weapons.[45]

The euphoria following the inaugural meeting—at which Russell, Foot, A. J. P. Taylor, Collins and Priestley, amongst others, spoke—was somewhat marred by the sit-down demonstration and subsequent arrests which took place at Downing Street immediately following the meeting. This was a portent of the divisions that were to plague the mass Movement throughout its turbulent life. Indeed, the problem was of immediate relevance to the new organisation: at its meeting on 28 January the Executive had had to decide its attitude to the DAC organised Aldermaston March due to take place in a few weeks' time over Easter. The Executive's statement that CND should "give its blessing to the Emergency Committee's plans and should publicise them, but should make it clear that at this stage of the Campaign they could not be very closely involved"[46] testified not only to the fact that the Aldermaston March was, initially, very much a DAC demonstration, but also to the reluctance of the CND Executive to become involved in 'street politics'. There is no doubt that the Executive would have preferred a more conventional, elite pressure group approach to the campaign. This most decidedly differentiated them from the young, militant, Gandhian-oriented activists of the DAC.[47] Far less prestigious, in fact comparatively obscure, the DAC nevertheless had an enthusiasm, conviction and dynamism which rendered it a cohesive and powerful group.

Following the huge and unexpected success of the first Aldermaston March (significantly *from* London *to* Aldermaston in accord with DAC's populist 'take the message to the people' orientation), the Movement entered into its 'mass movement' phase.[48] The March, which on its final day had between 5000 and 10,000 taking part, received wide press coverage and the Movement from then on became a nationally recognised (and much discussed) part of the political scene. The Ban-the-Bomb marcher entered into British folklore: the stereotype of the bearded, cranky intellectual pacifist, probably vegetarian and certainly amoral, may have been wildly inaccurate, but it stuck. The CND symbol, designed by Gerald Holtom, became internationally known and continues to symbolise protests against a whole range of iniquities.

The year 1958 marked the successful start of the Movement. The years 1959, 1960 and 1961 saw it reach its peak—but it also brought to the fore those inherent conflicts and divisions which were to be an important factor in the Movement's decline in the subsequent years. By the beginning of 1959 CND had a national network of branches, tens of thousands of active supporters[49] and an impressive array of public figures supporting its campaign. The 1960 Aldermaston March—organised since 1959 under the auspices of the CND Executive *from* Aldermaston *to* London—was a massive demonstration of support for the Movement's policies: estimates of the final day's crowd in Trafalgar Square varied between 30,000 and 100,000, an increase on the already large 1959 demonstration. The Movement was also gaining support in the Labour Movement: through 1959 and 1960 the TUs, under the powerful and determined lead of Frank Cousins and the TGWU, came more and more to support unilateralism. At the TUC Conference in 1959 the TGWU unilateralist resolution, although defeated, attracted 2,755,000 votes (whilst a motion protesting against the installation of missile bases was narrowly carried). After Labour's third successive General Election defeat in 1959 the division within the Labour Movement grew, and the issue of unilateralism became not only a matter of substantive difference on defence policy, but became also inextricably involved with the division between Left and Right in the Party and thus with the battle over the Party leadership. The Government's cancellation of the Blue Streak missile project effectively destroyed any realistic policy of *independent* nuclear deterrence, at least for the time being. This undermined the Party leadership's stance and this, coupled with more wholehearted support from the Communist Party for unilateralist policies, ensured that a number of key Labour Movement organisations gave backing to the unilateralist policy.[50]

The nuclear situation had now become more complex. The initial, simple, moral case of CND was no longer applicable. To all intents and purposes the British independent nuclear deterrent—always a somewhat tenuous and intangible concept—had ceased to exist. The Labour Party leadership amended its policy and adopted a stance which, whilst recognising that the BIND was no longer practicable, advocated a British defence policy based upon a full commitment to a nuclear NATO. Gaitskell, for principled as well as tactical reasons,[51] made British adherence to NATO the cornerstone of his strategy. (To this extent he shared the assumptions of other socialists—both Labour Left and New Left[52]—in the Movement that NATO and the future foreign policy of the UK was the central issue in the long term.) The moral imperative of unilateralism continued to dominate CND (and DAC and, later, the Committee of 100) but the more politically sophisticated agreed with A. J. R. Groom's verdict: "The protesters never fully grasped that the real unilateral act was to leave the alliance system and that this had nothing to do with giving up nuclear weapons, which was only a strategic disposition."[53]

Be this as it may, there is no doubt that the unilateralists scored a major and somewhat unexpected victory at the Labour Party Conference in Scarborough in 1960.[54] Both the TGWU and AEU resolutions were passed, largely because of mandated bloc votes from the major TUs, and the Party was, many thought, committed to a unilateralist policy.[55] Gaitskell's closing speech in which he promised to "fight and fight and fight again to save the Party we love" by reversing the decision, made it clear that this was by no means the end of the matter. After the Conference the leadership reasserted its position and counter-attacked through a new, revisionist organisation, the Campaign for Democratic Socialism.[56] The Parliamentary Labour Party supported the leadership's policy and rejected both the unilateralist programme and the attempt to defeat Mr. Gaitskell as leader.[57]

This was one of the central crises for CND activists. Could they, as those on the various socialist wings of the Movement urged them, unite and fight the battle in the Labour Party? They could not: the majority of CND supporters was simply not interested in the political struggle and regarded the Movement more as a moral crusade. It is unlikely that CND could have successfully resisted Gaitskell's offensive whatever policy it had adopted.[58] In the event, however, the response was disjointed, tentative and ineffective. The Labour Left too was divided over whether to hold out for Cousins' unilateralist position or opt for the so-called Crossman-Padley compromise.[59] By the summer of 1961 the rejection of the unilateralist position was assured and most of the big TUs had committed themselves to the leadership and its defence policy.[60] At the 1961 Labour Conference the TGWU resolution was defeated by 2,418,000 votes and, although the constituency delegates' opinions had in fact hardened by about 10% since 1960 against the leadership's policies, the battle for unilateralism within the Labour Party was, to all intents and purposes, over.[61]

The more politically aware sections of the CND leadership had been pursuing the Labour Party tactic actively from the inception of the Movement, and we analyse this perspective at length below.[62] The Direct Action wing of the Movement had, however, been pursuing their own, very different, campaign. In 1959 the DAC's 'Voters' Veto' got under way with the campaign against the anti-unilateralist Labour candidate for the S.W. Norfolk by-election. Such initiatives worried the Labour Left supporters in CND and, as with the later Independent Nuclear Disarmament Election Committee,[63] widened the already significant split between those who saw the way forward as exclusively through the Labour Party and those who saw the Movement as primarily extra-Parliamentary. The DAC, always critical and suspicious of both the motivations and the strategy of the CND leadership, nevertheless saw its relationship with CND as viable and, if not exactly harmonious, not mutually destructive. To a large extent the DAC's activities did not impinge upon CND; and Direct Action campaigns undertaken at North Pickenham, Harrington, Polebrook, etc., and the remarkable, consistent and courageous activism amongst industrial workers carried out by Pat Arrowsmith, were different in kind from those of CND and were small-scale and predominantly outside the large urban centres. The CND leadership was, of course, troubled by the confusion in the public mind between 'legal' and 'illegal' action, and Canon Collins in particular was constantly at pains to differentiate CND from the DAC and thus ensure a more respectable and acceptable image for 'his' organisation. There did exist, however, a *modus vivendi*.

The same could not be said once the Committee of 100 arrived upon the scene. From the time of the 1960 Aldermaston March onwards it became clear that the CND leadership had lost control of the Movement (or a substantial part of it) and that a new mood, more militant, more aggressive, and more concerned with 'Movement power' than with Parliamentary politics, was emerging. It was Ralph Schoenman, a young American militant supporter of the Movement,[64] who turned this general mood of frustration into organisational form. Schoenman's basic idea was simple: he proposed that the Movement, via *mass* civil disobedience, should compel the authorities to implement unilateralist policies. Schoenman was a dynamic, enthusiastic and persuasive man and he convinced Bertrand Russell—already impatient with what he considered to be the over-cautious attitude of the CND leadership—that his proposals were viable. Supposedly confidential letters were sent to leading figures asking them if they would be willing to take part in the formation of a Committee of 100 whose purpose would be to organise and stimulate mass non-violent civil disobedience to protest against "the ever-growing menace of nuclear war".[65] Russell had already intimated to Canon Collins his intention of speaking in support of Direct Action but Collins had asked him to refrain from making a statement of this kind in the period leading up to the 1960 Labour Party Conference. Following a meeting between Collins and Russell it was agreed, according to Christopher Driver, that Russell would postpone making his statement.[66] However, at no stage was any mention made of the proposed Committee of 100 nor of the letters which were about to be issued. All this complicated intrigue was to no avail, as could perhaps have been foreseen. A letter of invitation to join the Committee of 100, intended for John Connell, a friend of Compton MacKenzie's, was sent in error to John Connell the Tory military historian. He at once handed it over to the *Evening Standard* who, naturally, made great play of this schism in the Nuclear Disarmament Movement.[67] The CND Executive, outraged at what they regarded as the subterfuge and disloyalty of their erstwhile President, Bertrand Russell, who soon resigned his Presidency,[68] reiterated their view that the Campaign should "urge its policy only by legal and democratic methods. 'Individuals who advocate methods of civil disobedience, whatever their standing, do so without having consulted either the Executive Committee or the rank and file of the Campaign'."[69] Discussions between Russell and Collins continued on a formal and mutually suspicious basis: four meetings were held, each man was accompanied by a 'second', and all were tape-recorded.[70] This was all to no avail and, on returning from holiday on 23 October, Collins found Russell's resignation awaiting him.[71]

Henceforth the gulf between the two organisations was, at least at leadership and national level, unbridgeable.[72] The personal bitterness caused by the creation of the Committee of 100 was severe and, equally important, the ideological orientations of the two organisations were sharply differentiated as we attempt to show in Part III.[73] The Committee of 100 marked a decisive new phase in Direct Action politics and, with the dead-end of the labourist tactic becoming increasingly apparent through 1961, the Committee of 100 had the initiative, for good or ill, in 1961 and the early part of 1962. In many ways, however, the Committee was a continuation and expansion of the DAC. In terms of activists the DAC was very strongly represented in the Committee: Michael Randle (Chairman of DAC) became secretary of the Committee of 100[74] and all but two of the DAC moved over to active support for the Committee of 100:[75] the core of the Committee thus had considerable affinity with the DAC, although other ideological elements were also intermingled to a far greater extent than before.

The Committee of 100 held its inaugural meeting on 22 October 1960 but the DAC continued a separate existence for a further 10 months, largely in order to carry out a final project: a protest march, following the 1961 Aldermaston March, to Holy Loch to demonstrate against the stationing of a Polaris submarine there. In the event this was one of the DAC's most dramatic and successful demonstrations with more than 2000 taking part in the final march and protest.[76]

The Committee of 100 was, as Driver has pointed out, "the child both of the rocket-base demonstrations and of the Aldermaston Marches: it was Schoenman's contribution . . . to see that the two could be combined to forge a new weapon".[77] The acid test for the new organisation lay in its coercive potential—and thus in the size and militancy of its demonstrations.

On 14 December 1960 Bertrand Russell announced at a press conference that the first Committee of 100 demonstration would take place on 18 February 1961 outside the Ministry of Defence in Whitehall. Despite receiving considerably fewer than the declared minimum of 2000 pledges the Committee went ahead with the demonstration—which in the event attracted substantial numbers (estimates ranging from 1000 to 6000) and was generally hailed as a successful beginning. The 1961 Aldermaston

March—divided into two sections, one from Aldermaston and the other from Wethersfield, uniting on the final day—was larger than ever with some estimates of 150,000 for the final rally in Trafalgar Square. A small group, led by Schoenman, carried out a sit-down demonstration outside the US Embassy following the March. The next Committee of 100 demonstration took place on 29 April in Parliament Square. Over 2000 people took part and 826 arrests were made.

Outside events ensured that support for the Committee of 100 would grow during the late summer of 1961: persistent rumours of war over Berlin and the resumption of nuclear testing by both the USSR and the USA, on 31 August and 6 September respectively, gave real and undeniable force to the Committee of 100's contention that the nuclear holocaust was imminent and urgent action to avoid the catastrophe essential. Hasty and impromptu demonstrations were held outside the Soviet Embassy by both CND and the Committee of 100, but the major demonstration was undoubtedly that of the Committee of 100 scheduled for Sunday, 17 September in Trafalgar Square. In a quite uncharacteristic lapse of judgement the Government summoned thirty-six of the better known members of the Committee, including Bertrand and Edith Russell, and invited them at Bow Street to bind themselves over under the 1361 Act to keep the peace for one year. When thirty-two of the thirty-six refused, most were sentenced to 1 month's imprisonment (although Russell's sentence was reduced to 1 week).

The demonstration on the 17 September marked the highspot of the Committee of 100's success. About 12,000 people were in the Square and 1314 were arrested between 6 p.m. and 1 a.m. At Holy Loch, in a simultaneous demonstration, 351 were arrested. News coverage was enormous. Support for the Committee appeared buoyant and the strategy appeared to most activists at the time to be working. However, as Michael Randle and George Clark have both subsequently recalled,[78] the Committee was in the dangerous position of being committed to a virtual *geometric* progression in the size of its demonstrations if it were to achieve success. It was this need for ever greater and more spectacular demonstrations, combined with a rather facile optimism and lack of organisational and administrative experience on the part of a number of the leading activists, that led to the semi-fiasco of the demonstrations on 9 December 1961. The proposal was that, following the successful demonstrations in London, the Committee should now move ahead along its declared strategy and attempt to immobilise the 'war machine' of the State by bringing selected military installations to a standstill through civil disobedience. The major demonstrations took place at Wethersfield and Ruislip with supporting action simultaneously at Brize Norton, Bristol, Cardiff, Manchester and York.

The police, presumably acting on Home Office instructions, hardened their tactics. On 6 December the Special Branch raided the HQ of the Committee and the homes of five of its leading activists: on 8 December these five—Ian Dixon, Terry Chandler, Trevor Hatton, Michael Randle and Pat Pottle (and also Helen Allegranza)[79]—were arrested and remanded on bail under charges alleging conspiracy under the Official Secrets Act. This aggressive and unexpected action by the authorities undermined to the point of collapse the Committee of 100's organisation for the demonstration. It was already clear that seven simultaneous demonstrations, organised over a wide area with one of the major sites (Wethersfield) inaccessible to public transport, and all scheduled for the depths of winter, was an over-ambitious, if not positively foolhardy, project. With the arrest, on a serious charge, of the main organisers (and with other experienced Committee of 100 activists already in jail) the demonstrations were doomed to comparative failure.[80] According to Driver 5000 took part and 850 arrests were made:[81] *Peace News* estimated a total of some 6000 to 7000 participants, and was more sanguine about the success of the demonstration. An editorial was, however, very critical of the organisation at both of the main demonstrations: Ruislip was dismissed as "chaotic", whilst at Wethersfield, "the putting up of the fences and the last minute withdrawal of the coaches, both extremely foreseeable actions by the authorities, resulted in confusion about tactics, lack of facilities for briefing demonstrators, and a breakdown of communications on the spot".[82]

The Official Secrets Trial which followed in February 1962 resulted in sentences of 18 months imprisonment for each of the men and 12 months for Helen Allegranza.[83] The tactics of moderation and absorption having failed, the State had imposed heavy sentences in order to deter others from similar action. These heavy sentences, despite the spirited and intelligent case argued by the defendants and publicised through the media, combined with the sense of anti-climax if not failure following the December demonstrations to produce a decided downturn in the fortunes of the Committee.

By 1962 therefore the Movement had reached a stalemate: its support, measured in terms of the size of the Aldermaston Marches and the vigour of the branches, remained relatively stable.[84] But there seemed no conceivable way forward — and neither the established political parties nor public opinion (as measured by polls) showed any inclination to fall in with the unilateralists' demands. It was the Cuba missile crisis of October 1962 which broke the logjam. Bertrand Russell's role in the Cuba crisis and its resolution is well known and is recounted in detail in his book *Unarmed Victory*.[85] But the major impact of Cuba on the protesters, both CND and the Committee of 100, was to demonstrate the fundamental irrelevance of the Movement (at least in the immediate context) and indeed of Britain generally, to the life and death decisions that were being taken by the leaders of the two 'Super Powers'. Demonstrations could be, and were, held by the Movement's supporters both locally and nationally, but nobody could pretend that they had much if any impact on the situation.[86] Moreover, the peaceful resolution of the Cuban crisis demonstrated that the world's 'Super Powers' *were* able to pull back from the brink, and thus the desperate urgency which had characterised the Movement's activities (particularly the Committee of 100's) subsided.

The effects on the Movement were profound. The CND leadership realised that its hopes of converting the Labour Party to a full-blooded unilateralist policy were virtually non-existent — not least because of the imminence of a General Election and the consequent need for Party Unity. Stuart Hall, one of the leading intellectual activists of the New Left in CND,[87] wrote a detailed, closely argued and revisionist statement of CND's policy entitled *Steps Towards Peace*. The intention was to produce a policy which, in the new domestic and international political situation, would stand a good chance of influencing if not determining the Labour Party's stance on defence questions.[88] Sensible and practical these proposals may have been, but they clouded and compromised the original and clear commitment to British unilateral nuclear disarmament which had been the cornerstone — emotive and moral as much if not more than political — of the Movement since its inception. Psychologically, therefore, this was a disastrous move for CND, as both Canon Collins and Stuart Hall have subsequently agreed. For the mass of the Movement, however, it seemed a betrayal of the total and pure commitment to unilateralism. Fundamentally, of course, the problem arose because a realistic and comparatively sophisticated *political* programme was imposed upon a basically *moral* campaign. The tension between moral and political perspectives is a core theme of this study and is discussed in detail in Parts II and III.

The Committee of 100, weakened though it was by the events of late 1961 and early 1962, was very active in 1962.[89] The spontaneous activism of 1960/1 was replaced by a more serious and committed political stance which embraced a wider conception of objectives than purely nuclear disarmament. As a number of activists and analysts have noted the influence of anarchistic ideas was markedly increased within the Committee of 100 through 1962 and 1963. Going along with this was, naturally, a broader conception of appropriate Committee of 100 activities: decentralisation, community politics and community power, housing campaigns and other libertarian causes were taken up by the Committee.[90] By the beginning of 1963 CND and the Committee of 100 had thus moved farther apart than ever before: CND—at least as far as the leadership was concerned—more closely allied to the Labourist, 'Old Left' stance, and the Committee of 100 pursuing a generalised libertarian policy removed from the conventional political arena. The sense of urgency which had maintained some unity of purpose, if not of action, prior to the Cuban crisis had decreased and the Movement drifted apart—and began to lose momentum, and ultimately support, as a result.

For a complex of reasons[91]—including the Committee of 100's new stance—Russell resigned the Presidency in January 1963. In some ways, however, 1963 marked a resurgence of Committee of 100 activism: two events in particular caught public attention. The Aldermaston March of 1963—again, a huge demonstration—included a sensational protest at 'RSG6'[92] at Warren Row near Reading organised by the 'Spies for Peace' group. This group of libertarian socialists and Anarchists—who remained anonymous for obvious reasons[93]—had obtained details of the network of nuclear shelters that the government had installed throughout the country[94] and publicised them during the March. A large minority of the March split off to demonstrate at Warren Row, against the advice of the CND leadership of course. This was a considerable publicity coup by the Committee activists and was in accord with the Committee's developing hostility to the bureaucratic 'Warfare State' and all it stood for. The CND leadership was furious that this almost irrelevant issue, as it was seen, had diverted public attention from the real purpose of the March.[95]

A similar clash of perspectives occurred during the demonstrations organised by the Committee of 100 against Queen Frederika of Greece who visited London in July 1963. For the Committee this was an extension of the campaign against oppression and illegitimate authority—for the CND leadership it again diverted attention from the nuclear disarmament cause. The extraordinary Challenor episode—where, following Donald Rooum's accusations (first in the Anarchist paper *Freedom* and later in *Peace News*), the police were found to have 'planted' bricks on eight of the demonstrators on 11 July 1963—further complicated the situation.[96] The long-standing anarchist hostility to the police as the front-line representatives of the repressive State was now given full play; and CND's consistent policy of co-operation with the police and careful differentiation between political policies and law enforcement was challenged head-on.

The net result of these events—and of the growth of the aggressively militant *Resistance* journal of the Committee of 100—was to increase the militancy of the Committee but to decrease public support, not only for the Committee, but also for the

Movement as a whole. Symptomatic of the gradual but decided decline of the Movement was George Clark's decision to set up the itinerant 'Campaign Caravan' in order to stimulate, or *re*-stimulate, interest and activism amongst the 'ordinary people' in the country.

CND was deeply divided over the events of 1963. In June 1963 CND held a discussion conference to try, yet again, to bring together the two strands of the Movement into a united whole.[97] The result was the 'Tell Britain' series of actions which included projects run by CND, YCND, CUCaND and the Committee of 100, an autumn project Fallex '63, in which everyone combined, and a comprehensive plan of campaign for the coming General Election.[98] This was not to the taste of Canon Collins and the CND leadership: indeed, after 5 years of exhausting campaign leadership and the continual conflicts with the Committee of 100, the 'Spies for Peace' and so on, Canon Collins considered resigning the Chairmanship. In the event he decided against resignation and although opposed (for the first time) at the Annual Conference he was re-elected by a two-thirds majority. The Conference went on to accept the 'Tell Britain' proposals, however; the mood of the Movement was obviously at variance with Collins' own and, as Peggy Duff has recalled, "many of his public statements at that time reflected his doubts, uncertainties and hesitancies"[99] and he eventually resigned in May 1964 after the Aldermaston March. Olive Gibbs took over as Chairman and remained in office for several years: a popular, hardworking, enthusiastic and committed figure. It was, however, as Peggy Duff has observed, too late: the Partial Test Ban Treaty of 1963 further removed the sense of urgency from the Movement and many of the activists who had been campaigning for 4, 5 or 6 years could no longer keep up the enthusiasm and the pressure. Labour Party activists in the Movement—especially those in the hierarchy of the Parliamentary Party—rapidly disentangled themselves from CND in preparation for the 1964 General Election. In 1966 CND, no longer really a mass Movement and overshadowed in demonstrations and the public eye by the anti-Vietnam War Movement, "gave up the hard struggle to remain something different, adopted membership at last, and became an organisation rather than a campaign".[100] CND has of course continued to exist and has an important role to play, as we argue later,[101] but its period as a mass Movement had effectively ended by 1964/5.

The fate of the Committee of 100 was rather different: civil disobedience demonstrations were held in the mid-1960s (e.g. several demonstrations at Ruislip USAF base) but numbers declined and any prospect of *mass* civil disobedience disappeared. The Committee did have a number of important spin-off effects in a whole range of social and political contexts, however.[102] Peter Cadogan,[103] a political activist with experience of almost every conceivable left-wing organisation and ideology, who had been secretary of the International Sub-Committee of the Committee of 100 since 1962, became full-time secretary of the National Committee of 100 in 1965 and remained in this post until the Committee finally wound up in September 1968. The *raison d'être* of the Committee of 100 had been to organise mass civil disobedience against nuclear policies: by the mid-1960s this objective was clearly not likely to be fulfilled and, although the Committee acted as a valuable spawning ground for all sorts of libertarian initiatives, its central role had disappeared and, by 1968, it was by common consent time to disband.

The foregoing brief chronological account omits all but the most central events in the Movement's turbulent story, and it is not possible in this format to recapture the elan and sense of excitement created by the Movement at the time. For this, as was noted in the Preface, the Movement must await its historian. Our purpose here is rather to analyse and discuss the ramifications and importance of the Movement — arguably the greatest protest Movement in Britain since the Chartists. In many ways the 'CND years' of 1958 to 1965 marked a watershed in modern British politics: the experience of the Movement and the lessons to be gleaned from its failures (and its successes) constitute one important element in the development of contemporary British political structure and culture. The central focus of this study is thus political and sociological, and it is to this analysis that we now turn.

References

1. The Conservatives were returned with a majority of 17 in 1951 and 58 in 1955. Sir Winston Churchill remained leader of the Party until 1955, when Sir Anthony Eden succeeded him. Eden resigned in 1957 following the Suez affair and MacMillan, who became leader of the Party and Prime Minister, remained in office until 1963 when he was succeeded by Lord Home.

   The Conservatives were in office from 1951 to 1964, with General Election victories in 1951, 1955 and 1959.

2. India gained independence in 1947 under Attlee's Labour Government.

3. The first British colony in Africa to gain independence was Ghana (formerly the Gold Coast) in March 1957.

4. Principally, of course, the continuing conflicts in South East Asia, where the horrific suffering of the indigenous populations has become a commonplace over the decades.

5. It is perhaps not altogether fanciful to suggest that Freudian overtones could be read into Britain's determination to rectify her waning potency by indulging in the phallic parody of the nuclear cloud!

6. i.e. because of the inherent and long-term problems of the British economy, the growth was less spectacular and economic performance generally sluggish. (See, for example, G. D. N. Worswick and P. H. Ady (eds.), *The British Economy in the 1950s,* Clarendon Press, 1962.)

7. For graphic descriptions of the social effects of the economic depression in Britain see G. Orwell, *The Road to Wigan Pier,* Penguin, 1962; and W. Greenwood, *Love on the Dole,* Penguin Modern Classics, 1969.

8. Keynes has been the most influential economist in the Western capitalist world in the twentieth century. His writings are numerous but the 'classic' text is J. M. Keynes, *The General Theory of Employment, Interest and Money,* various editions, 1936.

   Keynes' contentions have been subjected to criticisms both from within the framework of capitalist economics (e.g. by the monetarist theorists of recent years) and from the Marxist perspective (e.g. Paul Mattick, *Marx and Keynes: the Limits of the Mixed Economy,* Merlin Press, 1971).

9. As a result of the seeming stabilisation of capitalism many argued that the new society marked the 'end of ideology' and that the old antagonisms and clash of perspectives were no longer relevant. (See, for example, Daniel Bell, *The End of Ideology,* New York, 1960; C. A. R. Crosland, *The Future of Socialism,* Jonathan Cape, 1956.)

10. Particularly TV and records. For an interesting analysis of the political and economic dimension of the media industries see G. Murdock and P. Golding, "For a Political Economy of Mass Communications" (in R. Miliband and J. Saville (eds.), *Socialist Register 1973,* Merlin Press, 1974).

11. For an excellent discussion and analysis of pop culture see G. Melly, *Revolt into Style: The Pop Arts in Britain,* Allen Lane, the Penguin Press, 1970.

12. For the Left in the 1940s and 1950s see R. Miliband, *Parliamentary Socialism* (2nd edition), Merlin Press, 1973; D. Coates, *The Labour Party and the Struggle for Socialism,* CUP, 1974. For the Right, see N. Harris, *Competition and the Corporate Society,* Methuen, 1972; also, the memoirs of leading Conservative politicians (e.g. Sir Harold MacMillan, Sir Anthony Eden, Lord Butler, Lord Home).

13. See Miliband, *op. cit.,* chap. ix.

14. *Ibid.*

15. *Ibid.,* chaps. ix and x; also see Coates, *op. cit.,* chap. 4; and Peggy Duff, *Left, Left, Left,* Allison & Busby, 1971 (section entitled: "Tribune and the Bevanites: 1949-1955").

16. See Miliband, *op. cit.*, and Coates, *op. cit.*

17. See Harris, *op. cit.*; also, see C. Pritchard and R. Taylor, *Social Work: Reform or Revolution?*, Routledge & Kegan Paul, 1978, chap. 3.

18. See Harris, *op. cit.*; also Lord Blake, *The Conservative Party from Peel to Churchill*, Fontana, 1972, for an account of Tory 'flexibility' over the years.

19. On Suez see: Sir Anthony Nutting, *No End of a Lesson: the Story of Suez*, Constable, 1967; A. Thompson (ed.), *The Day Before Yesterday*, Panther, 1971; Sir Anthony Eden, *Full Circle* (Vol. 3 of The Eden Memoirs), Cassell, 1960.
On Hungary see: P. Fryer, *Hungarian Tragedy*, Dobson, 1956; B. Davidson, *What Really Happened in Hungary?*, UDC, 1956; A. Anderson, *Hungary 56*, Solidarity Book, 1964; G. Mikes, *The Hungarian Revolution*, Andre Deutsch, 1957.

20. See, for example, I. Deutscher, *Stalin*, 2nd ed., Pelican, 1966; and the various writings of A. Solzhenitsyn.

21. Hence the formation of the *New Reasoner* component of the New Left (see Part III and Part IV). The crisis also resulted in the upsurge of the Trotskyist sects, however: in particular the *Newsletter* group, subsequently the Socialist Labour League (see P. Shipley, *Revolutionaries in Modern Britain*, Bodley Head, 1976).

22. Jimmy Porter, in John Osborne's *Look Back in Anger*, Scene I, Act III, Faber & Faber, 1957.

23. This account is based principally on the following sources: Christopher Driver, *The Disarmers*, Hodder & Stoughton, 1964; Peggy Duff, *Left, Left, Left*, Allison & Busby, 1971; A. J. R. Groom, *British Thinking about Nuclear Weapons*, Frances Pinter, 1974; R. A. Exley, "The Campaign for Nuclear Disarmament: its organisation, personnel and methods in its first year" (unpublished thesis, Manchester University, 1959); D. V. Edwards, "The Movement for Unilateral Nuclear Disarmament in Britain" (unpublished thesis, Swarthmore College, 1962); our discussions with surviving leadership figures.

24. Driver, *op. cit.*, p. 12.

25. *Ibid.*, pp. 18-19.

26. The Peace Pledge Union, founded by Canon Dick Sheppard, came to prominence in the 1930s and secured, by 1939, 136,000 signatures to the declaration "I renounce war and will never sanction another". By the 1950s the PPU had come to represent the individualistic and rather 'conservative' wing of the Pacifist movement. See Part III, pp. 75-79.

27. Driver, *op. cit.*, p. 20. The Commission's terms of reference were drawn up in 1949.

28. The DAC stemmed directly from 'Operation Gandhi' — Hugh Brock, editor of *Peace News*, being the guiding force in both cases.

29. These Conferences were named after the Nova Scotia village where the Canadian-American millionaire, Cyrus Eaton, had made his estate available for Conference discussions. For further discussion of Russell and Pugwash, see Part III.

30. Driver, *op. cit.*, p. 31. Miss Fishwick, a retired civil servant, a member of Finchley Labour Party and the Anglican Pacifist Fellowship, and an ex-Suffragette, "died exhausted by her efforts" 2 days before the Central Hall meeting which launched CND in February 1958.

31. Peggy Duff was secretary of NCANWT and subsequently organising secretary (1958-63) and secretary (from 1963-7) of CND. See Appendix III for biography.

32. Arthur Goss was proprietor of the *Hampstead and Highgate Express* and Clerk to the Middlesex Quarterly Meeting Peace Committee and the Society of Friends. He went on to become a member of the CND Executive and a leading activist in the Movement. See Appendix III for biography.

33. Cmnd. 124, para. 12, quoted in Driver, *op. cit.*, p. 34.

34. This soon changed its title to the Direct Action Committee Against Nuclear War and is referred to throughout the book as the DAC.

35. In the event Harold Steele arrived in Tokyo only to find that the test had already taken place.

36. Significantly, the Christian pacifist influence in DAC was considerably less than it had been in earlier organisations (such as the PPU).

37. However, she was sacked from her post shortly after the end of the March — largely because she was exhausted and unable to continue at the same frenetic pace. April Carter, who had organised the vigil after the 1958 March at the AWRE, took over her post. At the end of the summer, however, Pat Arrowsmith returned as Field Organiser and April Carter remained as secretary. (Source: Pat Arrowsmith, in conversation with Richard Taylor, January 1978.)

38. Sir Stephen King-Hall, a retired naval officer and former Independent National MP, was a strategist and military expert of some repute, who was both a non-pacifist and a non-socialist. His was an influential voice in CND and helped greatly to counter suggestions that CND was a 'subversive' and/or 'crackpot' organisation. The book referred to here was *Defence in the Nuclear Age*, Gollancz, 1958. See Appendix III for biography.

39. Subsequently published under this title by the OUP, 1958.

40. See Part III, pp. 58-62 and Part IV, pp. 114-121.

41. J. B. Priestley, "Britain and the Nuclear Bombs", *New Statesman*, 2 Nov. 1957. See Part III.

42. Driver, *op. cit.*, p. 43.

43. Driver, *op. cit.*, p. 44, notes that of the nineteen on the Executive of CND during the first year thirteen were in *Who's Who*. The Executive consisted of: Canon Collins, Bertrand Russell, Peggy Duff, Ritchie Calder, James Cameron, Howard Davies, Michael Foot, Arthur Goss, Kingsley Martin, J. B. Priestley, Professor J. Rotblat, Dr. Sheila Jones. During the first year Dr. Jones and Professor Rotblat resigned. There were eight cooptions: Lord Wilmot (who became Treasurer but later resigned and was replaced by Ted Bedford); Sir Richard Acland; Frank Beswick; Jacquetta Hawkes; Benn Levy; Lord Simon of Wythenshawe (who later resigned); and A. J. P. Taylor. (There was a deliberate policy, in these early days, of excluding MPs, in order to preserve the non-partisan ethos of CND.)

    The Executive Committee was reorganised in 1959 following pressure from those who felt that the original, self-selected, committee was insufficiently representative of the Movement as a whole. However, although CND frequently attempted to democratise its institutions they became, according to Peggy Duff, "large and unwieldy . . . (and) less disciplined, less friendly . . . (the institutions of the Movement) remained basically the same". Duff, *op. cit.*, p. 155.

    In 1961 a new Constitution was adopted: it provided for a Chairman, a vice-Chairman (later there were three), a treasurer, and ten individuals, nominated by CND groups and elected at Annual Conference. In addition, each Regional Council and each specialist section (i.e. Christian CND; Women's group; Press and Publicity Group; Scientists' group; Architects' group; CUCaND; YCND) were represented on the Council which met about four times a year. The Council elected an Executive Committee which had to include four representatives of the regions and, later, one from YCND. (Source: Duff, *op. cit.*, pp. 155-60.)

    The sponsors listed in the first year comprised: John Arlott, Dame Peggy Ashcroft, the Bishop of Birmingham, Lord Boyd Orr, Benjamin Britten, Viscount Chaplin, Count Michael de la Bedoyère, Bob Edwards, Dame Edith Evans, E. M. Forster, A. S. Frere, Gerald Gardiner, QC, Victor Gollancz, Dayan Dr I. Grunfeld, Barbara Hepworth, Patrick Heron, Rev. Trevor Huddleston, CR, Sir Julian Huxley, Edward Hyams, Doris Lessing, the Bishop of Llandaff, Sir Compton MacKenzie, the Very Revd. George McCleod, Miles Malleson, Denis Matthews, Sir Francis Meynell, Henry Moore, John Napper, Ben Nicholson, Sir Herbert Read, Dame Flora Robson, Earl Russell, Michael Tippett, Vicky, Professor C. H. Waddington and Professor Barbara Wootton. Professor J. Rotblat, Lord Simon of Wythenshawe and Lord Wilmot became sponsors after leaving the Executive.

44. Peggy Duff, *op. cit.*, p. 123. The text of the policy statement, deliberately 'moderate' in tone to pacify the United Nations Association, who were at this early stage involved in the Campaign, read as follows:

    "The purpose of the Campaign is to demand a British initiative to reduce the nuclear peril and to stop the armaments race, if need be by unilateral action by Great Britain. As a first step towards a general disarmament convention, Britain should press for negotiations, at top level, on the following issues:

    1. The stopping of all further tests of nuclear weapons;
    2. The stopping of the establishment of new missile bases;
    3. The securing of the establishment of neutral and nuclear free zones;
    4. The securing of the abolition of the manufacture and stockpiling of all nuclear weapons;
    5. The prevention of the acquisition of nuclear weapons by other nations;

    In order to underline the sincerity of her own initiative, Britain should be prepared to announce that, pending negotiations:

    (a) she will suspend patrol flights of aeroplanes equipped with nuclear weapons;
    (b) she will make no further tests of hydrogen bombs;
    (c) she will not proceed with the establishment of missile bases on her territory;
    (d) she will not provide nuclear weapons for any country."

45. *Ibid.*, p. 125.

46. Driver, *op. cit.*, p. 48.

47. The major activists in the DAC were Pat Arrowsmith, Hugh Brock, April Carter, Alex Comfort, Frances Edwards, Michael Howard, Sheila Jones, Michael Randle, Rev. Michael Scott, Allen Skinner,

Harold and Sheila Steele and Will Warren. Among the sponsors of the DAC were: Frank Allaun, Lindsay Anderson, Claude Bourdet, John Braine, Homer Jack, Dr. Winifred de Kok, George Melly, Spike Milligan, A. J. Muste, John Osborne, Dr. Linus Pauling, Sir Herbert Read, Archbishop Roberts, Ernie Roberts, Bertrand Russell, Bayard Rustin, Sydney Silverman, Rev. Dr. Donald Soper, Michael Tippett, and Philip Toynbee.

48. The Aldermaston March took place over the Easter weekend, leaving London on Good Friday, 4 April, with about 4000 taking part. Despite appalling weather the numbers never fell below 540 and the March was regarded by all concerned as a triumphantly successful beginning to the Movement. The March was followed by a vigil, organised by April Carter of the DAC, at the AWRE.

49. CND did not introduce a membership system, partly to avoid danger of proscription by the Labour Party, and partly to protect the self-elected and self-perpetuating CND Executive. The number of branches increased from 272 in 1958 to 459 in 1959. (Source: Driver, *op. cit.*, p. 93.)

50. i.e. the Cooperative Party, USDAW, and the AEU all passed unilateralist resolutions at their Annual Conferences.

51. Gaitskell was one of the most ideologically committed of Labour Party leaders and he believed passionately that CND's policy was mistaken. As a convinced social democratic revisionist he was virulently anti-Communist and anti-Marxist and a firm believer in the importance and value of the Atlantic Alliance. (This view of Gaitskell was confirmed by Sir Harold Wilson in conversation with Colin Pritchard, June 1978.)

52. This was especially the case with the New Left for whom 'neutralism' was the key issue. For discussion of Labour Left and New Left perspectives see Part III, pp. 58-62; 64-74; and Part IV, pp. 114-124.

53. A. J. R. Groom, *op. cit.*, p. 410.

54. See Part III. A number of our interviewees recalled how unexpected the unilateralist victory had been.

55. The fact that this was not so was formally due to the implementation of a rarely remembered clause in the Labour Party's constitution which stated that "no proposal shall be included in the Party programme unless it has been adopted by the Party conference by a majority of not less than two-thirds of the votes recorded on a card vote". More significant than the formal position, however, was the debate that ensued over the authority of the Conference *vis-à-vis* the Parliamentary leadership in the Labour Party. The issues involved here were of profound importance and are discussed further in Part III and Part IV.

56. The CDS, originally entitled 'Victory for Sanity', was established by a group of Gaitskell's supporters under the energetic secretaryship of William Rodgers (now a leading member of the Labour Shadow Cabinet).

57. Harold Wilson, who stood against Gaitskell on a 'party unity' platform (and who was never a unilateralist), was defeated by 183 votes to 81 votes in an election for leader of the PLP.

58. For detailed discussion of this point see Part III, pp. 58-61, and Part IV, pp. 117-121.

59. This policy, so called because it was drawn up and prosecuted by Walter Padley (General Secretary of USDAW and a senior figure in the Labour Movement), and R. H. S. Crossman (the noted intellectual Bevanite and, later, minister in the Wilson governments of 1964 to 1970), aimed to find a middle way on defence and so unite the Party. Briefly, the policy advocated was not unilateralist but argued for a radical reconstruction of NATO, an end to nuclear bases in Europe, including the UK, and rejected a NATO strategy based upon a threat to use nuclear weapons first. Canvassed throughout 1961 as an alternative to both the Cousins and Gaitskell policies, the policy was firmly rejected by the PLP leadership and its main effect was to divide those in the Party who opposed Gaitskell's policy and were sympathetic to CND. In this sense it can be seen as a contributory factor in the rejection of the unilateralist line at the 1961 Conference.

60. i.e. the AEU, the NUM, USDAW, and the NUR all reversed their previous position and backed the PLP leadership policy in 1961.

61. Part III deals in detail with this part of the Movement's history and analyses the political implications for those who hope to achieve socialist change through the Labour Party.

62. See Part III, pp. 58-62.

63. The Voter's Veto campaign, organised by the DAC, took place in 1958 and 1959, and argued that a commitment to unilateralism was more important than support for the Labour Party. Voters were thus encouraged to abstain if there were no unilateralist candidate, and to campaign against non-unilateralist Labour Party candidates. (The most notable by-elections where 'Voters' Veto' intervened were those at Rochdale and South West Norfolk.)

There was considerable discussion of an independent initiative following the 1960/61 debate over unilateralism in the Labour Party but those committed to the Labour Left were, of course, very hostile (most notably Michael Foot). The result was that, when INDEC was finally established, it received only minority support: INDEC was markedly unsuccessful in its attempts to win General Election seats (e.g. Michael Craft at Twickenham in 1964). Richard Gott's campaign in the Hull by-election in 1966, although enthusiastic and gaining considerable publicity, did not result in a high poll.

The whole experience of trying to create new electoral vehicles on this type of basis was singularly discouraging.

64. See Appendix III for biographical details.

65. From the circular letter inviting people to join the Committee of 100, signed by Bertrand Russell and Rev. Michael Scott.

66. Driver, *op. cit.*, p. 113.

67. This account is taken from Herb Greer, *Mud Pie: The CND Story*, Max Parrish, 1964, p. 48. Greer gives his source as Schoenman. Driver, *op. cit.*, p. 106, has a different version of this episode but we are assured by Nicolas Walter, in a review of Driver's book in *Solidarity* journal, Vol. 3, no. 7, p. 11, that it is Greer's version that is correct.

68. According to Collins, the CND Executive did not request Russell's resignation and the reports in the Press to this effect were malicious and inaccurate.

69. Driver, *op. cit.*, p. 114; the quotation is from the statement issued by the CND Executive on 29 Sept. 1960.

70. Details of this extraordinary affair are given in *Ibid.*, p. 114. Canon Collins and Arthur Goss both claimed that Russell was in fact being manipulated at these meetings by Schoenman. (Collins and Goss in conversation with Richard Taylor, January 1978.)

71. Quoted in Driver, *op. cit.*, p. 115: "I cannot countenance the Chairman of an organisation of which I am president permitting the policy of that organisation to be mis-stated in public statements which are said to come from him and have not been publicly repudiated by him."

72. Although, according to Dick Nettleton, this was certainly not the case at local/regional level. See Part III, p. 53.

73. Part III, pp. 75-83.

74. See Appendix III for biographical details of Michael Randle. Hugh Brock has recalled that Randle's secretaryship of Committee of 100 was a *sine qua non* of DAC support. Hugh Brock in conversation with Richard Taylor, January 1978. (See Part III, p. 80.)

75. Only Pat Arrowsmith of the leading DAC activists was notably ill at ease with the Committee of 100 in the early days. See p. 80.

76. Thirty-five DAC supporters set off immediately after the 1961 Aldermaston March on the 465-mile trek to Holy Loch. It took 7 weeks and ended with a march of several thousand from Dunoon to Holy Loch and an attempt by seventy demonstrators to board the *Proteus* while 200 others immobilised the pier at Ardnadam. This was, altogether, one of the most dramatic and successful of the DAC's demonstrations.

77. Driver, *op. cit.*, p. 117.

78. George Clark and Michael Randle, in conversation with Richard Taylor, January and May 1978, respectively.

79. Helen Allegranza was arrested at the Committee of 100 offices when the police raid took place. See Appendix III for biographical details of all six.

80. Although as Driver, *op. cit.*, p. 124, pointed out the 5000 he estimated as having taken part was about fifty times the number that the DAC had been able to mobilise 2 years previously.

81. This is an estimate of the total numbers taking part in all seven demonstrations.

82. Editorial, *Peace News*, 15 Dec. 1961. The paper also carried reports on each of the demonstrations and there was emphasis on the local impact made by the smaller protests which were hardly mentioned by the national media.

83. The trial produced some fascinating exchanges. Proceedings were fully reported in *Peace News* and a good account of the trial—"Official England versus Radical England"—is included in D. Boulton (ed.), *Voices from the Crowd: Against the H-Bomb*, Peter Owen, 1964.

84. Estimated numbers on the last day of the Aldermaston March, according to *Peace News*, were: 1962: 150,000; 1963: 70,000; 1964: 20,000.

85. Bertrand Russell, *Unarmed Victory*, Penguin, 1963.

86. Cuba demonstrations were reported in *Peace News*, 2 Nov. 1962, to have taken place at a large number of schools, colleges, and universities, and in several cities and towns throughout the UK (e.g. Bristol, Manchester, Liverpool, Paignton, etc.).

87. See Appendix III for biographical details.

88. The proposals were, first, that Britain, by renouncing nuclear weapons, nuclear tests and nuclear bases, opposing a European deterrent, and proposing disengagement in Central Europe, should initiate a move towards the withdrawal of strategic and tactical nuclear weapons by both the USA and the USSR from Europe. Second, Britain should initiate an extension of nuclear-free zones and negotiate an immediate test ban treaty. Third, Britain should encourage a strengthening of the UN whose Charter should take precedence over other national alliances and whose agencies should be used more for the distribution of foreign and military aid. Communist China and Eastern Germany should be admitted to the UN, and there should be a UN 'presence' in Berlin, guaranteeing West Berlin's freedom.

89. A Parliamentary sit-in was organised in January, and demonstrations in Parliament Square took place in March and at the US Embassy in April and July. Further demonstrations were organised at Holy Loch, Greenham Common and Honington.

90. For example, the Kinghill Campaign for the Homeless; support for those in the forces wishing to 'buy themselves out' (the troops movement); local tenants' associations campaigns, etc. Nevertheless, the central concerns of the Committee of 100 retained a strong connection with the nuclear issue.

91. See Part III, pp. 85-92 for a discussion of Russell's orientation in general.

92. Details of the RSG (Regional Seats of Government) system are included in "The RSG 1919-1963" by Nicolas Walter, *Solidarity*, Pamphlet 15. The full story of the 'Spies for Peace' has still to be made public, but reasonably detailed accounts appear in "Resistance Shall Grow", *Solidarity*, Pamphlet 14 (jointly produced by Solidarity, the Independent Labour Party, the London Federation of Anarchists, and the Syndicalist Workers' Federation), and in *Inside Story* No. 8, March/April 1973, and No. 9, May/June 1973, under the title 'The Spies that Got Away'.

  Although the individual identities of the 'Spies for Peace' have remained undiscovered it is clear that the group around the journal *Solidarity* was closely involved. (This was, and is, an anarcho-syndicalist grouping, very much opposed to Communism, Social Democracy and Trotskyism; its ideological stance is derived largely from the work of Paul Cardan.)

93. Given the close attention paid by the Special Branch to the Committee of 100 it is remarkable that no charges were ever brought against the 'Spies for Peace'.

94. As Driver observed, however, *op. cit.*, p. 153, Stevenson Pugh on 28 February in the *Daily Mail* had already publicised the outline of the system. Thus "the astonishment of the Campaign's rank and file was an indication of their youth and ignorance. . . ."

95. Peggy Duff, *op. cit.*, p. 220, writing about Canon Collins' reaction to the 'Spies for Peace' in a Panorama TV interview, revealed that Collins had gone against her advice in criticising the whole affair:"Always loyal to CND as he saw it, he was quite unable to see this as a part of the Movement, as a contribution to the Campaign. He didn't see it as a lift for morale when such a lift was urgently needed. He was blind to its originality, its ingenuity, its value in the fight against nuclear weapons. So he attacked it. What a row there was about that!"

96. Detective Sergeant Challenor was eventually discharged from the Police Force and, pronounced insane, when it was proved that he had been responsible for 'planting' the bricks on a number of demonstrators. (It took a year of appeals and enquiries, instigated by Rooum, to prove that this crime had taken place. It was reported in *Peace News* on 3 July 1964 that three policemen working with Challenor had been imprisoned for "conspiracy to prevent the course of justice".)

97. The purpose of this conference was, in Peggy Duff's words, "to bring the argument out into the open, to find a new, freer approach which might liberate the Movement and recapture its momentum". Peggy Duff, *op. cit.*, p. 221.

98. It was in fact the Conservatives—and especially Sir Alec Douglas-Home—who made the British nuclear deterrent an issue. Harold Wilson, elected leader of the Labour Party in 1963 following Gaitskell's death, played down the issue and succeeded in uniting the Party behind his non-unilateralist defence policy. CND made virtually no impact on the Election campaign.

99. Duff, *op. cit.*, p. 223.

100. *Ibid.*, p. 225.

101. See pp. 137-141

102. See Parts III and IV.

103. See Appendix III for biographical details.

PART II

"Where Have All the Marchers Gone?" The Protesters of 1958/65 and their Subsequent Development

THERE is no doubt that the Disarmament Movement of the 1958/65 period attracted very diverse support. The popular, media image of a campaign of eccentric, alienated, immature and irresponsible young people, led by an assortment of naïve clerics, impractical intellectuals and political subversives, was given further credence by the leading politicians of the time. This perception, however, was, as might be expected, a gross distortion and over-simplification of an astonishingly varied and complex movement.

What follows here is an attempt to define and analyse the complexity of the Movement's composition and to discuss the differing conceptions and motivations of activists between 1958 and 1965. Equally important, we shall discuss the subsequent activities and developments of the supporters over the following 20 years, and try to answer Peggy Duff's question "where have all the marchers gone?"[1]

In this Part, it is the ordinary supporters' recollections and views which are examined collectively rather than those of the prominent leadership figures of the Campaign.

The only previous study of Disarmament Movement supporters was carried out in 1965 by Frank Parkin,[2] who attended an Aldermaston March and questioned a sample of the marchers.[3] His study is of crucial importance to any *post facto* analysis of the Movement because it is the only work which attempted to explore empirically and in depth some of the sociological and political dimensions of the Movement. Parkin's study measured only *current* activities, attitudes, social backgrounds, etc., while our survey also measured activists' development over the 20-year period from the late 1950s to the late 1970s. Nevertheless Parkin's work is an essential baseline: it is only by comparison with his sample of the Aldermaston March in 1965 that any subsequent survey can determine its validity as a representative cross-section of the Movement.

The sample of activists we contacted was very similar to those analysed by Parkin on most of the appropriate variables: age, religion, education and social class (the latter based on the Hall-Jones scale[4]). The comparative details are given in the Methodological Appendix.[5]

Because of the similarity of our respondents to Parkin's it seems reasonable to claim that the sample on which the present study is based is as representative of Disarmament Movement activists as is feasible. Brief mention must be made here of how our respondents were reached. Supporters of the Movement between 1958/65 were invited — via letters to the press and to professional journals, and appearances on local and national TV and radio — to complete a detailed questionnaire (the questionnaire is reproduced as Appendix II). The effective response rate was 93% (nineteen questionnaires were returned too late to be included in the statistical analysis). It is obvious that the sample was self-selected and highly motivated and still apparently interested in the anti-nuclear issue and/or Movement. Equally, the method of contact, and the way of collecting the data, i.e. via the written word, made it more likely to be attractive to middle-class than to traditional working-class movement activists. Nevertheless, this survey accurately represents, it will be argued, the *core* activists of the Movement, and spans the whole range of diverse groups and perceptions present from the earliest years of the Direct Action Committee Against Nuclear War and the National Council Against Nuclear Weapons Tests which were the immediate forerunners of CND.[6]

To assist the reader handle the rather complex survey material which follows, it may be helpful to provide a short outline plan. The total sample is examined, in terms of age, sex and social class. The main thrust of our concern is to distinguish the differing ideological perspectives within the Movement and we have thus divided our sample as follows:

(a) the political protesters—those who saw the Movement in primarily political terms (i.e. Labour Party socialists, Liberals, Marxists, Anarchists, etc.);

(b) the moral protesters—those who had no particular political affiliation and whose protest was based on moral objections to nuclear weapons.

Over and above this basic division, we have also subdivided the total sample into those who pursued their objectives through extra-parliamentary and direct action campaigns, largely in the DAC and the Committee of 100, and compared their beliefs, attitudes and activities with others in the Movement. Similarly, we have compared those active in subsequent campaigns and activities of various sorts (e.g. the Anti-Vietnam War Movement; environmentalist campaigns, etc.) with others in the Movement. All these groups are compared with each other, *and* changes within and between the groups are analysed over the 20-year period (i.e. 1958-65 compared to 1978).

General Response*

Of the 403 respondents, 65% were male and 35% female. They were predominantly middle class; 51% were aged 45 or less, and 49% were 46 or more. (The detailed age breakdown was: 20% aged 35 or less, 31% aged 36 to 45, 20% aged 46 to 55, and 29% aged 56 or more.)

How strong was the respondents' support for CND? The vast majority came to CND in the years 1958 and 1959 (75%) and, by 1961, 96% of the sample was active in the Movement. There were no significant differences in terms of age or sex in this pattern.

As would be expected, the younger respondents came relatively late to the campaign, although only 1% after 1964. The length of respondents' commitment to the Movement was impressive, 97% being involved for at least 4 years, and 23% of the respondents being current members of CND. Interestingly, however, it was the older rather than the younger respondents who were involved for longer in the Movement. Such a general commitment to the Movement gives support to the contention that the respondents were very much core activists and representative of the keenest and most active sections of the Movement.

*Total raw scores are given in Appendix II.

EDUCATION

By 1978, 73% of our respondents had either a degree or professional qualification: only 19% of the sample had ceased formal education at minimum school-leaving age. As would be expected, the original 'youth group' had, over the 20-year period, been significantly* more able to utilise the greater range of educational opportunities available than had those respondents currently aged 46 and over. By 1978 only 11% of the whole sample had no educational qualifications. Women, as well as those from the working-class groups, did significantly less well in educational terms, reflecting the well-known discriminatory factors operating in the British educational system. It should also be pointed out that while the females were proportionately as 'middle class' as the men, they did not (either in 1958 or 20 years later) reach the higher social class groups 1 and 2 as often as their male counterparts.

Our study has also confirmed one of the findings of Parkin's survey that caused some surprise — and certainly contradicted the prevalent media image of the Movement's supporters. Parkin found that the youthful supporter in the 1960s was not alienated, anti-parent and anti-authority, but rather, on the contrary, generally well integrated and in fundamental accord with the radicalism of his (or her) parents.[7] This finding was substantially supported by our study which showed that these people were now well established occupationally and educationally, less than 4% of the ex-'youth group' having no educational qualification.

RELIGIOUS BELIEF

In 1958-65 over 41% of our respondents had a Christian religious belief (Parkin's study contained 40%). Our study contained similar proportions of the various Christian denominations to Parkin's: the Anglicans being the highest represented group, 35%, followed by a particularly high proportion of Quakers (28%). There were relatively few significant differences in regard to age, social class and sex distribution: there were proportionately more Methodists and Roman Catholics in the 'youth group' compared with the 'adult group'. By 1978, however, religious allegiance amongst respondents had fallen by almost 10%: only 32% (127) now declared that they held a Christian faith (the original 'youth group' respondents were significantly less religiously inclined than the older respondents). There was a slight shift in the levels of support for the various denominations: the Anglicans, Roman Catholics and Methodists lost proportionate support with the main 'increase' being in favour of 'other denominations'.

PACIFISM

Unlike all other previous British disarmament movements, CND was not fundamentally a pacifist body.[8] Many Pacifists were hostile to CND precisely because of this eclecticism: as Arthur Goss recalled,[9] the Absolute Pacifist organisations were amongst the hardest to recruit into CND's ranks. The dominant attitude to Pacifism in the

---

*By significant we mean 'statistically significant' and this will be shown on all tables as will the particular statistical test used. The specialist reader will appreciate that it is impossible to supply all results upon which the text is based within the limitations of space. In the text the term 'very significant' indicates at least a 1% level of confidence and 'highly significant' equals 0.1% level. Finally we follow the convention that all percentages quoted are rounded upwards to the nearest whole number.

Movement[10] was perhaps best exemplified by Russell who, although having a strong involvement with the pacifist cause in the earlier part of the century, had long since rejected Absolute Pacifism. His insistence that mankind faced an entirely new situation with the invention of nuclear weapons led many to adopt *nuclear* Pacifism — and to draw a sharp distinction between this and traditional, Absolute Pacifism.

It was a little surprising, therefore, to find 46% of our respondents describing themselves, in 1958/65, as 'Absolute Pacifists'. (The only significant variation, in terms of social class, age and sex, in this group was that 57% of the Absolute Pacifists were female.) A quarter of the Pacifists were supporters of the Peace Pledge Union, the 'traditional' pacifist organisation *par excellence,* and 14% supported the British Peace Committee, the British branch of the Communist-dominated World Peace Council.[11]

In both these latter cases there was significantly less support from the younger members.

OTHER MOVEMENT GROUPS

The two other major organisations in the history of the Movement (excepting the National Council Against Nuclear Weapons Tests which merged into CND on its formation) were the two 'Direct Action' oriented groups: the DAC and the Committee of 100.[12] Almost a third of our respondents had been DAC supporters, whilst over half had been involved to some degree in the Committee of 100. For the Committee of 100 there was a highly significant greater support from the ex-'youth group' among our respondents (compared with the former adult supporters).

The only other specifically disarmament movement group noted in our sample was the Independent Nuclear Disarmament Election Committee (INDEC) which was supported by 11% of the respondents, a surprisingly low figure given the furore created by the issue in the Movement.[13]

POLITICAL IDEOLOGY AND BEHAVIOUR

Political attitudes were inextricably intertwined in the whole Movement: even those who rejected a political conception of the Movement's role were, of course, taking a highly political stance — albeit a seemingly negative one. Most activists realised, however, that at some stage the political process was central to the achievement of the Movement's aims.

The Movement brought together diverse political groupings: many overlapped and some were incompatible. To disentangle these responses we shall begin by looking at actual or intended voting behaviour.

Table 1 shows how the respondents voted in the 1959 and 1964 General Elections and how they would have voted at the time of completing the questionnaire (1978). Only those findings of statistical variation will be commented upon.

Three themes emerge from these figures. The first, of course, is that the Labour Party attracted far and away the most support throughout the period: Conservative voters were in a very small minority, then as now, amongst our respondents. More interesting, however, is the growing number of our respondents who either did not or would not vote: this was particularly marked amongst the male 'youth group'. There was too a growth in support for both the Liberals and the other Parties, and a commensurate failure on the part of the Labour Party to attract younger voters. All these

TABLE 1

Voting Behaviour and Intention—General Response N = 403

	1959 (%)*	1964 (%)*	1978 (%)
Labour Party	54	65	62
Conservative Party	2	1	2
Liberal Party	2	7*	11*
Communist and other Marxist Parties	1	1	5
Did (or would) not vote	9[m]	11[m]	13[y]
Not eligible to vote	31	12	0
Other Parties—including Nationalists, Ecology Party, etc.	1	2	6

* indicates a statistically higher proportion of 'adult group' voters.
[y] indicates a statistically higher proportion of 'youth group' voters.
[m] indicates a statistically higher proportion of male voters.

trends reinforce the view, already demonstrated by other research,[14] that the Labour Party is losing its place as the natural home of radicalism. Other studies have concentrated on the melting away of working-class activists in the ranks of the Labour Party: this study demonstrates that the Labour Party may also be slowly losing the 'middle-class radicals'—the intellectual lifeblood of a social democratic party. It is most important to note, however, that this drift away from Labour does not appear to have benefited the Marxist Left (in any of its many guises): just as it has been argued that there is now a political vacuum amongst working-class activists formerly Labour Party members, there would now also appear to be a significant pool of politically homeless middle-class radical elements. This has resulted, not in the growth of a 'socialist alternative', but in a swing to the Centre, and, in some cases, in a disillusionment with and withdrawal from conventional politics of any sort. This is one of the major themes of our study to which we will return.[15]

The direct political affiliations over the twenty-year period were also very revealing (see Table 2). More than half of our respondents (51%) were members or strong supporters of the Labour Party between 1958 and 1965; if the 12% of Young Socialists are added to this, the total is substantial. However, it must be borne in mind that, generally speaking, the Young Socialists were far to the Left of the Labour Party and were dominated at different periods by Trotskyist groups of various types.[16] Although by 1978 Labour Party support had fallen to 40%, a considerable fall, Labour remained far and away the most widely supported political party. However, it would have been expected that most of the Young Socialists and those not eligible to vote would by 1978 have become Labour supporters: this did not happen. Support for the Communist Party was low in 1958/65 (7%) but has remained constant: the same applies to most of the other Marxist-oriented Left groups. The main growth over the 20-year period has been in support for the 'other Parties' (from 7% to 18%). Finally, it is important to note the large proportion (approximately one-third) who, throughout the period, did *not* support *any* political party or grouping. These findings conform again to the central pattern: a diffusion—slow but sure—of Labour Party allegiance, and a

TABLE 2
Political Affiliations—General Response 1958/65 and 1978
N = 403

	1958-65 (%)	1978 (%)
1. Labour Party	51	40
2. Young Socialists	12	2
3. Fabian Society	5	5
4. Liberal Party	3	5
5. Young Liberals	1	0
6. International Socialism/Socialist Workers' Party	3	4[y]
7. Socialist Labour League/Workers' Revolutionary Party	0	1
8. Institute for Workers' Control	0	3
9. Communist Party	7	7
10. Young Communist League	4	1
11. Solidarity	2	0
12. New Left Clubs	9[x]	N/A
13. Anarchists	7	4
14. Scottish National Party	0	1
15. Plaid Cymru	0	0
16. Conservative Party	0	1
17. National Front	0	0
18. (Vietnam Solidarity Campaign)	11	N/A
19. (British Campaign for Peace in Vietnam)	19	N/A
20. Other Political Groups	7	18
21. None	31[w]	34[w]

[x] indicates fewer women, $P = < 0.03$.
[w] indicates more women, $P = < 0.02$.
[y] indicates high support from 'youth group'.

(It should be noted that some respondents belonged to more than one party/organisation).

growth, not of Left-wing politics, but of support for minority, 'Centrist', groups (interestingly, however, the increased vote for the Liberal Party was not matched by any marked growth in Party membership or strong support).

In order to analyse the differing political orientations of the various perspectives in the Movement we subdivided the respondents into three separate political groups: the Anarchists, the Marxists and the Liberal Left.* The remainder of the sample (31%)

neither belonged nor gave active support to any of the political parties or groupings tabulated and were designated the 'non-politicals' (Table 2).

The groups were put together on the following criteria. All who described themselves as Anarchist were, irrespective of their membership of other political organisations, placed in this category; there were twenty-nine such people, 7% of the sample. The Marxist Left was composed of those who belonged to the various Marxist organisations (i.e. the Communist Party, Young Communist League, International Socialism, Socialist Labour League, Solidarity and New Left Clubs). There were seventy-one respondents in this group, constituting 17% of the total sample. Finally, there was the Liberal Left (comprising the Liberal and Labour Parties, Young Socialists, Young Liberals, and members of the Fabian Society), 42% (166) of the sample fell into this group.

How important were such political allegiances compared with the respondents' support for CND? Only seventy (18%) said that they would place their political interests, in 1958-65, ahead of the importance they gave to the Movement.[17] It is thus clear that, for the majority of those involved in the Movement, the prime loyalty was to the Movement. They were not 'using' the Movement to further their own political ends — though, of course, many would hold that the aims and objectives of the Movement could be achieved only within the wider political movement of which they, and the Movement, were a part.

There is thus a number of interesting political points to note: the extent of 'Far Left' influence in the Movement was *relatively* small (24% combining Anarchists and Marxists); more important, among this 'Left' group the vast majority put the Movement first and their own political allegiance second (this supports the contention of many of the leaders of the Movement that the nuclear issue was of paramount concern for almost everyone in the campaign — at least up until the Cuba crisis); the majority of the Movement's supporters were not, however, on the 'hard Left' — they were (*and by and large they remained*) moderates, owing allegiance either to the Liberal Left or to solely non-political, moral criteria.

There was evidence here of some overlap in terms of political allegiance and behaviour. However, this tendency became much more apparent when respondents' belief-systems were analysed. It is not only the bi-partite (or sometimes tri-partite) electoral system of Britain which obscures people's real ideological orientations: the nature of the political parties themselves, particularly the Labour Party, serves to mask quite incompatible ideological stances that are artificially united under one banner. Thus there can co-exist in the Labour Party, albeit unhappily, old style nonconformist socialists, Fabians, neo-Liberal social reformers, 'post-capitalists' à la Crosland, working-class sectionalists, Marxists, populist socialists, 'apolitical' pragmatists . . . and, of course, political careerists.

In order to try to probe the real ideological orientations of our respondents, we listed a number of systems of belief with opportunities to give a range of responses. There were fascinating variations as well as overlapping coincident views. The results are presented in Table 3; as there are major differences between the ex-'youth' and

---

*Because of membership of more than one political organisation, respondents were grouped according to that perspective which is the most radical — thus someone belonging to the Labour Party but describing himself as Anarchist would be placed in the Anarchist group for further comparisons.

'adult' groups, the sample's responses are shown accordingly.

TABLE 3
Response to Systems of Belief—'Youth' vs 'Adult' Groups
(N = 206 and N = 197)

	Strongly Agree and Agree	Neutral	Disagree and Strongly Disagree	Total Sample	
				Strongly Agree and Agree	Strongly Disagree and Disagree
	(%)	(%)	(%)		
System of belief	Youth — Adult	Youth — Adult	Youth — Adult	(%)	(%)
Christian $x^2 = 21.9$ d/f3 $P = <0.001$	34 - 52	21 - 24^w	45 - 24^w	43	35
Marxist $x^2 = 11.31$ 4d/f $P = <0.03$	52 - 36	21 - 33	27 - 30	44	29
Social Democratic $x^2 = 13.01$ 4d/f $P = <0.02$	51 - 53	22 - 33	27 - 14	52	20
Conservative $x^2 = 11.91$ 3d/f $P = <0.01$	2 - 5	9 - 19	90 - 77	3	84
Liberal Humanist $x^2 = 3.23$ n.s.	46 - 46	30 - 36	24 - 17	46	21
Apolitical $x^2 = 9.66$ 4d/f $P = <0.05$	9 - 8^w	19 - 28	73 - 64	8	69
Libertarian-Anarchist $x^2 = 15.11$ 4d/f $P = <0.01$	34 - 20	15 - 25	51 - 54	28	52

^{w} indicates significantly higher female response.

One immediate point of interest arising from these figures is the fact that, with the exception of Conservatism, all the categories received over a fifth of neutral responses whilst only the Social Democratic position had an absolute majority of support (the Conservative and the Apolitical perspectives being almost totally repudiated). On the other hand, there was a range of sympathy with the Christian, Liberal Humanist, Marxist and Libertarian-Anarchist perspectives, the latter being the least well supported with 28% whilst the other three categories gained at least a 40% level of sympathetic agreement. This would seem to indicate a blurring of perspectives and ideologies, even though party membership and voting intentions were much more clearly defined. It also indicates, in conformity with our earlier comment, a lack of ideological clarity or certainty. For the majority of Movement activists the reference point was the nuclear issue: whilst they were interested in wider ideological issues they did not, or were perhaps unable to, commit themselves whole heartedly to any single ideological framework. Arguably this was illustrative too of the classical 'liberal' elements of middle-class radicalism: the ability to see the other's point of view and to share something of the 'opponent's' analysis. This eclecticism is further demonstrated by the 16% of respondents who 'wrote in', in the space provided for 'other belief' systems. These included expressed sympathy for Buddhism, Hinduism, Islam, etc., not to the *exclusion* of the more traditional perspectives but *in addition* to them, thus emphasising the ethos of tolerance, acceptance, and, perhaps, ideological uncertainty.

The cross-sympathies were clearly demonstrated as well as the overlapping anti-pathies. Although Social Democracy was the only category to obtain over half the sample in agreement, three other major belief systems all achieved very high rates of support (i.e. Christian 43%, Marxist 44%, and Liberal Humanist 46%). Particularly surprising is the very high rate of agreement with Marxism, compared to the very low figures for both Marxist group voting *and* membership of Marxist organisations. There is a major discrepancy here perhaps suggesting both that many of the Movement activists who support the Labour Party would like to see a change to a more Marxist orientation, and that the existing Marxist organisations (the CP, IS/SWP *et al.*) lack credibility and/or appeal. Alternatively, perhaps it reflects a 'romantic' tolerance but falls far short of active commitment. Bearing in mind our earlier findings (and the tendency of Movement activists to drift to the Centre, or out of conventional politics), and the high rating gained here by Christianity and Liberal Humanism, it may also be reasonable to interpret the whole response to this section as a desire for a move towards a more *idealistic* socialism. On this reasoning there is a desire here, not for orthodoxy—whether Christian, Marxist or Social Democratic—but for the reassertion of a *socialist humanism,* bringing together the idealistic impulses, rather than the overall analytic structures, of these ideologies: significantly, the support was for ideals and ideas embodied in these ideologies and not for the institutions which claim to represent them in organisational form. This whole ideological orientation and its implications is a major theme and will be returned to later.

There are two final points on this general response résumé of the various constituent elements in the Movement. Women supporters were consistent in their relatively apolitical perspectives: they more often had a more neutral view and indeed significantly favoured the apolitical more than did the males. It is also very important to note that working-class respondents—except for a tendency to be more in favour of or neutral towards the social democratic perspective—were not statistically differentiated from the middle-class respondents. It would thus appear that the working-class section of the Movement did not constitute a separate group with its own perceptions and objectives. The dominant ethos of the Movement—an amalgam of various types of middle-class radicalism—encompassed the minority, working-class elements too. This is not to say, of course, that all those in the trade unions who gave their backing in 1959, 1960 and 1961 to the policies of unilateralism were identical in orientation to the activists of the CND Movement. On the contrary, it seems reasonable to assume that the unilateralist trade unionists' extreme reluctance to become involved with or give any support to CND *per se* (let alone the more radical disarmament groups) is explicable in large part in terms of the fundamental antipathy between the middle-class radical ethos of CND and the conventional machine politics of Labourism which characterised the trade unions, then as now.

RESPONDENTS' OBJECTIONS TO NUCLEAR WEAPONS

Asked about their major reasons for objecting to nuclear weapons, the respondents answered as follows: moral-religious reasons, 39%; political reasons, 13%; and equally moral and political, 48%.

The respondents' reasons for the renunciation of the Bomb were sought in an open-ended question. While the major reasons given combined the moral, the political and the moral/political criteria there were also other important motivating factors in Movement support: a straightforward fear of attack and fear of the consequences of nuclear tests and proliferation, and a concern about the dangers of over-dependency upon the USA. (The latter two reasons found particularly strong support amongst the 'youth group'.) For full details see Table B, Appendix II.

CND ACHIEVEMENTS

Based again on an 'open-ended' question the respondents' views on CND's achievements were sought (full results are presented in Table C, Appendix II). A quarter of all the sample believed that the Movement had achieved some of its major objectives. The responses fell into four broad areas: on the nuclear issue itself (predominantly moral); on the raising of public awareness and radicalisation (predominantly political); on the Movement as a prototype for later protest movements (e.g. anti-Vietnam war organisations); and finally on the impact of the Movement experience itself (e.g. realisation of the political power of ordinary people, and the camaraderie engendered by the Movement). That 25% believed that CND achieved much, was perhaps to be expected, as was the higher proportion of the former 'youth group' who believed that CND 'radicalised' people. The fact that almost a third of the adult members believed more strongly that CND achieved its goals reflected, in part, the natural tendency of those who have been involved in a movement for a long period, and have invested considerable political, personal and emotional capital in working for it. Whatever the realities of the achievements and failures of the Movement there is a likelihood that the activists will have a more sanguine view of the Movement's success than more 'detached' observers!

THE MOVEMENT'S FAILURES

Various opinions have been offered over the years to account for what has been seen as the Movement's failure. In order to analyse Movement activists' perceptions a set of fifteen statements was devised and respondents were asked to express their level of agreement on a five-point scale. Only five gained a majority agreement, with four views being repudiated by most of the sample. There was general agreement concerning the difficulties of maintaining the momentum of a mass movement, and the apparent psychological barrier of reaching out to the non-committed, while external events and the gap between apparent aspiration and achievement compounded the sense of failure. The rejected statements seemed to reflect the marchers' knowledge of their own good will and optimism, and the value they placed in democratic persuasion. They *dis*agreed strongly with the contentions that the Movement was inherently unpatriotic, or that such movements were bound to fail, or that the Movement had been taken over by subversives or extremists.

Table 4 shows the results and the variations that occurred between the youth, adult and women's groups' perceptions.

The differences of opinion between the former 'youth' and 'adult' groups reflected

TABLE 4

I believe that the Disarmament Movement failed in its major objectives between
1958 and 1965 because:

Reasons for failure	Total Sample			
(N = 403) ('Youth' vs. 'adult' groups (N = 206, N = 197)	Strongly Agree and Agree (%)	Neutral (%)	Strongly Disagree and Disagree (%)	x^2 (with 4d/f) and P value
1. CND failed to devote sufficient attention to winning over the Labour Party to its policy	35	24	42	
2. The CND leadership was out of touch with the radicalism of the rank and file	30[y]	25	45	23.39 $P=<0.001$
3. The leadership concentrated too heavily on winning the Labour Party's support	25	26	49	n.s.
4. It failed to win the support of ordinary people	69[y]	11	20	9.71 $P=<0.05$
5. The Movement was split by the creation of the Committee of 100 in 1960 and its subsequent activities	35	24	40[y]	19.51 $P=<0.001$
6. The Movement was increasingly taken over by political extremists	25	21	53[y]	12.17 $P=<0.02$
7. The single issue of unilateral nuclear disarmament could not for long unite so many conflicting groups	58	16	26	n.s.
8. The Left failed to convince the Movement that the achievement of socialism was indissolubly linked to the specific issue of nuclear disarmament	42	28	30	n.s.
9. The Movement became too political	16	21	63[y]	16.36 $P=<0.01$
10. The Movement ceased to be a centrally moral campaign	36	24	40	n.s.
11. CND's campaign declined naturally as a result of changes in circumstances external to the Movement (e.g. relaxation of world tension 'post-Cuba'; the Partial Test Ban Treaty; the changes in the Labour Party's defence policy)	84	7	9	n.s.
12. It became obvious that the policy of CND was ultimately unpatriotic	7	8	85	n.s.
13. Gradually, "we have learned to live with the Bomb"	66	14	20	n.s.
14. The Movement failed to develop sufficient international momentum	55	26	19	n.s.
15. All social and political movements of this kind are doomed to failure from the outset	13	14	73	n.s.

[y] indicates a significantly higher frequency from the 'youth' group than the 'adult' group.

the tensions in the Movement: the 'youth group' expressing impatience with the leadership, a feeling that there was a lack of understanding as to why the ordinary people did not join, and denying more strongly that the Movement was in any way taken over by extremists or became too political.

Other 'reasons for failure' were spontaneously mentioned by the respondents and offer additional views on what is obviously a complex issue. Three other features emerged: the sense of distress following apparent public apathy; the hostility of the media, the government and the 'establishment'; and the damage done to the image of the Movement because of its association, in the public mind, with a bohemian lifestyle (drugs, sexual permissiveness, etc.).

(In Table D of Appendix II the spontaneously offered reasons for the Movement's failure are given.)

To gain some overall understanding of respondents' views, the answers to the set questions were factor-analysed to identify the main themes.

The first, and most important, factor was the notion that the Movement's failure was attributable both to the public perception of the Movement as being 'extremist' and 'subversive', *and* to the belief that, to a greater or lesser extent, the Movement was in reality too much influenced by those with 'extreme' political views (e.g. categories such as the campaign's being "increasingly taken over by political extremists", and being "split by the creation of the Committee of 100 in 1960 and its subsequent activities", etc.). This factor accounted for 39% of the variance.

The second and third factors posed the opposite point of view: that the Movement failed because it was not political enough! (Examples of the constituent categories concerned being that "the CND leadership was out of touch with the radicalism of the rank and file", that "CND failed to devote sufficient attention to winning over the Labour Party to its policy", etc.)

Thus the main factors illustrated one of the central tensions in the Movement: there were, on the one hand, those who saw CND as a single-issue campaign which should have no general political overtones or loyalties, and, on the other, those who saw the objectives and the tactics of the campaign as essentially political and who were thus concerned with the political struggle in one form or another. In other words, the factor analysis confirmed the basic division of perception between those in the Movement who had a predominantly *moral* view and those whose orientation was predominantly *political*.

Just what effect and influence their involvement in the Movement has had upon the marchers is difficult to determine: however, only 7% of the whole sample said that it had had no influence upon their subsequent attitudes. Equally, many stated that their political interest had increased over the 20 years (23%) or stayed the same (23%): though 41% felt that their political *activity* had decreased or was much reduced.

There is little doubt that their experience in the Movement had a deep and lasting influence on Movement activists. Over 20% of our respondents were involved in one or more of the Anti-Vietnam War organisations and in 1978, 43% were active in Community Politics, 57% in Single-issue Campaigns, 37% in Environmentalist groups and 14% in Women's Liberation. As three-quarters of all respondents said that CND had strongly or very strongly influenced their attitudes it would seem that, for many, their disarmament movement experience started them on a lifelong concern and activity with many social and political issues and had a lasting impact on their perspectives.

Perspectives in the Movement

THE POLITICAL PROTESTERS

We have seen that while over a third of our respondents were apolitical, the other two-thirds had some distinct political affiliation—in effect, along the Left continuum, unless the apolitical are conceived of as belonging to the Right. However that may be, it seems logical to explore views amongst those who have a political perspective, especially from the Liberal and Marxist Left.[18]

It will be remembered that the 1958/65 Liberal Left contained respondents who belonged to the Labour and Liberal Parties, the Young Liberals, the Young Socialists and the Fabian Society. These were juxtaposed with the Marxist Left, consisting of those belonging to the Communist Party, the Young Communist League, International Socialism, the Socialist Labour League, the New Left Clubs, and Solidarity. The Anarchists were classified on their own. Of course in both major Left groups there were important variations of emphasis but the main division, we would argue, was (and is) primarily along the Marxist/Non-Marxist division (although it is important to note the ambivalent, and somewhat conservative, role and stance of the Communist Party in this context. This is discussed below, in Part III.)

Liberal Left versus Marxist Left. There were 166 respondents who belonged to the Liberal Left compared with 71 on the Marxist Left. The only socio-economic variable of note was that the Marxists contained a higher proportion of under-25s in the 1958-65 period; also, as would be expected, fewer Marxists had a religious belief (21% of Marxists against 42% of Liberal Left) and fewer were Absolute Pacifists (17% to 39%). By 1978 the Liberal Left was supported by 162 (40%) of respondents and the Marxist Left was reduced to 51, that is 12% of all respondents. Within the present Liberal Left group 20 (13%) had originally belonged to a Marxist party, while of the remaining 1978 Marxists, 43 of the 51 survivors were of the original Marxist Left. Thus it would seem that, although there was some drift between the two groups, neither Marxists nor the Liberal Left were very successful in 'attracting converts'. More striking than this, of the original 1958/65 groups, 16% of the Marxists and 21% of the Liberal Left are now (in 1978) non-political! Thus, not only would it seem that the Left failed to win over the majority of the Movement's activists to the Left perspective over the intervening 20 years, it also appears that a substantial section of the Left (particularly those originally in the Marxist Left) has become disillusioned about politics altogether.

Over the 20 years the voting behaviour of the two Left groups has been along lines that would be expected; the Marxist Left has, when possible, more often voted for Communists or other Marxist candidates, while in 1959 and 1964 Marxists, in comparison with the Liberal Left, more frequently did-not-vote (or in 1978, would-not-vote). However, an important and highly significant difference was that 40% of the Marxists placed their political commitment before their allegiance to the Movement—compared with only 17% of the Liberal Left. Interestingly, the same proportion of commitment was found in the 1978 Left groupings.

SYSTEMS OF BELIEF

Table 5 shows the adherence of both Liberal Left and Marxist Left to different ideological perspectives.

TABLE 5
Belief Systems—Liberal vs. Marxist Left 1958/65
(N = 166, N = 71)

	Strongly Agree and Agree %		Neutral %		Disagree and Strongly Disagree %	
	Lib. Left	Marx. Left	Lib. Left	Marx. Left	Lib. Left	Marx. Left
Christian $x^2 = 19.69$ 4d/f $P = <0.001$	49	20	21	23	30	57
Marxist $x^2 = 41.17$ 4d/f $P = <0.0001$	43	68	31	20	26	11
Social Democratic $x^2 = 20.38$ 4d/f $P = <0.001$	60	49	26	12	14	39
Conservative $x^2 = 11.78$ 3d/f $P = <0.01$	3	0	18	6	80	94
Liberal Humanist $x^2 = 5.67$ 4d/f n.s.	39	36	38	31	23	32
Apolitical $x^2 = 10.32$ 4d/f $P = <0.04$	6	2	24	16	70	82
Libertarian Anarchist $x^2 = 4.74$ 4d/f n.s.	20	32	21	22	59	46

It is apparent from the results that those on the Marxist Left were much more *decisively* for or against the various ideological perspectives: they were more strongly opposed to Conservatism, to an apolitical stance and to Christianity, though less opposed to Libertarian-Anarchist views, than the Liberal Left. Nevertheless the Marxists were not as inflexible in their attitudes as is perhaps the common perception: most of the perspectives attracted some degree of support from the Marxist Left. The Liberal Left, as would be expected, had a considerably wider degree of sympathy with all the perspectives—excepting both the apolitical and the Conservative, which both they and the Marxists rejected heavily.

This ideological eclecticism[19] certainly helped to bring together the disparate groups in the Disarmament Movement coalition: their willingness to have some respect for, and sympathy with, other viewpoints was a very positive advantage. Moreover, as we have seen earlier, most of the activists (though not the Marxists) regarded the single issue and their allegiance to the Movement as being of more importance than their political/ideological adherence. On the other hand, this very eclecticism, and the surprisingly high rate of dual or treble ideological allegiance, signified to the extent of ideological uncertainty, confusion and lack of direction.

THE MOVEMENT'S ACHIEVEMENTS AND REASONS FOR FAILURE

The Left groups did not differ greatly in their estimation of the Movement's achievements, about a quarter of both groups believing that the Movement achieved at least some of its major objectives.

The inherent difference of approach emerged in the groups' analysis of why the Movement failed. The Marxists were much firmer in their affirmation of the *political* causes of the Movement's failure than was the Liberal Left, and were much more opposed to any suggestion that the Left of the Movement was in any way to blame for the Movement's decline and disintegration. Fifty-seven per cent of Marxists as against 30% of Liberal Lefts disagreed that the Movement had been damaged by the creation of the Committee of 100; 69% to 48% disagreed that CND had been "taken over by extremists", and 81% to 65% denied that the "Movement became too political". These tendencies were even more emphatic when the 1978 Marxist/Liberal Left groups were examined, thus demonstrating the underlying consistency of these political perspectives.

The Movement greatly influenced both groups' attitudes in subsequent years, only 4% saying that the campaign had had no influence upon them. Political interest and activity was proportionately similar: almost half of both groups have lessened their political activity though a third stated that their political activity had increased.

Of the various activities in which our respondents were subsequently concerned, the Anti-Vietnam war organisations (a section is devoted to this link, see pp. 46-50) included 35% of the Marxists and 20% of the Liberal Lefts. Although this was a significant difference, there was, however, little variation in other activities: in Single-issue Campaigns, 58% cf. 54%; in Community Politics 52% cf. 45%; in Women's Liberation 17% cf. 9%; and in Environmentalist groups 27% cf. 39%. What is noticeable is that *both* politically oriented groups were more active in these areas than those respondents who had no political allegiance.

THE ANARCHISTS

It is important to compare these two socialist-oriented groups with the other major political grouping in the Movement—the Anarchists. In many ways the life-style and culture which the Movement came to symbolise found its most accurate and coherent political and ideological representation in the Libertarian-Anarchist perspective. Yet only 7% (29) of our respondents described themselves as Anarchists. However, it must be remembered that over a quarter of the Left groups had some sympathy with the Libertarian-Anarchist perspective—even if it could be better described as a romantic attachment rather than a coherently thought-out belief. The Anarchists were younger than the Liberal Left and were proportionately more involved in the Direct Action Committee (41% of the Anarchists), Committee of 100 (97%) and, another significant variation, the Peace Pledge Union (44%).

Predictably, the Anarchists more frequently declared either that they did-not or would-not vote (or gave electoral support to 'fringe' groups). However, this did not mean that Anarchists eschewed all involvements with Left groups: nearly 30% of the Anarchists in our sample were involved with the Labour Party and the Young Socialists; 27% of the Anarchists were linked to Marxist groups and 17% were members of the New Left Clubs.

The only other interesting points of difference between the socialist groups and the Anarchists were that proportionately more Anarchists (62%) than Socialists were Absolute Pacifists—and, in some ways more surprising given their wide involvement with a range of Left groups, the Anarchists were the most strongly anti-Marxist of all the 'political' groups.

How can we describe the Anarchists in our study? It would seem that if we consider the results we obtained, the Anarchists were even more 'active' than the Socialists and had a distinctive 'direct democracy' quality in their concentration upon the need to reach the general supporter and the 'man-in-the-street'. They were a small section but wielded an influence out of all proportion to their size: in part because of their activism and in part because of the dramatic nature of their involvement, and the links between their ideology and the tactics and techniques of civil disobedience. The Anarchist ideology and tradition is distinctive and should never be seen exclusively in relation to Marxist (or other varieties of) Socialism. This applied with particular force in the context of the Disarmament Movement.

Interestingly, 21% of the original Anarchists of 1958/65 now declare themselves to be wholly non-political. This perhaps indicates not only that attachment to Anarchism is often a passing phase of political adolescence, but also that Anarchism (at least in the context of contemporary Britain) more often entails an attitude of mind rather than an allegiance to a political 'organisation'.

The Moral Protesters

For the majority of the Movement, however, political considerations — whether in the context of Marxism, Anarchism or the more conventional Liberal Left perspective — were not the main motivating force. One of the great original strengths of CND was that it cut across political, religious and age barriers (but not perhaps class ones . . .[20]) because its central message was clear, simple, urgent and couched in straightforwardly *moral terms*. This group of moral protesters is more amorphous and thus more difficult to subdivide and analyse than the 'political' group. Nevertheless there appear to be some clear divisions: we shall discuss here those respondents who classified themselves as Absolute Pacifists, those who professed a Christian religious affiliation, and those who had no political affiliations. (These groups obviously overlapped considerably but, by looking at the total for each group in turn, we shall be able to analyse their distinctive approaches.)

THE PACIFISTS

Forty-six per cent (186) of the sample described themselves as Absolute Pacifists. In comparison with the rest of the Movement, they were significantly more often older (the majority now being over 56), had a higher proportion of women, and had a greater number who had supported CND from the outset. They more often had a Christian religious belief (59%): a significant proportion belonged to the Quakers, and 45% were non-political. Interestingly, of those other organisations associated with CND (i.e. Committee of 100, etc.), only in relation to the Peace Pledge Union did either the Pacifists or the Non-political respondents differ from the rest of the marchers — yet again a finding that suggests that despite the many inherent variations within the Movement, the experience of common involvement created a relative structural cohesion that minimised, at least for a time, the apparently incompatible ideological differences.

PACIFISTS AND POLITICS

Pacifists were to be found amongst all the political groupings: 39% of the Liberal Left described themselves as Pacifists, as against 17% of the Marxists, and 65% of the Anarchists.

Not surprisingly the vast majority of the 186 Absolute Pacifists placed the Disarmament Movement before any political interest. However, in terms of voting behaviour the Pacifists in the 1959 and 1964 elections were indistinguishable from the Non-pacifists and it was not until 1978 that significant differences emerged; in 1978 the Pacifists were more inclined than the rest of the sample either not to vote or to support the Liberal Party.

The Pacifists were against the Bomb *primarily* on moral-religious grounds: only 6% of Pacifists placed major importance on political reasons. Amongst the various other reasons for being anti-Bomb, the Pacifists were especially strong on the "sense of moral outrage in response to Hiroshima and Nagasaki" and less concerned with ideas about nuclear weapons being a "futile strategy".

These responses would seem to indicate clearly that Pacifists did not, on the whole, see the Movement in political terms, and were not generally involved for reasons relating to the specific dangers facing the UK (because of her possession of nuclear weapons, US bases and so on), but were motivated by a general belief in the moral basis of the nuclear disarmament case which was unrelated to specific self-interest and self-preservation.

SYSTEMS OF BELIEF

Apart from their commitment to Pacifism itself, what did the Pacifists believe in? We know that there was a large measure of Christian ethical influence but, as this study demonstrates in numerous contexts, almost all the ideological groupings in the Movement expressed a high degree of sympathy, and in some cases agreement, with the principles of those who would normally be thought of as their political and ideological opponents.

Table 6 shows that the Pacifists were no exception to this pattern. We have also included a comparison of Pacifists and Non-politicals within Table 6 as this demonstrates clearly the very close comparability of the two groups. The similarities between the two groups are quite striking—particularly when it is borne in mind that 35% of the Non-politicals were not Absolute Pacifists. Interestingly, 27% of the original Non-political group had, by 1978, moved to political activism within the Liberal Left ambit, thus translating their attachment to Liberal Humanism into action.

Of the Pacifists, half expressed agreement with the Christian perspective whilst a quarter disagreed. Almost half the Pacifists were in agreement with the Liberal Humanist and social democratic ideologies, with 20% disagreeing. Surprisingly high proportions of Pacifists expressed agreement with Marxism and Libertarian-Anarchism—36% and 26% respectively, thus indicating perhaps the strength of political radicalism within pacifist circles in the Movement. Thus yet again the theme of coalition emerged with major variations of perspective *within* ideological groupings consequently making possible the cooperation of seemingly disparate groups of activists.

TABLE 6

Belief Systems—Absolute Pacifists (N = 186) vs. Non-pacifists (N = 217) and a Comparison of Non-politicals (NP) (N = 126) with Pacifists

	Strongly Agree and Agree		Neutral		Disagree and Strongly Disagree	
	Pac. (%)	Non-pac. (%)	Pac. (%)	Non-pac. (%)	Pac. (%)	Non-pac. (%)
Christian $x^2 = 20.53$ 4d/f $P = <0.001$	52* (NP = 53)	36	24	21	25	44
Conservative $x^2 = 4.23$ 3d/f n.s.	3	3	17	10	79 (NP = 82)	86
Social Democratic $x^2 = 16.71$ 4d/f $P = <0.003$	49 (NP = 48)	54	36*	20	14**	26
Liberal Humanist $x^2 = 2.26$ 4d/f n.s.	46 (NP = 62**)	45	35	31	18	24
Marxist $x^2 = 17.89$ 4d/f $P = <0.002$	36** (NP = 37)	51	34	21	30	28
Libertarian Anarchist $x^2 = 9.87$ 4d/f $P = <0.05$	26 (NP = 25)	29	25	15	49	56
Apolitical $x^2 = 27.48$ 4d/f $P = <0.001$	10 (NP = 16)	7	32*	16	58** (NP = 61)	78

* = Pacifists score proportionately higher.
** = Pacifists score proportionately lower.
NP = Non-politicals.

THE MOVEMENT'S ACHIEVEMENTS AND REASONS FOR FAILURE

The Pacifists' relatively weak emphasis on structural and political analysis was demonstrated in their views of the Movement's achievements and the reasons they gave for its failure. On the one hand, they were much more optimistic than the rest of the sample that the Campaign had achieved some of its aims (particularly "alerting the general public to the nuclear issues"), whilst on the other, they appeared indifferent to the suggestion that the Movement needed an adequate political outlet other than the Labour Party. Similarly, they put relatively little stress upon the need to win over the Labour Party, while they were completely divided about just how much the Committee of 100 had helped or hindered the campaign. This mirrors earlier observations about the Pacifists' orientations: their activism was largely moral in impetus and they were uninterested in Labour Movement politics. It is difficult, though, to explain how these results match up to the Pacifists' 36% agreement with Marxism: perhaps, as Michael Randle has argued, whilst the *radical* pacifists were wholly opposed to Stalinist Communism (as they were to Labour 'machine politics'), they were attracted to the idealistic, humanistic aspects of Marxism (especially in the manner in which these found expression in the New Left).

SUBSEQUENT ACTIVITIES

Pacifists were, as might be expected given the socialist/communist orientation of both anti-Vietnam war organisations in the UK, less active in these movements than were most of our respondents (this is particularly true of the Vietnam Solidarity Campaign (VSC)). However, by 1978, for whatever reasons, the pacifist respondents had renewed their enthusiasm for socio-moral issues and were even more active than most in other causes, such as the various Single-issue Campaigns (66% cf. 50%), with over 40% being active in Community Politics and in the Environmentalist groups.

By 1978 the Pacifists' levels of political interest and activity had followed the same pattern as the rest of the sample (i.e. political *interest* had increased for 44% of Pacifists, whilst political *activity* had decreased for an approximately similar proportion).

For many Pacifists, the Disarmament Movement experience was uplifting and liberating and appeared to offer real hope of gaining general acceptance for their views. Their feelings towards the Movement were very positive though a small but significant proportion of them (9%) felt that the Movement had in no way influenced them. This would seem to reflect the position of the older, traditional, long-term committed member of the Pacifist Movement, who always regarded CND as less than pure because it was not fully pacifist in its policy. The majority of Pacifists, however, both gave a lot to the Movement and gained a lot from their involvement. For the majority, the Movement marked a watershed between the old, individualistic pacifism of the Peace Pledge Union (PPU) and the new pacifism of the nuclear age—far more politically involved, heavily influenced by radical Gandhian ideas and by the experience of Civil Rights campaigners in the USA. For these Pacifists, radical political ideologies were highly relevant—but were re-interpreted within what they were agreed was the overridingly important context of the age: the nuclear arms race.

THE CHRISTIAN BELIEVERS

The remaining element amongst the primarily moral protesters was those who had a Christian religious faith; 167 (41%) of the sample in 1958/65 had such a belief. By 1978 only 110 (27%) of the original believers retained their faith; but this was not all net loss as some who had previously been 'non-believers' had become Christians. Taking all this into account, 32% of the sample were, in 1978, in agreement with Christian belief. In many areas they were, as might have been expected, in agreement with the Pacifists. There were, however, some disagreements—most particularly in the area of political affiliation.

Religious beliefs and political attitudes. Of the Liberal Left, nearly half (42%) had a religious faith whilst amongst the Marxist Left the figure was as high as 21%. Thus over half of the Christian believers had a specific and major political affiliation. Nevertheless, only 13% of them, similar to the general sample, placed their political allegiance before that to the Movement (whether such people should be considered mainly amongst the 'politicals' is an open question, though obviously the two perspectives are not mutually exclusive).

It was the Christian believers who, over the 20-year period, were the most loyal politically, especially to the Liberal Left. There was an actual increase in their intention to vote Labour as well as a significantly improving Liberal Party support over the period. This position was emphasised when the Christian believers' responses to the 'systems of belief' were analysed: 60% supported the Social Democratic position, 43% the Liberal Humanist view, and a surprisingly high 38% expressed sympathy for Marxism. (Despite a 20% Christian believer agreement with Libertarian-Anarchism, 52% were opposed to this view.) However, what is especially important is not that the Christian believers appeared relatively strong on the Liberal Left but that they were 'political' at all, albeit in a secondary sense.

The Christian believers' ideas about the achievements and failures of the Movement differed very little from the rest of the sample: as might have been expected they placed greater emphasis on the explanation for the failure of the campaign on the fact that the "Movement ceased to be a centrally moral campaign"; a significant number also mentioned their belief that the Movement lost the "support of the moderates".

The Christian believers' 'activity' over the 20-year period appears to have been as constant as those 'non-believers' who are characteristically active in so many 'causes'. (A fifth of the believers were involved in the Anti-Vietnam War Movement, a third in Environmentalist groups and two-thirds in Community Politics.)

The Christian believers' remarkable consistency was again emphasised by the fact that, of all the groups, their level of political interest and activity had changed the least over the 20 years; only a third of the Christian believers recorded a decline in political activity over the 20-year period. By 1978, however, the group showed an even stronger tendency towards political moderation.

That the Movement influenced their subsequent attitudes cannot be doubted, three-quarters saying they were strongly or very strongly influenced by the experience. Their influence upon the Movement, not least at leadership level, was profound, whether for better or for worse is a matter of debate. Middle class, respectable, committed, constant, centrist, the Christian believers at the head of the Movement were a counterweight to those of a strongly structural and political persuasion, and were an extremely important influence on the policies, attitudes, and 'image' of CND (though perhaps rather less so in relation to other Movement organisations).

THE EXTRA-PARLIAMENTARY GROUPS

So far we have examined those respondents who, despite their varied perspectives, were generally agreed that any political initiative emerging from the Movement would have to be, ought to be, channelled through the existing, conventional Parliamentary political system. (This 'Parliamentarism' applies neither to the Anarchists nor to some sections of the Marxist Left, however.) The importance of Direct Action politics within the Movement can hardly be overemphasised, however. In the context of Movement politics itself the fundamental cause of friction appeared to the participants to be along the Parliamentarist/Direct Action division. The decision on whether to 'march with Collins or sit with Russell' assumed an almost theological importance in some circles within the Movement, and the dispute came to symbolise far more fundamental tensions over objectives and ideological perspectives than were inherent in the actual tactical issue of civil disobedience itself. In the wider political context the Direct Action politics of the Direct Action Committee Against Nuclear War (DAC), and later the Committee of 100, had a profound effect on subsequent political activity and attitudes. It is thus in this area that the Movement can justifiably claim to be a watershed in the development of a 'new politics', and it is to the analysis of DAC and Committee of 100 perspectives that we now turn.

THE DAC

In our study 29% (118) respondents had been supporters of the DAC. Naturally, DAC supporters were significantly more active in the Committee of 100 than were the rest of the sample (77% cf. 41%): and of those backing INDEC, half were DAC supporters, thus demonstrating that, whilst they were not wholly opposed to electoral politics (as the pure Anarchist must be) they were for the most part not committed to Labour Movement or Socialist politics.

DAC politics, beliefs, and activity. Politically the DAC was significantly different from other extra-parliamentary groups: it appeared to eschew political parties more than any other group (save the Non-politicals) — only 27% of DAC belonging to the Liberal Left and 20% to the Marxist Left. There was, however, a discernible 'Anarchist' flavour with 10% of DAC supporters having Anarchist commitments although, in 1958/65, a larger number (over one-third) was non-political; 13% were members of the New Left Clubs. Over the years, ex-DAC people have moved even further away from politics, nearly a half stating that their political activity has decreased, while some have moved to other minority political parties and some to the Liberals. DAC members shared a mixed moral and political objection to nuclear weapons. Their 'belief systems' were numerous and eclectic — their unity coming from their strong, some might say almost obsessive, commitment to the nuclear issue as the central reference point. Thus there was a wide range of sympathy from DAC supporters for most of the ideological perspectives listed (excepting Conservatism). Only in their greater support for Liberal Humanism and Libertarian-Anarchism were the DAC supporters more committed to particular perspectives, and even here the level was not dramatically higher. Their opposition to Marxism was, however, quite marked (45% cf. 27% of the rest of the sample). This again highlights the nature of DAC's radicalism; although committed to radical methods of protest, and although opposed to the existing form of society, opposition was centred on the concept of the need for the *violent* society to be changed to the *peaceful* society. The central concerns of socialism were not, for most DAC supporters, of particular interest or relevance, and the *practice* of Soviet communism with its militaristic and nuclear weapons policies was enough to convince them that the conventional Left was not the vehicle for accomplishing the social changes they sought.[21]

DAC supporters were slightly less involved in the Anti-Vietnam War Movement than the rest of the sample, perhaps because the nuclear and peace issue was not central, and had been replaced by the more traditional socialist/capitalist antagonism. DAC supporters were, however, well represented in subsequent activities in Community Politics, Single-issue Campaigns, and particularly in the Environmentalist groups.

Their views concerning the Movement's success and failure were similar in most respects to the general sample although they strongly repudiated the suggestion that the Campaign had been "split by the creation of the Committee of 100 in 1960 and its subsequent activities". However, a factor analysis of these results emphasised the DAC's orientation towards populist politics, by-passing the established institutions of the political system (parties *and* Parliament) and going straight to the people.

On a similar theme, the DAC was the only sub-group to have reduced its *interest* as well as its activity in politics. The commitment was, and perhaps remains, to hard-line, radical pacifism which rejected 'conventional politics' and has found expression in activities since 1958/65, more in social and single-issue campaigns than in Left politics. What is beyond doubt is that the DAC activists formed the core of the highly distinctive radical wing of the Movement which, after 1960, found its expression in the Committee of 100.

THE COMMITTEE OF 100

The Committee of 100 brought together those various radical groupings within the Movement that were hostile to the tactics, strategy, objectives and policies of the CND leadership. The immediate issue of dispute may have been civil disobedience and illegality but more fundamental ideological issues underlay the conflict.[22] The Committee of 100 was a disparate coalition, united only in its belief in the primacy of the nuclear issue, its conviction that civil disobedience was the correct method, and its deep antipathy towards the CND leadership. The DAC may have formed the core of the Committee of 100 but the new organisation also attracted, albeit briefly, many other groupings. The complex of objectives — ranging from publicity for the cause to quasi-anarchist revolution — arose from this disparate structure.

Over half of the respondents (206) were supporters of the Committee of 100. An immediately striking feature is that almost two-thirds of them were, in 1978, still aged 45 or less, thus illustrating the relative youthfulness of the Committee of 100. Nearly a third of these Committee of 100 respondents were, in 1958/65, non-political. The political complexion of the Committee of 100 can be seen from the fact that 43% of the Liberal Left in our sample were Committee of 100 supporters (surprisingly high in view of the Labour Party's antagonism) and nearly two-thirds of the Marxist activists also supported the Committee. Moreover, of the admittedly fairly small number of Anarchist respondents, virtually all were Committee of 100 supporters; 13% of the Committee of 100 respondents were members of the New Left Clubs. The 'Left' orientation of the Committee of 100 was thus much more marked than was the case with the DAC.

By 1978 there had been a significant drop in political activity among our Committee of 100 respondents: about half of the group had decreased their political activity — on the other hand, almost half had increased their *range* of political behaviour. Their cynicism and/or lack of interest in conventional politics was clearly demonstrated by the fact that, of all the groups, the Committee of 100 scored higher in the 'would-not-vote' and 'did-not-vote' categories. The current political energies of the Committee of 100 supporters appear to have been channelled into minority political parties.

The Committee of 100's objections to nuclear weapons were similar to those of the general sample. However, nearly one-fifth of the Committee of 100 respondents spontaneously commented that they feared dependency upon the USA and its possible international repercussions: and 10% commented that, for them, the Movement was part of a "general protest against an unjust society".

The beliefs of the Committee of 100 again appear to reflect the coalition aspect that the Committee itself comprised, a third having sympathy for Christianity, while 42% disagreed; the Social Democratic and Marxist positions both attracted majority support, whilst they were rejected by a quarter in both cases. Most noteworthy of all was the Committee of 100's agreement with the Libertarian-Anarchist perspective. Table 7 gives the detailed results.

TABLE 7

Belief Systems

Committee of 100 (N = 206) vs. Non-Committee of 100 (N = 197)

	Strongly Agree and Agree		Neutral		Disagree and Strongly Disagree	
	C. 100 (%)	Non-C. (%)	C. 100 (%)	Non-C. (%)	C. 100 (%)	Non-C. (%)
Christian $x^2 = 12.03$ 4d/f $P = <0.02$	35	51	22	22	42	27
Marxist $x^2 = 15.31$ 4d/f $P = <0.01$	52	35	22	32	26	33
Social Democratic $x^2 = 5.96$ 4d/f n.s.	52	52	23	32	24	16
Conservative $x^2 = 8.74$ 3d/f $P = <0.04$	3	4	10	18	88	78
Liberal Humanist $x^2 = 2.16$ 4d/f n.s.	45	47	35	31	20	21
Apolitical $x^2 = 6.23$ 4d/f n.s.	7	9	25	22	68	69
Libertarian-Anarchist $x^2 = 56.60$ 4d/f $P = <0.001$	41	13	18	22	41	65

The Committee of 100 respondents were enthusiastic and optimistic about the Movement's achievements. They significantly more frequently mentioned that the Movement had "demonstrated the political potential of the man-in-the-street" and had "radicalised the marchers" than did the rest of the sample. Undoubtedly there is much in this *perceived* and subjective view, and it is indicative of what the Movement experience meant to a large number of individuals, though whether this was valid in reality must remain a matter for conjecture.

In response to the 'set-questions' concerning the Movement's failure, the Committee of 100 respondents varied from their non-Committee of 100 fellows more markedly than any other of the groups: it was clear that the Committee of 100 was very much opposed to the leadership of CND and felt that the Movement's potential for radicalism was being thwarted by an over-conventional stance. These respondents not unexpectedly denied vehemently that the Committee of 100 had been responsible for splitting the Movement.

In terms of subsequent activities the Committee of 100 supporters have been significantly more active than the remainder of our respondents in Community Politics, Single-issue Campaigns and Women's Liberation. Much more surprising, however, was the relatively low level of involvement of Committee of 100 respondents in the Anti-Vietnam War Movements. As with the DAC, this may be explicable in terms of the contrast in orientation between the predominantly moral Disarmament Movement and the more socialistic Anti-Vietnam War Movement, or merely have been the result of post-campaign deflation.

There can be no doubt of the importance of the Committee of 100 in the Movement. Whether the influence of the Committee on the Movement's development was for good or ill depends upon the analysis of the nature, objectives and ideological perspectives appropriate to the Movement, and this is discussed in some detail in both Parts III and IV.

THE NEW LEFT CLUBS

The New Left—whose main organisational formation was in the New Left Clubs established throughout the country in the late 1950s and early 1960s—was a most important development, both in the specific context of the Disarmament Movement and in the more general area of post-war British politics. The significance of the New Left was, in our estimation, very profound, and the issues, objectives and dilemmas posed by the New Left for the development of a radical Left politics are central themes is Parts III and IV of this study.

Thirty-eight of the respondents (9%) were members of New Left Clubs.

As a group there were a number of significant variations in their social backgrounds, an atypical finding compared with all the other subgroups. They tended to represent a particular age group—the 20- to 30-year-olds—had a higher proportion of males, and more graduates than any other group. They were, more frequently than the rest of the sample, found to support the Committee of 100, and INDEC. The group contained fewer Pacifists and, while not at a significant level, fewer Christian believers.

Despite a high Labour Party membership (86% of all our New Left Club group were originally in the Labour Party) they were, obviously, very critical of the Party. By 1978 only 55% were active supporters or members of the Labour Party, and, as a group, they appeared to have lost interest in the nuclear issue: only one or two were still involved with CND (compared with 23% of the rest of the sample).

Examining their responses to 'systems of belief' perhaps yielded the best profile of the group: they were significantly more anti-Christian, anti-Conservative and more opposed to the apolitical perspective. (This was reinforced by the fact that both in 1958 and 1978 they had significantly fewer non-politicals amongst them, only 1% and 11% respectively.) Their attitude to the social democratic ideology was split by a particularly high 'for' and high 'against', confirming the political ambivalence which characterised the New Left: it could never make up its mind about its attitude to social democracy and the problem for Marxists of whether or not to work in and through the Labour Party.

Activities of the New Left groups of respondents after 1958/65 declined substantially. Although significant minorities of these respondents belonged to the Institute for Workers' Control and to the Fabian Society, 55% of the New Left group said that their political activity had decreased and 29% that their political *interest* had declined (cf. 12% of the rest of the sample). On the other hand, the New Left group maintained its rejection of the apolitical perspective and was slightly more active in Community Politics and minority political parties than the remainder of the sample.

The overwhelming impression by 1978, however, is of a *demoralised* group. Their former high allegiance to the Labour Party had declined dramatically after 20 years. They were split along the extremes that the campaign had "failed to win over the Labour Party", and significantly split about the Movement's "concentrating too much upon the Labour Party"; in both cases the disagreement view was the stronger, whereas they most vehemently denied that the Movement had "been split by the Committee of 100".

The New Left found that their vision of the Disarmament Movement as an embodiment of a new, democratic, socialist politics, eventually disintegrated. Unable to solve the 'problem of the Labour Party' and not finding any suitable or viable alternative vehicle for their politics, the New Left has tended to disperse—back into the Labour Party or out of politics altogether.

THE SCIENTISTS AND ENVIRONMENTALISTS

By extrapolating those respondents with scientific training in either Physics or Chemistry (scientific journals in both the UK and the USA published our letter) we obtained a group we could reasonably designate as Scientists: there were thirty-eight in all. Confidentiality prevents our naming them, but many hold important posts in universities and industry. Although a quarter of them was non-political, the majority belonged to the Liberal Left, an affiliation that continued at more or less the same level into the late 1970s. Compared with the rest of the sample they contained similar proportions of Pacifists and Christian believers, but few were supporters of the DAC and the Committee of 100. Generally, they seem to have been 'middle-of-the-roaders'— their science-based objection to nuclear weapons being shared by the rest of the Movement. Amongst the Movement supporters at any rate, the scientists were able to get their message across very effectively. Their importance to the Movement was considerable, not least in providing expert argument and information on the complex nuclear issue itself, thus in effect becoming the 'educational arm' of the Movement.

There has been both popular and academic conjecture that the present Ecology and Environmental Movement has links, or is indeed the heir to, the former CND Campaign. Over a third (148) of our respondents was active in 1978 in various areas of Environmental pressure group activity. The Environmentalists (extrapolated from those respondents who were active in 1978 in this field) were, surprisingly, significantly older as a group, compared with the rest of the sample, and were more closely affiliated to the DAC than other respondents. Not unlike the DAC, over half the current Environmentalists were Absolute Pacifists, and over a third had a Christian faith. Politically, again there were similarities with those 'tough-minded pacifists' of the DAC. There had been a growth in the 'non-political' perspective in this group from a third to two-fifths between 1958/65 and 1978. Of the 'political' respondents in this group, by far the greater number were supporters of the Liberal Left (and particularly of the Liberal Party). Support for the Marxist Left had declined from 20% to under 10% between 1958/65 and 1978.

Thus, generally, the Environmentalists might be described as active moderates with an element of anti-party politics about them. Their constellation of 'belief systems' included majority support for Christianity, Social Democracy and Liberal Humanism, with only a third expressing some sympathy for the Marxist and Libertarian-Anarchist positions. Only Conservatism and the Apolitical perspective received a majority rejection.

The Environmentalist view of the achievements of the Movement was on the optimistic side, a significantly higher proportion than the rest of the sample believing that it achieved its major objectives, but with a higher proportion believing that the Movement had been undermined by public apathy.

In terms of subsequent activities, the Environmentalists were involved to the same degree as other respondents in Community politics, but were significantly more active in Single-issue Campaigns.

There are thus strong connections between the Disarmament Movement of 1958/65 and the Environmentalist movement of the 1970s. However, although the Environmentalists might be thought to have some of the same problems — for example they are a disparate coalition struggling against both very powerful entrenched interests and public apathy — they do not have many of the *advantages* of the Disarmament Movement; there is no equivalent, single, unifying and emotively attractive issue to draw the Movement together, and there is no real potential for political access as there was with the CND and the Committee of 100. Ultimately, though, there is a strong case for arguing that the two Movements are part of the same basic struggle — for human, rational control over the high technology created by advanced industrial society.

THE ANTI-VIETNAM WAR GROUPS

On one view of the history of the British Left from 1956 to the early 1970s, the Disarmament Movement of 1958/65 was a staging post on the road to socialist awareness and maturity (whose culmination, however, is still awaited). According to this perspective, the first New Left and the CND, the DAC and the Committee of 100, represented the first, idealistic, unstructured and ill-fated moves towards the growth of an extra-parliamentary, Marxist revolutionary formation which would spearhead the advance towards socialist revolution and the transformation to a socialist society. On this view, the real contribution of the 1958/65 Movement was largely the radicalisation of a section of the middle-class intelligentsia (particularly amongst the young), and the growth of extra-parliamentary activity (marches, 'sit-downs', etc.) as a strategy of protest. Its shortcomings were seen as its lack of a developed, coherent socialist analysis, and its failure to attract working-class support. Because of these factors its potential as the basis for a new revolutionary movement was virtually non-existent. From this perspective the Anti-Vietnam War Movement was a significant step forward: here, the issue was much more centrally concerned with the ideological struggle between the 'imperialism' of the United States and the 'resistance' of the socialist National Liberation Front (NLF) (or so it was seen). Although there were undoubtedly overtones of the threat of the involvement of the 'Super Powers', in a conflict which might eventuate in the use of nuclear weapons and lead to the outbreak of World War III (and it was on this basis that CND itself justified its involvement in the Anti-Vietnam War Movement) — this theme was very much subsidiary to the overriding ideological conflict. The Anti-Vietnam War Movement thus mobilised support on a *socialist* platform and, particularly through the Vietnam Solidarity Campaign (VSC), provided the springboard from which the Marxist groups of the late 1960s and beyond grew and flourished. International Socialism, the International Marxist Group and a host of other sectarian, quasi-Trotskyist organisations emerged as relatively important political formations from the VSC and the huge demonstrations of the Anti-Vietnam War Movement.[23] After 1968 — and the rapid decline of the Anti-Vietnam War Movement — the 'serious work' of building the party in the working class began in earnest.[24] None of those involved in this process would deny the crucial importance of the Disarmament Movement of 1958/65 but they were not centrally interested in the declared objectives of the Movement so much as in its potential for building the foundations of the socialist party.

There is, however, another interpretation of the Anti-Vietnam War Movement, which, for good or ill, was more common amongst Disarmament Movement supporters. For the majority — both the non-politicals and the DAC hard-line pacifists — the central feature of the Disarmament Movement had been the nuclear issue itself. From their very different perspectives there had been agreement that the overriding need was to rid Britain, and ultimately, of course, the world, of the threat of nuclear annihilation: peace and disarmament were the objectives, and in so far as 'socialism' (or any other political perspective) had relevance it was as a *means* rather than an *end*. From this viewpoint the Anti-Vietnam War Movement was a regression to a variation on the Cold War theme. The acceptance of the use of violence, the strongly partisan stances of both the BCPV (British Campaign for Peace in Vietnam) and the VSC, and the subjugation of nuclear and peace issues to the overriding concern with socialist advance, rendered the Movement unacceptable to a large number of CND/DAC/Committee of 100 activists. The socialist analysis of the Anti-Vietnam War Movement groups, and the Marxist groupings which subsequently emerged, failed to convince the mass of the Disarmament Movement. Their activities, after 1958/65, were not, as we have seen, for the most part concerned with Far Left politics but with humanitarian issues, community politics and the like — and to some extent with the 'orthodox' Liberal Left. For many, however, the decline of the Disarmament Movement meant the effective end of political involvement: the progressive degeneration, as they saw it, of radical protest through the Anti-Vietnam War Movement and the *Annus Mirabilis* of 1968 to the Marxist groupings of the late 1960s and early 1970s, disillusioned them with politics altogether, and they ceased political activity.

The information which follows relates only to those Disarmament Movement supporters who went on to become activists in the Anti-Vietnam War Movement and should not be taken as representing a profile of the typical Vietnam protester. However, there is no doubt that there were strong links between the two Movements and that the Disarmament Movement activists provided a large part of the core of experienced protesters who were at the heart of the BCPV and the VSC.

Over 25% (122) of these Disarmament Movement supporters belonged to one or both of the major anti-Vietnam war groups, seventy-eight respondents were members of the BCPV and forty-four of the VSC. It has been suggested that the BCPV was essentially a Broad Left (i.e. Labour Left and Communist Party) movement and there is some evidence from our respondents to support this. Similarly, our information supports the contention that the VSC was composed of those more inclined to the quasi-Trotskyist, extra-parliamentary Left.

The only significant socio-economic variation for the anti-Vietnam war group (AVWG) as a whole was the age range. In 1978 almost a third was aged 35 or less, and over 40% 56 or over. This suggests that the section of the Vietnam movement that is being considered was composed predominantly of experienced, committed Left campaigners, combined with a high proportion of young activists motivated by outrage at the successive horrors of nuclear weapons and US 'aggression' in Vietnam.

In 1958/65, 38% of the subsequent AVWG were members of the Marxist Left, 37% of the Liberal Left and 24% were non-political. This suggests that, although it was the Disarmament Movement Left that moved on into the AVWG, they were probably *less* aligned to the Far Left than were the majority of the AVWG. However, no empirical study of the AVWG has yet been undertaken so this must remain pure conjecture: it may well be, for example, that the AVWG was far *less* political than we are assuming and that the majority followed the leadership—which undoubtedly was of the Marxist Left—because of the intrinsic appeal of the issue, and despite the leadership's Left political commitment.

Whatever the truth of the situation there is no doubt that the respondents who subsequently became active in the AVWG were more involved with the Marxist Left than were the rest of the sample. Table 8 shows their past and present political associations in detail.

TABLE 8
Political Affiliation of the Anti-Vietnam War Group vs. Rest
(N = 102 and N = 301) 1958/65 and 1978

	AVWG %	Rest %	x^2 with 1 d/f	P value
International Socialism (Socialist Workers' Party)				
1958-65	7	1	6.83	<0.01
1978	9	2	9.62	<0.002
Communist Party				
1958-65	15	4	11.16	<0.001
1978	18	3	23.89	<0.001
Young Communist League				
1958-65	9	3	5.72	<0.02
1978 N/A				
Non-Political				
1958-65	25	34	—	n.s
1978	12	41	27.66	<0.001
Political activity increased	45	25		
Political activity decreased	32	45	2 d/f 14.957	<0.01

The most striking feature about the AVWG's politics is that activists have gone against the general trend found amongst other Disarmament Movement supporters: they have 'hardened' their politics moving not towards a centrist position but to the Left. The BCPV respondents were associated predominantly with the Communist

Party over the 20-year period, while those Disarmament Movement supporters who were associated with the VSC were linked to the International Socialists in particular (21% cf. 0%), and also to the CP. As would be expected *no* IS members were involved with the BCPV.

Interestingly, almost a third of the AVWG placed their political loyalties higher than the anti-nuclear cause, easily the highest frequency amongst all the groups in this study. Of those organisations associated with the Disarmament Movement only with regard to the British Peace Committee did the AVWG differ; significantly more were members than the rest, 30% cf. 8% (not a surprising finding, bearing in mind the strong CP influence in the BPC). There were also significantly fewer Pacifists amongst the AVWG, indicating the move away from 'Peace and Disarmament' as central concerns, as argued earlier.

Their responses to questions concerning various belief systems, while confirming the strong Marxist, tough-minded position, nevertheless revealed not only the 'coalition' theme already noted, but also the relative split between the two Vietnam groups. The BCPV followed the more traditional line associated with the CP, whilst the VSC respondents were much more pro-Marxist, anti-Christian and relatively less opposed to the Libertarian-Anarchist position. As a whole group, however, the AVWG respondents showed their relative 'hard-line' attitudes by either rejecting or being neutral towards Liberal Humanism (only a third of the AVWG group had any sympathy for such a position compared with over half of the rest of the respondents). Moreover, their objections to nuclear weapons were significantly more 'political' and less 'morally' inspired than the rest of the respondents.

In their analysis of the Movement's achievements the AVWG supporters differed only in that they mentioned less frequently the value of the Movement's 'camaraderie' and more strongly denied the suggestion that such movements were "doomed to failure from the outset", perhaps indicating that the AVWG, whilst being less sanguine about the middle-class 'cosiness' of the Movement, was also, as a Marxist group, more conscious of its potential role in the political process. The VSC members laid greater stress than the BCPV on the Movement's influence on the subsequent growth of the AVWG, and argued that the Movement was a prototype for subsequent protest movements. Their general views about the reasons for the Movement's failure were, as would be expected, similar to those of the Marxist Left. They vehemently denied that the Movement "became too political" or that it was "taken over by extremists". Again, conforming to the pattern of the internal split in the AVWG, the BCPV respondents were more in agreement with the suggestion that "the Movement was split by the creation of the Committee of 100 in 1960 and its subsequent activities" than were the VSC.

The AVWG among the respondents was more active than the rest of the sample in Community Politics and many supporters asserted that they had been strongly influenced by their Disarmament Movement experiences. Perhaps most significantly of all, the AVWG respondents have increased not only their political interest but their political activity. (And only 5% of the AVWG, cf. 20% of the rest of the sample, reported a 'much reduced' political commitment.)

The AVWG was, of course, a successful movement whilst the Disarmament Movement was not. The success of AVWG, however, lay more in its activities in the USA, and the British groups' effect must be adjudged marginal. However, to be a part of a successful movement may well encourage activists to maintain their activism and optimism — whilst the converse certainly applies. This may explain in part why the AVWG activists have been more persistent than the rest in their political commitment. It is also true, though, that those active in the AVWG were, in their Disarmament Movement days, far more politically committed to the Marxist Left than the rest of the sample. Their activism in subsequent movements can thus be interpreted as a progressive and continuing commitment by an atypical group, rather than a direct result of their radicalisation through their AVWG involvement.

Whatever the correct analysis the fact remains that, from the point of view of the Marxist Left, the AVWG produced a higher degree of subsequent political involvement and activism than any other group.

CONCLUSION

Before moving on to assess and analyse the major themes emerging from this empirical evidence we must consider in some detail the ideological bases and the varied perspectives on the Movement of the different leadership groups. The eclecticism, the overlapping beliefs, the mutual tolerance and, above all, the commitment to the central single issue on the part of the rank-and-file activists of the Movement might be thought, on the basis of the evidence presented here, to have been sufficient to keep the Movement united. Amongst the leadership groups the tensions were that much greater, the conflicts (personal as well as ideological) that much harsher, and the different ideological perspectives that much more clearly differentiated; the result was that the fragile unity of the Movement could not be preserved for long, if indeed at all. It is to an examination of these disputes and divergences amongst the leadership groups that we now turn.

References

1. Peggy Duff (secretary of CND in its heyday, see Appendix III) dedicated her book *Left, Left, Left*, Allison & Busby, 1971, "most of all (to) the Aldermaston Marchers, whom I loved — I wonder where they're gone?"

2. Frank Parkin, *Middle-Class Radicalism: A Study of the Social Bases of the British Campaign for Nuclear Disarmament*, MUP, 1968. (A survey of Committee of 100 activists was also carried out by Nicolas and Ruth Walter via the Committee's journal *Resistance*. See *Resistance*, Vol. 3, No. 6, 15 June 1965.)

3. The 'youth group' was contacted on the Aldermaston March and was sent questionnaires later. In Parkin's estimation, the sample of 550 (of which 445 questionnaires were returned) represented approximately 10% of the March. The 'adult group' was contacted via local branch secretaries, and of the original 505 contacted, 358 returned questionnaires. Parkin, *op. cit.*, pp. 6-7.

4. i.e. Hall, J. and Jones, D. C., "Social Classification", *British Journal of Sociology*, Vol. 1, No. 1, p. 516 (1950).

5. See Appendix I on Methodology.

6. See Part I.

7. Parkin, *op. cit.*, Chap. 7, *passim*.

8. See Part III.

9. Arthur Goss in conversation with Richard Taylor, January 1978.

10. See Part III for a discussion of Pacifism.

11. The CP, in Britain as elsewhere in Europe, had been active in campaigning for 'international peace'. See, for example, the Stockholm Appeal of the early 1950s.

12. See Part I and Part III.

13. This may be held to lend weight to Young's contention that INDEC came too late — the crucial time was in 1961 following the Labour Party's rejection of unilateralism — and anyway fell between the two stools

of Labourism and Anarchism. See Nigel Young, *An Infantile Disorder? The Crisis and Decline of the New Left,* RKP, 1977, p. 74.

14. See, for example, Barry Hindess, *The Decline of Working-Class Politics,* MacGibbon & Kee, 1971.

15. See Part IV.

16. At various stages the YS were dominated by the Trotskyists of the Socialist Labour League, and, after their expulsion from the Labour Party, by the International Socialists. For the detailed history of this complex organisation in the 1960s, see Peter Shipley, *Revolutionaries in Modern Britain,* Bodley Head, 1976.

17. Of these seventy, forty-five belonged to the Labour Party or the Young Socialists, ten were Anarchists and six Communists, and there were nine others.

18. We use the term 'Liberal Left' rather than Social Democratic because the group includes a substantial minority who would not consider themselves as 'socialist' in any sense.

19. Although this measures current (1978) ideological perspectives, it may reasonably be assumed that an approximately similiar ideological eclecticism characterised the respondents' attitudes from 1958 to 1965.

20. Our findings certainly confirm Parkin's (*op. cit.*) central thesis that the Movement was, fundamentally, composed of middle-class radicals.

21. For a detailed discussion of DAC ideology, see Part III.

22. As various CND leaders have testified—see Part III. For detailed discussion of the Committee of 100, see Part III, pp. 79-83.

23. Although our findings here do *not* suggest that a great number of Movement activists went on to become Marxist converts in subsequent years. The implication of this important aspect of our study is discussed in Part IV.

24. For a good general account of this process see Peter Shipley, *op. cit.;* see also David Widgery, *The Left in Britain, 1956-1968,* Penguin Books, 1976.

PART III

Leaders, Tactics and Strategies — A Case of Lost Direction?

ALL single-issue campaigns are characterised by the diversity of the support they receive. This is both a strength and a weakness. The ability to attract support from a wide range of opinion in society is a distinct advantage. On the other hand, the wide discrepancy, and consequent conflict, between the various factions can seriously hamper the unity of such campaigns. At its worst, such disagreements can divert attention away from the common objectives and concentrate energies instead on the internal divisions. The most successful single-issue campaigns, judged in terms of how far they managed to achieve their specific objectives, have been those which combined access to those in power with a relatively homogeneous area of support.

The Disarmament Movement was not only one of the largest single-issue, extra-parliamentary movements this century, it was also one of the most diverse both in terms of its range of support and the divergent sources from which it originated. In terms of age, social background and religious and political attitudes the Movement contained a very wide variety of people. As we have seen in relation to the rank and file there were identifiable, though sometimes overlapping, ideological groupings within the Movement. These groups had very different perspectives on both the general issues of ideology and the specific policy questions of the Movement itself, and it is very important to analyse these positions to appreciate the alternatives open to the campaign. Often these 'categories' intermingled and interacted: in a movement of this size and dynamism there is necessarily a high pace of change and fluidity. But in the course of the twenty-five in-depth interviews conducted for this study with the whole range of the leadership, a number of consistent perspectives on the Movement did emerge. The following discussion thus represents what, in our view, were the main currents of thought and opinion in the Movement. In all cases it was the prior ideological attitudes combined with the experience within the Movement that moulded these perspectives: the purpose here is not to argue which, if any, of these is 'correct', but to describe and analyse how and why these differences occurred. Yet it is important to remember that despite the extent and depth of the differences, there was a considerable degree of unity. In the early years, the 'pull' of the central issue, the urgency and the enthusiasm of the campaign, blended the CND and the DAC and their constituent ideological groupings into a common endeavour.

Amongst the leadership sections there was some considerable friction — in particular the resentment, suspicion and anger felt by the DAC leadership for Canon Collins and the CND executive following the first Aldermaston March[1] — but in the Movement as a whole there was considerable tolerance and inherent ideological schisms were not initially a major impediment to action.[2] It was only later, in 1960/1, that the Movement began to polarise overtly over both strategy and objectives. It was during this crucial period that the divisions beneath the surface began to emerge; consequently the remarkable initial apparent unity of the Movement was necessarily temporary and illusory. It was at the leadership level that all the component variations in ideological perspectives first appeared and were most marked and most clearly understood and articulated. As Dick Nettleton has said: "The division was at the Centre—in London, between the few individuals at the centre of the Campaign. But everywhere else, in the regions, in the rank and file—in fact in the proper Movement—amongst the people who actually carried out the work of the Campaign—everyone worked quite harmoniously together." But this co-operation 'on the ground' became more difficult as time went on: the direction and orientation (and hence the priorities and the objectives themselves) of the Movement depended from the outset on the ideological perspectives of the various groups. In this section we outline and develop the various 'tendencies' within the Movement as characterised by the leadership figures themselves.

The Campaign as 'Moral Protest'

THE CND LEADERSHIP

From the outset of the Campaign the keynote was 'moral protest'. In their very different ways both the Direct Action Committee Against Nuclear War (DAC) and the National Council for the Abolition of Nuclear Weapons Tests (NCANWT) were essentially expressions of moral revulsion against the effects, and indeed the very concept, of nuclear weapons. The leadership of CND was principally motivated by a similarly moral credo. In Canon Collins' view: "The balance of those in the spearhead of CND was not political as such . . . but certainly the bulk of the Executive . . . were left of Toryism—but it was (based) on moral principles uncompromisingly. . . ."

In what did these 'moral principles' consist? Why did nuclear weapons arouse such strong feelings of revulsion? First of all there is the obvious difference in degree—the unimaginable increase of the destructive power that was provided by nuclear weapons made the scale, and the indiscriminate nature, of the killing quite different from previous conflict contexts. There was, it was argued, a qualitative moral change as a result of this massive quantitative increase in destructive potential. The realisation that the world might to all intents and purposes be destroyed through nuclear war led many to argue for a recasting of traditional moral categories.[3] "The mere willingness to *risk* a war that could annihilate civilisation . . . is a wickedness without parallel, a blasphemy against creation."[4]

The major thrust of the leadership's campaign was thus to publicise this moral case against nuclear warfare. Interestingly, although many of the early leaders of CND were pacifists (Collins himself, Arthur Goss, Donald Soper and others) they, unlike the DAC, were very clear that they did not want to see CND as a *pacifist* group. The CND Executive was, according to Canon Collins, very concerned from the outset "to commend nuclear disarmament to non-pacifists as well as to pacifists, to statesmen, to politicians, to military experts and civil servants as well as to idealists".[5] Their attitude to nuclear weapons was thus clearly and openly distinguished from their views on the general questions of the immorality of war. Although this was based, as we have noted, on the contention that nuclear weapons changed the moral parameters in fundamental and drastic ways, it was also the result of the tensions within the single-issue campaign: the leadership realised that if it restricted the Campaign to the traditional pacifist constituency then it would gain neither the wider public support nor the serious attention of the politically powerful. Talking of the DAC, Collins claimed that "on its own it would never have made a really big public appeal . . . (it was not) the sort of group that was likely to make any real sort of organisation in fact". The focus on moral outrage at nuclear weapons, and not on absolute pacifism, alienated the 'traditional' Pacifists of the Peace Pledge Union (PPU),[6] but it was essential for providing the basis of the Campaign's strategy. Just as full-scale pacifism would have greatly diminished the Campaign's appeal, so would a thoroughly political orientation. It was only the moral basis that could bring in the wide support, stimulate public interest and concern, appeal to the Labour Party and act as a unifying platform.[7] By keeping the focus on moral protest the leadership avoided, for a time, the clashes of perspective inherent in the Campaign. As Stuart Hall has claimed, it was not only that the leadership was motivated by moral concern, it was also that it realised that the Campaign would be "most effective if *kept* as a moral issue, if the appeal was left on the moral plane".

Of all the early leaders of the Campaign it is perhaps J. B. Priestley, and his wife Jacquetta Hawkes, who best exemplify the content and the tone of this moral approach to the issue. Indeed, it is generally agreed that it was Priestley's *New Statesman* article in November 1957[8] which provided the immediate impetus for the creation of the CND. This was written, as Jacquetta Hawkes recalled, in response to Bevan's denunciation of unilateralism at the 1957 Labour Conference: a response in the "heat of this emotion" to Bevan's desertion of the moral crusade against nuclear weapons and nuclear policies (and, for Jacquetta Hawkes the unilateralist case "was almost entirely moral"). The article set the tone of the Campaign in a unique way: its language was emotive, urgent and straightforward. It appealed to the common sense of the 'ordinary people' and was contemptuous of the "VIP - Highest - Priority - Top - Secret - Top - People Class, men now so conditioned by this atmosphere of power politics, intrigue, secrecy, insane invention, that they are more than half-barmy".[9] Combined with the populist appeal to common sense was the firm rejection of pacifism: "This (unilateralism) is not pacifism. There is no suggestion here of abandoning the immediate defence of this island."

Still less was Priestley concerned with Left politics; he explicitly accepted that Britain was, and should continue to be, allied with the Americans against Russian Communism, and, implicitly, he accepted the existing political structure. What was envisaged was rather the creation of a large, morally based, popular movement gathering strength from all sections of the community (with the exception of those Priestley described as the "few uncertified lunatics" who were in control of the military machine). To rid Britain of nuclear weapons, and thus lessen the danger of "universal catastrophe and apocalypse", required, Priestley argued, a change of policy on the one specific issue — nothing more, and nothing less. To him, and to the CND leadership as a whole, at least in the early years, it was a simple message: unilateralism was the only sane policy — to rely on the British nuclear deterrent was immoral, irrational, and suicidal. (As A. J. P. Taylor has observed: "One of the difficulties was that we were all so absolutely convinced that unilateral nuclear disarmament was sensible, morally right, wise—we simply could never make contact with our opponents, who seemed to be thinking in old-world terms.")

Closely entwined with this moral rejection of nuclear weapons was the affirmation of Britain's potential role as a world leader through moral example. Aside from the moral issue itself, the case for moral leadership through unilateral renunciation was the argument, at once radical, emotive and chauvinistic, that went farthest in unifying the Campaign. In one important sense the Campaign was the last fling of those who wanted to see Britain occupying world power status: if Britain could no longer rule by force then surely she might exert moral and cultural, and therefore, political, influence. The early leadership laid great emphasis upon Britain's unique position as the third nuclear power who could therefore make the unilateral gesture and thereby encourage multilateral disarmament whilst making Britain less likely to suffer nuclear attack as a result of having no nuclear bases. In the article already referred to, Priestley stressed this aspect of unilateralism and, combining a number of central anti-nuclear motivations—moral revulsion, fear of attack, and a pride in the British system "of parliamentary democracy"—he argued that "There is nothing unreal in the idea of a third nation, especially one like ours, old and experienced in world affairs, possessing great political traditions, to which other and smaller nations could look while the two new giants mutter and glare at each other . . . our bargaining power is slight; the force of our example might be great." There was, moreover, on the part of the majority of the leadership, a firm belief in the validity of the deterrent theory as operating between the two 'Super Powers': they did not advocate total unilateral disarmament (although this later became CND policy, against the leadership's wishes; and the DAC always argued unequivocally for total unilateralism). Thus, for example, Jacquetta Hawkes has observed: "I think we did . . . feel that unilateral disarmament by the whole West really would be disastrous." The policy was thus in many ways relatively *conservative*—and was a long way from the politics of the New Left and the (later) Committee of 100, in terms both of specifics and of general ideological overtones. The CND leadership was on the whole loyal to the Western alliance: Jacquetta Hawkes stated categorically that the leadership "very much disapproved of the idea of leaving NATO". And even those, like A. J. P. Taylor and Arthur Goss, who were opposed to NATO, believed that CND should remain wholly and only concerned with British unilateral nuclear disarmament. Unlike the more radical supporters of the Movement, the CND leadership accepted the general theory of deterrence, and was 'loyal' to the NATO alliance: the leadership was, in essence, arguing about a *specific policy commitment* and not a whole structure and style of politics. The implicit, and highly conservative, assumption was made that the existing political and strategic framework was given and almost immutable, and that the unilateralist Campaign involved no more than a change of mind (and heart) on the part of the existing political leadership.

Although the notion of 'moral example' was strongly held it was, in most cases, sharply differentiated from the radical neutralism of others in the Campaign. The moral example was quite unconnected with the ideological commitment to a 'third way' of mediation between the two 'Super Powers'. It rested on the assumption that Britain, as a "third nation . . . old and experienced in world affairs",[10] could act as a trusted older colleague—an honest broker between the USA and the USSR (although *why* the USSR should place any trust in a Britain unequivocally committed, politically, economically and culturally, if not militarily, to the USA, was never made clear).

It may, however, be fairly claimed that this is to portray an apolitical stance in political terms. The perspective of the early leadership was, in the broad sense and with some qualifications, generally and genuinely non-political. As the more astute members of the Executive foresaw, any major deviation from or extension to this policy would have caused dissension and dislocation in the Campaign. The central emotive appeal of Priestley's original article set the tone — a mass moral campaign of the people to prevent the greatest immorality of all, nuclear destruction of mankind — that was the demand. And it was that rallying call to the British people who were waiting "for something better than party squabbles and appeals to their narrowest self-interest"[11] that brought out so many of the previously non-political thousands behind CND's banners. It was the ability of the Campaign to provide the mixture of moral indignation, fear, humanitarian concern and, above all, a single, simple, solution to an increasingly urgent problem that fired the enthusiasm of so many.

And yet it would be wildly incorrect to see the CND leadership as an inexperienced, apolitical and a somehow 'pure' group who were led astray or overwhelmed by the political hardliners and the 'wild men' of the Left. In reality, despite their very genuine moral basis of concern, those at the heart of the leadership were the 'Protesting establishment'. Most of the leading figures were veteran campaigners on humanitarian causes dear to the heart of the moderate Left — capital punishment, foreign affairs issues in the 1930s, anti-apartheid movements and so on. As Stuart Hall observed, "They were people who knew how to operate; how to lobby, how to influence people in the Labour Party and/or Government . . .". In a very important sense the early leaders had intended to keep CND firmly in this small pressure group role: "to make it an issue and then build a Fabian-style infiltration . . . feeding Royal Commissions with the right sort of evidence and talking to the right sorts of people and mobilising the majorities . . .". And they were at a loss when the campaign they had seen as a *pressure group* developed into a huge *mass movement*. The origins of the CND organisationally were precisely of this elite pressure group type: Jacquetta Hawkes has recalled how the idea was born, following Priestley's article, at "the rather famous little gathering at Kingsley Martin's flat with Kennan, Russell, Kingsley and his wife, and Jack (Priestley) and myself and probably one or two others . . .". As such diverse authorities as Stuart Hall and Lord Home have pointed out, the elite pressure group, which CND was at the very beginning, always works more effectively 'from the inside', rather than on the streets. There was in fact some reluctance on the part of the early CND leadership to give support to the first Aldermaston March (which was of course planned, organised and publicised by the DAC not CND). Having been persuaded into giving rather grudging support to the March, Hugh Brock recalled that he and Frank Allaun had had "a terrible job to persuade Canon Collins to come and speak in the Square when the March moved off", the leadership found itself involved in a populist politics which it found distasteful and at which it was inexperienced. After the success of the March it had no alternative but to espouse a political style that was at least partially alien. Lord Home readily confirmed that the eminence of the Movement's leadership would have guaranteed them access to any Prime Minister. By 1960 the March had become so large and so immersed in a new style of politics that the leaders realised, in George Clark's words, "that they weren't in charge any longer".

Viewed from the inside, as it were, Jacquetta Hawkes saw this development from elite pressure group to mass movement as disastrous:

As far as the leaders of the Campaign at that early stage (were concerned) — when it really was a compact sort of little campaign it depended very considerably on friends . . . we all knew one another . . . for some time it did keep that sort of atmosphere, and it had a very good middle period when it was coherent, cohesive and friendly but large — and then it began to disintegrate.

The elite nature of the early campaign leadership was inextricably linked to an espousal of the *moral* basis of its perspective. Jacquetta Hawkes and others "really quite strongly disapproved once the Labour Party and further Left had weighed in and it became a *neutralist* thing". Both Arthur Goss and A. J. P. Taylor rejected explicitly and with some vigour the notion that CND should have developed a democratic structure appropriate to a mass movement: as Arthur Goss put it: ". . . we were criticised as being a self-selected, self-perpetuating body — and we were . . . we didn't want membership, either people supported us or they didn't support us: this was the Campaign *we* were running, *we* decided to run it. . . ."

For the early leadership, then, CND was a single-issue, morally motivated Campaign consisting of a relatively small group of well-connected, mildly radical public figures backed by public opinion. Most of the original initiators were already linked to one another — personally, professionally or through their common involvement in past moral, social or political campaigns. 'Politics' was a central concern only in the sense that Collins and others realised that the translation of their moral campaign into national policy would require the winning over of a major political party — to all intents and purposes this meant the Labour Party of course.[12] Given this situation, there was a willingness on the part of some of the leadership, especially Canon Collins, to work with and through the Labour Party as much as possible. (Although perhaps more typical of the early leadership's 'distance' from politics was Jacquetta Hawkes who was "absolutely astonished" by the 1960 Labour Conference vote and was quite "unaware" of what was happening outside the Campaign leadership itself.) However, given this necessary political involvement at the level of winning over support, it is important to stress the absence, in the leadership, of any wider political commitment in the ideological sense. Canon Collins, shrewd tactician and negotiator though he was, was firmly committed to the concept of the pressure group, and the "short, sharp, vigorous campaign". Not only did he and the Executive reject the notion of a mass movement — they did not appear to *comprehend* the idea. The numbers and (diverse) radicalism of the growing Movement, through 1959, 1960 and beyond, was thus in a very real sense an embarrassment to the leaders, and they, with increasing difficulty, continued to run what had become a mass movement as if it were still the small, coherent, elite group of early 1958.

There were, as Stuart Hall has said, two styles of politics operating, conveniently symbolised by the Front and the Back of the March. The only intersection of these two perspectives lay in the issue of the Bomb itself. But this unanimity on the issue was more apparent than real. In essence those in the leadership saw the Bomb, enormously important though it was, as a monstrous mistake by a society which was fundamentally sound in structure and attitudes: what was needed, therefore, was a change of policy on this particular issue. As the obverse of this, the "back end of the March", so to speak, enormously varied though its ideology was, saw the Bomb as the final, absurd and obscene product of a society which was based on irrational if not insane assumptions.

The ideological gap was reinforced by both a social class *and* a generation gap; private correspondence has shown that there was mutual antipathy on the personal, lifestyle level between the CND leadership and the younger, more militant leaders of the regional CND groups (to say nothing of the Committee of 100!). Moreover, there is considerable evidence, from confidential sources, that this divergence found expression in persistent criticism of Canon Collins' leadership. Those on the early CND Executive Committee were at the very height of professional and public life — and many of them were also 'household names', in itself a part of CND's attraction.[13] This was indeed a charmed circle. In fact, as Canon Collins has recalled, the CND leadership intermingled socially with the highest in the land: "I knew Hugh Gaitskell quite well — and Wilson and Callaghan — (and) I would say in some senses that Gaitskell was a more lively character, and a person that I found myself drawn to — excepting on this (CND) issue".

The CND leaders, as they claimed, based their arguments and their campaign on the moral issue and the moral arguments: but, in many senses more important were their conservative, 'single-issue', ideological assumptions, and the natural elite nature of their leadership grouping. As Canon Collins implied, on all important criteria the CND leadership tended far more towards the 'Gaitskellite establishment' and had little in common with the inherent radicalism of the mass movement which they had, almost unwittingly, been instrumental in creating.[14]

The Campaign as 'Labour Movement Pressure Group'

THE LABOUR PARTY

From the outset, the Movement against nuclear weapons had strong support within the Labour Party and the wider Labour Movement. There is, of course, a strong tradition of both pacifism and anti-imperialism in the Labour Movement, stretching back to the ILP's opposition to World War I and beyond.[15] In the 1950s there had been muted but slowly increasing opposition to nuclear weapons, culminating in the Labour Hydrogen Bomb Campaign Committee.[16] By the time of Bevan's notorious 1957 Conference speech when he denounced, forcefully and aggressively, the unilateralist case,[17] the strength of the unilateralist movement in the Party was considerable.[18] *Tribune* had supported the unilateralist argument through 1957, and continued to do so even after Bevan's speech.

Both the *New Statesman's* editor, Kingsley Martin, and the *Tribune's* editor, Michael Foot, were founder members of CND itself. CND was thus deeply involved with the Labour Movement from its very beginning. Leading Labour activists and politicians in both leadership and rank and file[19] were in the Campaign from the beginning: and, equally important, the CND leadership had, as Jacquetta Hawkes recalled, "all been Labour Party voters, though most, not, I think, actual Party members". Thus, even for those with a predominantly moral motivation, the Labour Party appeared as the natural political outlet for CND, as for other previous progressive campaigns.

Just as the Disarmament Movement was, for the DAC, part of the wider struggle to create a non-violent society, so, for Labour activists — especially those in the Parliamentary Labour Party — it was a part of the struggle to win over the Labour Party to socialist policies. This is not to say that those on the Left of the Party saw CND solely, or even primarily, as a means of opposing and, ultimately, unseating Gaitskell from the Party leadership. Contradicting the popular view[20] all the leading Labour figures we interviewed[21] explicitly rejected the idea that the Labour Left used the Campaign as a means of opposing Gaitskell, and was only marginally, if at all, involved with the issue itself. Both Michael Foot and Ian Mikardo have testified to the "very strong feeling in the Labour Party on the side of unilateral disarmament . . .". As Ian Mikardo has pointed out: "If we'd wanted to try to change the leadership, that wasn't the way to do it; we'd have done it in the Labour Party, not joined an outside organisation." There can be no doubt that the Left of the Labour Party did have a genuine commitment to unilateral nuclear disarmament: the old ILP traditions rendered CND the most appealing of causes.[22] It is thus a more correct view to see the Labour Left's opposition to Gaitskell as being *intensified* by his reaction to CND's policy and activity on perfectly genuine ideological grounds. Not only was he seen, by the Labour Left, as being an unacceptable leader because of his explicit and radical revisionism on the Party's commitment to common ownership:[23] his inflexible support for the British independent deterrent and the NATO alliance confirmed its view that his ideological position was far to the Right. After his refusal to accept the Conference decision of 1960, which rejected the leadership's defence policy and accepted a quasi-unilateralist TGWU resolution and a straightforward unilateralist resolution from the AEU,[24] the Left of the Party was incensed at what it saw as his undemocratic and unconstitutional behaviour.

To the Labour Left, then, the CND issue and campaign were of intrinsic importance — *and* they also formed part of the struggle for a socialist policy within the Party. There was nothing sinister or underhand (or even particularly complex) in this: it was another episode in the long struggle between Right and Left in the Party[25] and it ranged over foreign affairs and defence as well as over 'socialist commitment' and domestic policy.

Everyone on the Labour Left viewed the CND's chances of success as being wholly dependent on winning Labour Party support. Sympathetic as they might be to the moral impetus of the Movement, and understanding as they might be of the 'impetuosity of youth' in wanting to by-pass the constitutional channels, most agreed with Mikardo that "*the only* political force capable of effecting such a change was the Labour Party. . . . The fact of the matter is that the battleground *was the Labour Party*. It was the only arena in which the Campaign could ride." Similarly, Frank Allaun saw CND as fundamentally a pressure group to push the Labour Party into becoming "the 'Peace Party' . . . that would attract not only the best people to it, but also (ensure) that the Labour Party would *mean* something".[26] Theirs was, ultimately, a wholly political view of CND — the problem was quite simple to define in these terms, although of course to reach the solution was considerably harder. On this perspective, the Right-wing leaders of the Labour Party (whose views are, as Allaun commented, "in many cases, similar to those in the Conservative Party") had taken their normal firm and inflexible stand against the progressive measures advocated by the Left: in this case, the unilateralism of CND. Again, as in most cases, the progressive policy had the support of a substantial proportion, arguably the majority, of the activists in the Party. The task was therefore to translate this rank-and-file support in the constituency parties into pressure to change Party Policy, and to mobilise the TU movement in support too. It was thus essential, arguing from this perspective, for there to be as

much CND/Labour Party integration as possible. Thus, this position entailed an opposition to other, non-political or 'extremist', perspectives and a reassertion of the
primacy of Labourist, electoral politics: hence the Labour Left's fierce opposition to
ideas such as Voters' Veto and the Independent Nuclear Disarmament Election Committee (INDEC).

To an extent the CND leadership, as we have seen, supported this Labourist
perspective. But, as Canon Collins himself has remarked, he was not a "good party
man", and it is quite clear that the CND Executive as a whole were, quite simply, not
'party political' people.[27] Had they, and the Movement as a whole,[28] been more
politically attuned, the outmanoeuvering of CND, and Gaitskell's easy and final victory in 1961, might not have been achieved.[29]

Whether or not the Labour Left perspective was correct in its assertion that the only
way for CND to achieve its policy aims was to win over the Labour Party for a Left
leadership, is not a question to be discussed at this stage. But, even assuming that this
was the correct perspective the outlook for success was bleak: not only had CND itself
at best an ambivalent attitude to Labourist politics, the Left in the Party was and
always had been, deeply hostile to its minority Left wing. Again, we do not here need
to explore *why* this has been the case[30] — but in a significant expression of fatalistic
frustration Mikardo described the situation for the Left succinctly: "If I were to put up
a motion to the PLP that the sun shines by day and the moon by night some of them
would vote against it, on principle, because it was from the Left. . . . They would say
'It *sounds* all right, but there must be some hidden motivation'."

From the Labour perspective there were, in retrospect, only two possible ways in
which CND could have won over the Party following the 1959 election defeat; either
they would have had to win the support of the leadership of the Party, via the replacement of Gaitskell and the Right by a Left leadership, or they would have to have
secured the permanent and overwhelming support of the TU Movement, thus making
it impossible for the Right-wing leadership to pursue its declared policy. The first of
these alternatives never got off the ground; Bevan unequivocally rejected the
unilateralist case in 1957 and never had any contact with CND[31] — and, by 1960, he
was in any case soon to die. For many on the Labour Left, Bevan's death removed any
real chance of CND's succceeding. Without a political figure of Bevan's immense
charisma and experience it was indeed unlikely that the pro-CND lobby on the Left of
the Labour Party could have triumphed. But, if the TUs had remained solid for
unilateralism through 1961, as the majority of them had in 1960, the political leadership would have been forced to change its policy or, more likely, resign. The extent of
TU support, and working-class support generally, has been a matter of some debate:
all the surveys of the Movement (including our own of course) have shown a relatively
low level of working-class activism and involvement. But in Michael Foot's opinion
there was "very strong working class backing", and both Frank Allaun and Dick
Nettleton have expressed similar views,[32] whilst both Dick Nettleton and George Matthews made the important point that working-class support tended to find expression
in activities other than marching, demonstrating, etc. There can be no doubt,
however, that TU support was based on activist rather than rank-and-file opinion, on
a moral rather than a political perspective, and on a hostility to the Party leadership.
None of these motivations was, however, strong enough or deeply held enough to
withstand the Gaitskellite campaign of the CDS through 1961: Gaitskell's appeal to

party unity, to loyalty, was well formulated to appeal to the TUs. As Sir Harold Wilson has said: "This was in 1961 and by this time we were beginning to think of winning the next election and some of the Unions must have switched sympathies." Moreover, Gaitskell managed skilfully to outmanoeuvre Frank Cousins on the policy issues that were debated in the Labour Movement through 1960/61.[33] There was, too, crucially, a distance and a coolness between the TUs and CND: in Michael Foot's view the CND leadership did not "always have the best way of conducting it (i.e. the relationship with the TUs)". A. J. P. Taylor was more critical: "Frank Cousins *never* worked with us in any way: he simply took his own line and expected us to follow him." Frank Cousins himself — he was incidentally the only major figure to decline the request for an interview — confirmed that in his view there was never "a clearly fixed and defined attitude on the subject of unilateralism and/or the CND within either the political or TU Movements. Therefore opinions become simply personal or at the best a limited collective view."[34]

From both sides, so to speak, there was thus insufficient unity of purpose and political determination to resist the Gaitskellite campaign to reverse the 1960 decision. The TUs were the crucial arena of struggle — and neither the Labour Left (i.e. the PLP *Tribune* Left) nor the CND leadership, had sufficient strength and influence at either the 'national officer' or the rank-and-file level to establish a firm basis in the Labour Movement. In retrospect it is tempting to agree with one of the (few) CND leaders avowedly *un*interested in converting the Labour Party:[35] in A. J. P. Taylor's view the 1960 Conference vote was "really almost a distraction; it was a misfortune that it was carried in this way and gave an illusion that the Labour Party had been carried for unilateral nuclear disarmament: it hadn't — something had been carried by the mass vote of the TGWU". And this, as has been pointed out, did not represent a genuine movement of rank-and-file opinion to the unilateralist line, or even to the Left in general: the swing was due to an extent to the succession of Frank Cousins to the General Secretaryship of the TGWU.[36]

The attitude of those who held a Labour Movement perspective towards the Direct Action of the DAC and the Committee of 100 was, as might have been anticipated, at best one of tolerating an outburst of youthful impetuosity which had little relevance to the real political battle, and, at worst, a hostility and annoyance that such tactics distracted attention from serious politics and undermined attempts to get the Movement taken seriously. None of the leading Labour figures supported the Committee of 100 (although Frank Allaun had been active in the earlier DAC), and, although Foot, Mikardo and Allaun expressed 'tolerant' views of the Committee of 100, none of them viewed the development of civil disobedience as desirable or useful.[37] Others in the Labour Movement, like Olive Gibbs, were considerably more critical: it was, she stated, "Direct action pure and simple" that had resulted in the failure of CND to consolidate its 1960 Conference victory; it was Direct Action which had "lost the support of trade unions, we lost the support of the rank and file of the Labour Party, because above all I think people join the Labour Party because . . . they believe in democratic decisions, and they don't believe in Direct Action." At all events, whatever their public utterances, there was little contact between the perspectives of the Labour Left and the extra-parliamentary movements of the Committee of 100 (and the DAC): they moved in different ideological universes and there was as little hope of converting

Labour activists to quasi-anarchist politics as there was of interesting the Committee of 100 in the intricacies of Labour machine politics.

Viewed in retrospect, and with at least a degree of objectivity, it seems likely that even a CND fully committed to the Labour perspective would have been unsuccessful in deposing the Right-wing and installing a Left-wing leadership which had unilateralism as a cornerstone of its policy. The inbuilt structure of the Party, the constitutional arrangements, and the inherent weaknesses of Labour's Left wing, combined with the Gaitskellites' determination, efficiency and media support, would, probably, have proved too strong for any offensive mounted within the parameters of Labour machine politics.[38] Nevertheless, it would have been far more of a battle than in fact it was, had the Movement been committed to working through the Labour Party. As it was, CND was, in Stuart Hall's phrase, "bizarrely unprepared" for the 1960 Conference victory; and, as Hall also observed, nobody realised that after the 'victory' CND still had to face "exactly the same hard-faced Labour agents up and down the country with the apparatus at their command, who were not suddenly going to start putting out anti-NATO propaganda! We were not strategically prepared for victory when it came." But this was by no means entirely the result of inexperience and political inefficiency; there was always an "ambiguity (in CND) about the Labour Party". There is indeed more than a little truth in Nicolas Walter's hostile (to the Labour Movement) analysis of the Disarmament Movement:

> . . . the unilateralist movement is essentially pacifist and anarchist, and was begun by people normally regarded as cranks . . . the real question is: Does the Committee of 100 belong to the official Labour Movement? And the answer is surely: No . . . what cannot be valid is any pretence that the Committee is in some way part of the Socialist Movement . . . socialists must stop being either patronising or possessive about unilateralists. . . .[39]

This is certainly true of the Committee of 100 — but in modified form it is true too of at least a substantial section of CND. Whatever attempts were made by those whose ideological framework and primary loyalties lay with the Labour Movement, there was little chance of turning the priorities and perspectives of the Disarmament Movement towards the well-established channels of 'conventional' Left politics. This mutual impasse is of central significance in the analysis of the Movement's political importance and forms a major part of the discussion in Part IV.

THE COMMUNIST PARTY

Before turning to look at the extra-parliamentary Left in the Movement, we should discuss briefly the attitude and role of the Communist Party. Whilst most of those in the Labour Movement would firmly repudiate the ideology of the Communist Party, there can equally be no doubt that the CP was viewed with hostility and suspicion by the other sections of the Left who together comprised the extra-parliamentary grouping: indeed one of their central defining characteristics was their *rejection* of Old Left (i.e. CP) politics.[40] The CP's own orienation was firmly Parliamentarist in strategic terms,[41] but, of course, equally firmly Marxist in ideological analysis: their perspective was thus unacceptable to the Labour Party (as it has been since the 1920s[42]) and to both the New Left and Anarchist/Direct Action sections of the Disarmament Movement, and to the wider non-political sections of the Movement. Throughout their association with CND the CP thus endeavoured to cultivate a responsible and moderate image (much as they have tried, unsuccessfully, to create a similar image with the Labour Party); the corollary of this was the CP's 'distance' from the extra-parliamentary wing of the Movement.[43] At the same time, the CP's long-term commitment to Marxism differentiated the CP membership strongly from the Social Democratic Left (hence our categorisation of the rank and file earlier).

It would thus be inaccurate to place the CP in either the Labour Movement or the extra-parliamentary category. Moreover, far from straddling the divide the CP seems ultimately to have fallen between the two stools, being viewed with some hostility and suspicion by both camps.[44] Be that as it may, there can be no doubt that the Party played a significant, though not a crucial, role in the Movement.[45]

The CP's attitude to CND was at first sympathetic but not fully supportive. Having campaigned for world peace through their own British Peace Committee the CP regarded the CND's initial stress on unilateralism as diverting attention from the main business of multilateral disarmament through international summit negotiations. The CP's main misgiving about CND was that it failed to ally itself closely enough with the aspirations and ideology of the Labour Movement and made a commitment to unilateralism the sole criterion for support. It thus attracted, so the CP argued, sections of the bourgeoisie who were arguing for unilateralism on unsocialist and non-progressive grounds: thus "unilateralism wasn't automatically a fully progressive demand"[46] in the CP's view. The CP changed its policy from sympathetic but critical interest to full support during 1959 and 1960. This was due to a number of factors: the growing popularity of CND and the development of a genuine mass movement obviously played its part; the shift in CND policy itself, in particular, the adoption of an explicit opposition to Britain's remaining in NATO; and above all the change of opinion in the Labour Movement to support for unilateralism over the summer of 1959.[47] For the CP, as for the Labour Left, success for CND could come only through Labour Movement support:[48] for the CP, its attitude to CND was, according to George Matthews, "a question of tactics, of estimating what was the best campaigning demand". Once the Labour Movement appeared to be swinging behind a unilateralist campaign the CP had no doubt that it should support the CND policy, and the CND Movement. The basic strategy of the CP[49] was and is to build Left unity through an alliance on all issues between the Left of the Labour Party and the Left of the Trade Union Movement to challenge the Right-wing control. Given the assumptions of this strategy, it was logical for the CP to *react to* increased TU and Labour support for CND by changing their own policy (or "changing their emphasis" as George Matthews of the CP would have it).

Fundamentally, then, the CP saw CND as part of the Left pressure group on the Labour Movement. As with the Labour Left, they were less concerned with the Mass Movement *per se* and concentrated primarily on building Labour Movement support. Their antipathy to the extra-parliamentary style of Disarmament politics was most apparent in their attitude to the Committee of 100—"we were never terribly keen on that" (George Matthews); it was not so much that the CP was hostile to the Committee of 100 as that it never understood the unstructured, populist, approach of the Direct Action wing of the Movement. The CP perspective on the Disarmament Movement conforms to the generally conservative tenor of European CP politics and strategy since the last war. Just as the French CP was one of the major conservative forces during the 'May events' in France in 1968, so the British CP threw its weight behind the solidly Labourist tendencies of CND's centre and showed no sympathy with the various revolutionary strands of thought which existed within the Movement.

THE DISARMAMENT MOVEMENT AS THE BASIS OF A 'NEW LEFT' POLITICS

The CP was not the only, nor indeed the most important, Left political force within the Disarmament Movement. The same complex of events in the mid-1950s which gave rise to CND itself gave rise too to a 'New Left'. The first New Left looked for a time as though it might become a major force in British politics. The persistent, but as yet unsuccessful, attempts to build an alternative Socialist Movement outside the confines and constraints of the Labour Party has been a feature of considerable importance in post-war Britain. The extent to which this first New Left interacted with, and indeed was a constituent part of, the Disarmament Movement would alone justify our spending some time analysing its nature and role. However, in the long term more important are the reasons for the New Left's failure to build the alternative mass movement for Socialism: as with the Disarmament Movement itself, the life of this first New Left was relatively short and dramatic. The fates of the two movements were inextricably connected and arguably neither could have survived, let alone succeeded, without the other.

Unlike other political groupings associated in various ways with the Disarmament Movement the New Left put unilateralism as a policy and CND as a Movement, at the centre of its political programme. For the editors of the *New Reasoner* CND provided the essential catalyst which could free the stagnant socialist movement and establish the beginnings of a new revitalised Socialism: "At last it is beginning to move. The frozen formations of the Cold War are beginning to break up . . . all talk of sweeping socialist advances in the next few years is unrealistic unless it starts from this premise: *there is no way forward until the international deadlock is broken.*"[50] The New Left felt strongly that, in the British context, CND provided the vehicle for this advance. A number of questions thus arises: what was the distinctive policy of the New Left and how did this integrate with that of CND? In what ways was the NL so much more in harmony with the overall ethos of CND than other Left groups? How did the NL relate to the radical wing of the Disarmament Movement? And, most important of all, why did the NL, despite all its influence and commitment, fail to change the nature and course of the Movement?

It is important to begin by defining precisely what is meant by the New Left. In this context the term New Left refers to the groupings associated with the *New Reasoner* (*NR*) journal and the *Universities and Left Review* (*ULR*), which merged in 1959/60 to form the *New Left Review* (*NLR*), and the informal network of New Left clubs around the country which were associated with the *NLR*. This New Left was not an orthodox political party or group—differing from the International Socialists, the Communist Party and, for that matter, the Labour Party. The NL had no formal membership, no constitution, no official 'party' programme (and no aspirations to become the Leninist vanguard party . . .). The NL was thus very much like CND in its organisational format—or perhaps one should almost say *lack* of organisational format. As D. G. Arnott pointed out in the *New Reasoner,* in a rather different context, "nuclear disarmament is a continuing state of mind or it is nothing. That it is which makes the campaign   so   much   greater   than   any   comparable   political   movement: it cannot succeed unless Man assumes control over his own evolution."[51] The same could be said of the New Left, which was as much a generalised ethos, an attitude, as a set of specific political theories and policies.

Of what did this 'ethos' consist and how did it relate specifically to the Disarmament Movement? The explanation lies in the two mainsprings of NL development: the group of ex-CP members around the *New Reasoner,* and those 'unattached' young radicals of the *ULR.*

The *New Reasoner* evolved from *The Reasoner,* a duplicated journal published by two university lecturers from Yorkshire, Edward Thompson and John Saville, both members of the Communist Party. The first two issues of the original journal had been published following Knischev's 1956 'exposure' of Stalin's régime and had contained articles critical of the Communist hierarchical structure, and this had led to censure by the CP leadership. Whilst the third issue was in preparation the Russian suppression of the Hungarian uprising took place and *The Reasoner* urged its readers to dissociate themselves from their leaders' support for this action. The Party was not prepared to tolerate such open opposition: Thompson and Saville resigned from the CP, and the first issue of the *NR* appeared in 1957. The Hungary crisis brought to a head already existing tensions within the CP: some sections of the Party "sought a return to a more rigorous Leninism. . . . This desire eventually led many disillusioned Communist militants . . . to the Trotskyist movement, which . . . became an important ideological antagonist of the New Left".[52] In contrast, other sections in the Party "demanded an end to the organisational and theoretical 'monolithism' which distinguished Communist methods from the more open practices of the non-Communist left".[53] It was this latter strain that was represented by the *NR* group, emphasising the humanist and democratic aspects and aspirations of the Marxist tradition. Edward Thompson, in particular, was highly critical of the British Communist Party for its sectarian defence of Stalinist theory and practice, and its tendency to dismiss the democratic traditions and liberties of British political culture as 'bourgeois democracy', and thus a sham. In a key article on 'Socialist Humanism'[54] Thompson argued that the 'base/superstructure' model of Marx had been misapplied and distorted by Stalinism: it had been used "not as an image of man changing in society, but as a mechanical model, operating semi-automatically and independently of conscious human agency". A fundamental objective of the anti-Stalinist New Left was "to reject mechanical Marxism, to reinstate human agency in Communist theory and practice, and to eliminate bureaucratic inhumanity . . . its primary aim would be a *'return to man'*: from abstract formulations to real men: from deceptions and myths to honest history".

Nevertheless, despite these fundamental, central, and consistently emphasised criticisms of the Communist Party, the CP legacy was tremendously important in the evolution of the *NR*'s perspective.

A crucial aspect of this CP legacy, in practical political terms rather than theoretical framework, was the adherence of the *NR* to a Labourist strategy. The strategy of the CP — the Parliamentarist programme of the 'British Road' so reviled by other sections of the Marxist Left — was implicitly accepted by the *NR,* and every effort was made to forge a link with the "theoretically inclined sector of the Labour Left".[55] The *NR* never deviated from its belief in a reformed, left-oriented, Labour Party as the vehicle for a socialist transformation. For the *NR*, the New Left was based firmly on revolutionary reformism — a radicalising of the *existing* structures (the trade unions and the Labour Party), plus the long-term development of an appropriate socialist theoretical analysis. The *NR*, operating within the ideological parameters of the or-thodox Labour Movement, saw its role as filling what it took to be the ideological vacuum that existed between "the conceptual sterility of the traditional polarity be-tween the evolutionary model of Fabianism and the cataclysmic model of the Leninist tradition".[56] Nevertheless it is clear that in both practical and theoretical political terms the *NR*'s concept of revolutionary reformism was considerably more reformist than revolutionary — and "despite its incorporation of New Left vocabulary, (it) was . . . essentially an old left concept".[57]

Of particular concern, in our context, obviously, is the *NR*'s concern with unilateralism and the Disarmament Movement. From the beginning the *NR* was in favour of British withdrawal from NATO, unilateral nuclear disarmament, and the adoption of a neutralist foreign policy. The *NR* linked up the international theme — the need to end the Cold War and develop a neutralist bloc — with the inter-national role of British Labour — the opportunity for Britain to take the lead through unilateral nuclear disarmament, a withdrawal from NATO, and the espousal of a neutralist foreign policy. The *NR* realised from the start that underlying the Labour leadership's rejection of the CND's unilateralist case was the far more fundamental commitment to NATO. "The fig-leaf which Mr. Bevan holds on to so desperately turns out to be — not the H-bomb at all — but NATO and the American alliance . . . we must make a choice between NATO and the unmapped policy of positive neutrali-ty. . . ."[58] One of the major contributions of the NL to the Disarmament Movement was to bring home the connection between unilateralism and membership of NATO. In 1960 CND officially adopted the withdrawal from NATO into its statement of aims — and the influence of the NL in this process of persuasion was central.[59] The *NR*'s consistent advocacy of positive neutralism and the potential British role in this process was intimately linked to its belief in the deep-rooted and valuable radical democratic socialism inherent in British political culture.

The actual form of neutralism advocated by the *NR* and, later, by others in the NL was, with the hindsight of 20 years or so, all too sanguine in its implicit assumptions of the good (socialist) faith of many régimes, subsequently seen to have been anything but progressive, let alone dedicated to the humanistic Marxism of the *NR*.

The mainspring of the *NR*'s neutralism lay, as already stated, in its vehement rejec-tion of both Western capitalism and Eastern totalitarian Communism,[60] and in the assertion that the Left in the West and the dissident communists of the East should and would converge on the common ground of Marxist humanism — and thus forge a genuinely new and socialist society, East and West. The "NL . . . while it draws much from both traditions, stands apart from sterile antagonisms of the past, and speaks for what is immanent within both societies. It champions a new internationalism which is not that of the triumph of one camp over the other, but the dissolution of the camps and the triumph of the common people."[61]

The fullest statement of the *NR*/NL position on 'positive neutralism' is contained in Peter Worsley's *Imperialism in Retreat:*

> (Britain could) generate immense pressure, in alliance with India, Ghana, Yugoslavia and backed by the uncommitted countries, for world peace and active

neutrality. And most of these uncommitted nations are countries which could, under such stimulus, move towards Socialism . . . India, Austria, Israel, Indonesia, Ghana to name a few . . . not forming another frozen bloc, but trading and communicating freely, gradually breaking down the barriers on both sides. . . .[62]

Similarly, the *NR* argued that the neutralist position as "expressed in the diplomacy of the uncommitted Afro-Asian nations, Yugoslavia, etc.", had, in common with the 'revisionist' neutralism of the dissidents from the Eastern bloc, "a common enemy not only in the tensions of the cold war, but also in the strategic postulates and partisan ideology of the (cold) war".

The *NR* thus envisaged an internationally linked movement for positive neutralism — with a European neutralist bloc "with the Scandinavian countries, Yugoslavia, Austria and Poland as possible entrants"[63] linked to similar Asian and African movements.

The *NR*/NL policy of positive neutralism tied in closely with the logic of CND's own position. If unilateralism entailed withdrawal from NATO — as for all Socialists it surely must; and if, like all except the CP and the Trotskyists of the Socialist Labour League, the USSR and its alliances were rejected too, then the logical next step was to define a role for a neutralist Britain. As Thompson outlined,[64] the implications of such a policy were not confined to major changes in international relations and foreign policy; it was quite possible too that on a domino theory scenario the adoption of a unilateralist/neutralist policy might lead to the Socialist revolution. And, with varying degrees of enthusiasm and for differing reasons, many of those in CND and the Labour Left were prepared to follow this policy lead and combine their demand for unilateral disarmament with a commitment to the achievement of a neutralist change in foreign policy.

Before considering why this 'escalation of socialist demands' failed to take hold of CND in the way envisaged by the *NR* we should return to consider the other component of the New Left of 1957-1962, the *Universities and Left Review* (*ULR*). If the *NR* was still firmly within the Marxist tradition, albeit emphasising a 'new' humanistic, non-aligned version, the early *ULR* was not of such orthodox lineage.

Peter Sedgwick[65] has characterised the *NR* as the representative of the 'political' concerns of the NL "as against the pretensions of its chief rival, which may be called Socio-culture". The *ULR* concentrated "on the exploration of the cultural mass media and their effects on popular moral and social consciousness . . . it theorised upon the role of the mass media in a class-divided society, and on the relationship between a critique of the media and the overall Socialist case against capitalism". Politically *ULR* was, from the outset, "highly sceptical of the legacy of both the Communist and Labour Parties and saw as its primary goal the construction of a completely new body of socialist thought . . . its Socialist humanism therefore remained essentially a more intellectualized expression of wider middle-class radicalism and the unprecedented youth revolt. . . ."[66]

The *ULR* was far more eclectic and less "doctrinaire" than the *NR*, as Stuart Hall recalled:

> it included Marxists and non-Marxists, it included people on the left of the Labour Party, and it included people of no affiliation; it included some pacifists . . . and it included quite a lot of Third World people. . . . It was a lot of tenden-

cies and what held them was a notion that it wasn't the post-capitalist era, and that, on the other hand, the traditional (Marxist) analyses of capitalism didn't account for all that had happened. So, in the sense, it was 'Left' but 'New'. And similarly, about our political organisation, it was both very anti-Leninist, anti-the Vanguard Party, anti-democratic centralism, because this was very tied up with Stalin, (and), on the other hand, it was very aware of the weaknesses and compromises of the Labour Party. But it functioned very much *in relation to* the Labour Party: I think on the grounds that this continued to be, whatever its faults, the major organisation of the working class, so you had to be in there somehow. . . .

The *ULR* was, however, less interested in organisation, tactics and 'orthodox' political action and more attuned, both to the development of socialist cultural analysis,[67] and to the more dramatic 'demonstration' politics of the Disarmament Movement.

The activists of *ULR* were largely student or radical-intelligentsia based (the *ULR* was edited initially from Oxford—and its editorial board was exclusively student/academic in composition). And, to that extent, the group was a part of the 'Aldermaston generation' to which Thompson referred:

> (those who) never looked upon the Soviet Union as a weak but heroic Workers' State; but, rather, as the nation of the Great Purges and of Stalingrad . . . their enthusiasm is not for the (Labour) party, or the movement, or the established political leaders . . . they prefer the amateur organisation and the amateurish platform of the CND to the method and manner of the Left-Wing professional.

As Thompson went on to imply, this was a generation "alienated not from 'life', nor even from 'politics', but from the established institutional movements of modern politics—West *and* East, capitalist *and* Communist".[68] The point need not be laboured but it is important to emphasise the degree to which Labour Movement *and* Marxist politics generally were discredited in the eyes of the radical young in the late 1950s and 1960s.

The *ULR* was thus in many ways the natural nucleus for disaffected students and other young radicals. If the *NR* provided the Labour Movement and Marxist experience, and, substantially, the bedrock of *political* theory for the NL, the *ULR* fulfilled the equally vital role of providing a bridgehead to students and radicals and to the rapidly growing radical pacifist movement.

Many of the people who flocked to the 'Partisan' Coffee House and to the NL Clubs in the early days were drawn not to Marxism, humanistic or otherwise, but to a 'new kind of politics'. This was an essentially middle class, morally motivated, almost apolitical movement appalled at the enormity of the H-Bomb in particular, but also at the general lack of any *morality* in politics.

NATO was in many ways the key issue for the NL—British membership of NATO was the major link between the predominantly *moral* campaign against nuclear weapons—and the predominantly *political* analysis of the NL which argued for a change to socialism and a rejection of the entanglement of the UK in the American system of alliances. By persistently raising the NATO question the *ULR* was able to relate its broader political concerns to CND audiences that had been hitherto outside the Socialist ambit. In that way, as Stuart Hall has pointed out, *ULR* "was involved in political education—in further radicalising people who were in your tendency. . . . And it's not quite true . . . that we just flowed in on CND's terms and were lost to it . . . we were trying to move on in a certain direction. . . ."

The merger of *NR* and *ULR* took place in late 1959, following discussions initiated by *NR*; the first issue of the *New Left Review* (*NLR*), under the editorship of Stuart Hall, appeared in January 1960.[69] In relation to the Disarmament Movement the *NLR* pursued its policy of positive neutralism with some enthusiasm. Peter Worsley, for example, believed that "the emergent peoples (were) the makers of a new synthesis which may contain the germs of a shared and enriched world—culture".[70] There is no doubt that the concern with a more 'conventional' politics as exemplified by the *NLR*'s neutralist policy, contrasted with the *ULR*'s earlier and less structured approach: and even more, of course, with the whole decentralised, quasi-anarchist perspective of the Committee of 100. The *NLR* politics was conventional, not in the sense of supporting conventional political objectives (NATO and so on), but rather in the sense of the conceptual framework of political thought within which policies were formulated—in this context, thinking in nation-state, diplomatic and international relations terms. The legacy of the CP perspective on foreign policy, and politics generally, was writ large in the NL: again, the political arguments, whilst not acceptable to all on the Labour Left, were couched in the same political context. For very different reasons, both the Far Left and the Committee of 100 rejected the suppositions of the argument, as well as the specific policies themselves.

This drift back to a more orthodox politics is even more evident in the discussion and policy documents produced by the *NLR* in the early 1960s on the specific problems and orientations of CND itself. John Rex, in one of the fullest statements of NL policy on the Bomb,[71] followed the same line of analysis of CND as the leadership:[72] although to some Aldermaston was a means for converting "the shock-troops of this or that political sect . . . (for the majority) . . . Aldermaston means nothing else than and nothing less than the moral response of British people to the facts of Hiroshima and Nagasaki, and to the possibility of their recurrence". Rex then made the normal NL argument in favour of withdrawal from NATO and advocated the following foreign policy for a unilaterally disarmed and neutralist Britain: the priorities for Britain should be to take an independent initiative for the achievement of comprehensive disarmament; and to put its "whole weight and authority . . . behind the UN General Assembly". Britain should also "devote the maximum possible part of her resources to the economic development of under-developed territories through UN agencies, because such a policy is right in itself, because it is in her economic self-interest, and because the maintenance of her authority in the World depends on her doing so". Thus the NL was by this stage considerably distanced from the radicalism of the Committee of 100: the sentiments of Rex's pamphlet could have come from the Labour Left, and George Clark's 'new kind of politics' seemed a long way off.

Significantly, the NL never committed itself wholeheartedly to the Direct Action tactics of the Committee of 100. The *ULR* had had some flirtations with Direct Action in its early days, but the whole range of Committee of 100 thinking was alien to the Marxist tradition—from the aristocratic individualism of Bertrand Russell, through the radical (individualist) pacifism of Michael Randle, April Carter *et al.*, to the bitterly anti-Marxist syndicalists and anarchists, there was very little common ground between the Committee and the NL. This distance was increased as the NL became, through 1961 and 1962, more and more wedded to a Labour Left perspective — and the Committee, after the relative failure of the Wethersfield demonstration, and the subsequent Official Secrets trial, came more and more under anarchist influence.[73]

As the Committee and the NL drew further apart, so the relationship between the NL and the CND — or rather those socialists in or near the centre of CND policy-making who were sympathetic to NL thinking — became ever closer. The rejection by the Labour Party Conference in 1961 of the previous year's unilateralist resolution resulted in a whole range of alternative strategies being put forward. The credibility of the traditional CND policy of 'working through the Labour Party' had been severely, if not fatally, weakened by the reversal of the Scarborough decision. The NL provided the theorists in this situation, not so much through design as because there were "too few others in CND ready with the will and the capacity to transform the Movement in-to a different and more political entity".[74] The NL became, in Peggy Duff's words, "CND's think-tank" — but it was a very different NL from the old *ULR*, or even from the massive radicalising force which Edward Thompson had envisaged in the *New Reasoner*. Stuart Hall produced, in 1962, one of the most controversial of CND statements, *Steps Towards Peace*. Hall's statement, adopted by the Executive, reneged or appeared to renege on the unilateralist commitment. In retrospect Canon Collins saw that this was a mistake: ". . . we must never seem to be departing from our basic policy. It was, perhaps, our failure in this respect which led to the poor reception by the bulk of the campaign of the *Steps Towards Peace* programme."[75] In influencing CND to abandon, or demote and hedge around with qualifications, its central com-mitment to unilateralism, Hall was trying to bring CND policy 'up to date' — to develop its politics to take into account both the changed nuclear situation in the years since CND's inception, and the changed political climate in the UK which, after 1960, had to mean a reoriented campaign, with a new strategy, to obtain its objectives. The motivation was, no doubt, genuine, but Young is surely correct when he claims that the "NLR showed the same fundamental misunderstanding of the nuclear disarma-ment movement that had first led them to advocate a Labour Party tactic".[76]

By 1962, then, the NL had changed — its influence on the Disarmament Movement was no longer (if it had ever been) on its 'radical' Committee of 100 wing, and it was no longer a radical influence on CND. The NL/Socialist pressure on CND had achieved the commitment to withdrawal from NATO in 1960, and to positive neutralism in 1961, but, in the new situation, the NL pressure was towards 'moderation'.

As the Disarmament Movement began to disintegrate after 1963 the NL lost both interest and influence. The decline of CND and the Committee of 100 as mass movements came coincidentally with the 'takeover' of the *NLR* by Anderson *et al.*: from then on the *NLR* showed no interest in the Disarmament Movement — and precious little in any contemporary socialist campaign or movement. The originators of the NL "dispersed to catch up on their research, emigrate, help run CND, or just vanish".[77]

The central problem raised by the history of the CND/Committee of 100 relation-ship with the NL is thus, why, given all the innate and considerable advantages with which the NL began, and the virtual political vacuum of CND, the NL failed, and in the end failed totally, to develop the Movement into the wider popular socialist crusade that had originally been envisaged.

In Peggy Duff's view CND was a mixed blessing for the NL: "In one way, CND did them no good. It swallowed them up as a political force in Britain."[78] And yet the Socialists of the *NR* had seen the youth of Aldermaston as the mass of the new socialist movement: the *NR* had envisaged the coming together of a new generation, grouped around the issue of the Bomb, but also fundamentally committed to a wider, new politics which embraced neither East nor West, but instead would evolve a humanistic socialism of its own. The catalyst of the NL failed to produce, through CND/Committee of 100, the new mass Socialist movement.

There are several aspects of the makeup of the two movements which go some way towards explaining this failure. First and foremost the NL never developed a mass base of its own — hence the relevance of Peggy Duff's remarks. Initially the NL movement, very largely through the *ULR*, had a promising network of regional and local 'New Left Clubs and Groups': for a short time there appeared to be some substance in the expectation of a new socialist movement, but this soon faded: the early emphasis on 'Youth' — "The bureaucracy will hold the machine; but the New Left will hold the passes between it and the younger generation"[79] — produced few results. "The only section of young people among whom the movement made any progress was its own further-educated juniors . . . among the thousands of youngsters who marched with CND the New Left never established an independent socialist presence."[80] Why was this? The rarefied university language in which New Left perspectives were transmitted certainly did not help: the level of political sophistication in Britain is notoriously low — and the lack of familiarity with the Marxist tradition of thought was, until the later 1960s, very widespread. Much of what the New Left was saying was therefore both complicated and to some degree alien, especially to those young people in CND/Committee of 100 not involved in higher or further education. Ironically, there was a communications failure by the New Left: the fundamental need was to establish the idea that the moral campaign of CND was necessarily linked to a structural analysis of modern society which would demonstrate the inherent connection between the abolition of the Bomb and the need to create a socialist society. The New Left failed to concentrate sufficiently on driving this analysis home: not only was its presentation too abstract, its concerns were, understandably, very much wider than this central issue. Indeed, the NL never really committed itself to activism, to building up a new movement: given the occupations, outstanding intellectual abilities, and temperaments of the leading NL figures it is not surprising that, despite its early rhetoric, the NL (both *NR* and *ULR*) remained primarily a *forum for discussion* of Marxist and other NL ideas. Neither did the NL leadership make much attempt, outside the universities, to build a mass membership.

In the most crucial area of all for any Marxist organisation — the attraction of support from the working-class — the NL made virtually no progress at all. "Shop stewards and rank-and-file worker militants were rarer here than in any left-wing grouping in Britain."[81] In a movement claiming to provide the potential political and ideological backbone which would transform the Disarmament Movement from a single-issue, moral campaign into a mass socialist movement, this failing was absolutely crucial.

This leads into the second major reason for the NL's failure in relation to the Disarmament Movement. The NL, for all its theoretical sophistication, had a hopelessly ambivalent attitude to the Labour Movement, to the Labour Party and to Labourism.

Eventually, as both Sedgwick and Young[82] point out, the New Left opted for a tactic of pressurising the Labour Party into pursuing socialist policies. With some prescience, Sedgwick, in 1964, wrote: "What is particularly staggering is its failure to imagine that it might be outmanoeuvred: pursuing a tactic of total theoretical entry, all its eggheads have marched into the single basket of Left reformism. . . ."[83] The total failure of this tactic, from a Marxist viewpoint, during the disastrous 1964-70 period of Labour rule is all too obvious to those on the Left more than a decade later.

This was, however, a relatively late decision by the NL: and it represented the orientation of the new *NLR* editors post-1963. In the key years from 1958 to 1962 the NL pursued a variety of different tactics at different times: the *NR*, whilst being committed for Marxist reasons to the Labour movement, envisaged, as we have seen, a new mass movement which would by-pass the bureaucratic party machine (and, presumably, eventually supersede it); the *ULR* flirted with Direct Action, and had little specific political strategy prior to the merger in 1960, apart from its (student-centred) attempts to build up an eclectic, discussion-oriented movement around the 'Partisan' in London. As early as 1961, however, there were significant indications of the fundamentally 'Labourist' orientations of the NL. Michael Barratt Brown, for example, argued strongly for Left unity *inside* the Labour Party. A new socialist party would, he wrote, take years, "even generations", to establish. "In the meantime Gaitskell would have won what he desired, a Labour Party minus a Left and the establishment of the American political position in Britain. . . . What we need is not a new organisation but more unity and coordinated action among the Left groups in the Labour Party."[84]

In 1959 the New Left had fought many disparate local campaigns on the fringes of central political activity in the orthodox sense (like George Clark's campaign for David Pitt in Hampstead and St. Pancras in 1959) for a 'new kind of politics'. The emphasis was at that time very much on building a new movement through the New Left Clubs and, more importantly, through the Disarmament Movement. This was combined through 1959 and 1960 with the campaign, following the election defeat, to convince the Labour Party to pass a unilateralist motion at the 1960 Conference. Through this period the *NL* became, *de facto*, and with no real strategic justification being made, committed to working through CND to influence the Labour Party. The NL's *strategy*, though not of course its *ideology*, was not very different from that of the CND leadership.

As Holden[85] has concluded:

> The first NL . . . became more a left-wing lobby, seeking to influence Labour policy from a position neither entirely inside nor entirely outside the conventional channels of party politics . . . one can today view the first NL as the last serious attempt to give traditional British Social democracy a coherent, long-term perspective which could lead to the eventual fulfilment of the Labour Party's official socialist goals . . . (it) remained dependent upon an established old left party to implement its socialist humanist ideas.

Symptomatic of the ambivalence of the NL was the debate over CND's putting up independent candidates for election on a unilateralist 'ticket'. Frustrated at the lack of progress through the Labour Party there was a move in 1961 to persuade CND to put up occasional candidates at by-elections: this was thrown out, Michael Foot denouncing the proposal as "poison". The proposal had been strongly supported by Peggy Duff and Stuart Hall of the New Left, and in the aftermath, and at the instigation of "The New Left and various other groups and individuals . . .",[86] INDEC (the Independent Nuclear Disarmament Election Committee) was set up.

The NL, characteristically, fell between two stools with this proposal. It came under attack from both wings of the movement: "the libertarians of the Committee of 100 and the Labour Left of the CND Executive, anxious about proscription, the first wrote it off as an irrelevance, the second condemned it as a threat".[87] The whole initiative thus went off at half-cock. Thompson claimed that putting up independent peace candidates was " 'the right, the only response' . . . to the Berlin crisis, the Blackpool rejection of unilateralism in the Labour Party and the massive Trafalgar Square demonstrations".[88] But the New Left did not consistently work for the creation of such a movement: instead it 'retreated' into more 'realistic' discussions on strategy, CND objectives and so on, culminating in 1962 in the *Steps Towards Peace* statement.

Whether the NL would have been able to create a new political force through independent candidates if it had campaigned for this strongly is, to put it at its most optimistic, very doubtful. But it does demonstrate, again, the divisions within the NL over the Labour Party question.

Reduced to essentials there were, for the NL, three possible strategies, all of them hinging critically on attitudes to both CND/Committee of 100 and the Labour Party: to back the militant, radical wing of the Committee of 100 in the hope that this might eventually form the nucleus of a new mass Socialist Movement outside, and opposed to, the Labour Party; to back the Labour Left perspective and work for CND policy to become official Labour Party policy, and, in the process, to agitate for the Labour Party developing a far more Left stance generally; or to try to activate a new mass movement, free of 'Labourist' or 'moralist' illusions, based upon the Disarmament Movement, and possibly fielding independent candidates, but soon broadening out into a generalised revolutionary socialist formation.

In the event, in the crucial years from 1957 to 1962, the NL flirted with all three, never concentrating fully on any one, although the second, Labourist, perspective was perhaps dominant throughout. By 1962/63, when the NL had moved decisively to the Labourist perspective, the mass Disarmament Movement was on the decline — the moment for action was past.

If the NL had opted for the last of the three alternatives given above it would have faced tremendous difficulties: as Peggy Duff has said: "So *many* people in the Campaign weren't political — at least not in that sort of way (i.e. a New Left/Marxist way) . . ." and: "What they (the New Left) came up against in the Campaign was that a lot of people, when it came to the point, were not prepared to challenge the Labour Party."

The dilemma of the NL thus comes back, ultimately, to the continuing problem of the Labour Party: Marxists' attitudes to the Labour Party in a society where the Party is indisputably the only mass working-class party, and where Marxism is so weak generally, has been a matter of keen, not to say vitriolic, debate, throughout the twentieth century, and has perhaps become particularly bitter during the decade and a half since Labour came to office in 1964.[89] The debate in the later 1960s and 1970s has been conducted largely in the context of the Communist Party/Labour Left (the so-called 'Broad Left') perspective as against the various Trotskyist or quasi-Trotskyist organisations of the Far Left (i.e. IS/SWP, SLL/WRP, IMG *et al.*). What differentiated the NL/CND/Committee of 100 debate of 1957/63 so crucially from this general division, was the existence of a *mass* movement: at its peak CND was attracting up to 150,000 people to demonstrations. This has never been equalled since 1945 — and, as has been repeatedly argued, neither CND nor the Committee of 100 had any coherent, consistent ideological position. The Disarmament Movement *was* a *mass* movement but it remained at the same time a single-issue pressure group. Had the NL been able to harness this tremendous "movement power" as George Clark referred to it, then the possibility of the socialist transformation so long fought for and so long desired on the Left, might have become a realistic possibility, as the *New Reasoner* had hopefully prophesied in the early NL days.

When asked why the NL had failed to convince the Disarmament Movement of the need for the wider socialist struggle along the lines it advocated, Peggy Duff replied: "They did *try* you know — they did try."[90] Maybe so. But they did not unite around a particular perspective for action and work for that. The very eclecticism which was one of the major elements of their appeal also motivated against any *unity* of action: and, despite their intellectual sophistication, they were unable to come to a clear decision about the most central problem of all: the attitude to Labourism. They acknowledged the centrality of the Labour Movement to CND's effectiveness — and they were aware of the need to build both inside and outside that movement — but they had no detailed plans for achieving such links, and showed no serious practical intention of working to convert the industrial and political sections. There were of course enormous political and cultural barriers to building such links; and, in purely organisational and numerical terms, the NL was never a major force *vis-à-vis* the Labour Movement. Nevertheless the almost total lack of a *serious* attempt to realise what was, after all, the cornerstone of their framework and hence of their strategy, would seem to testify to the view that they regarded themselves as in some ways above the rough and tumble of political in-fighting. Psychologically they thought of themselves as something of an elite — not altogether unlike the Fabians' self-perception *vis-à-vis* the Trade Union Right of the Labour Movement. In terms of CND, too, there was a similar failure to come to grips with the perspectives of the 'ordinary supporters', which, as we have seen, were to a significant extent apolitical. The task of a mass conversion to a New Left, socialist, politics was a major political task requiring unity, determination, organisational ability and, above all, hard and often mundane political work. The NL failed to take seriously the task of converting to a socialist perspective a mass organisation based on a moral, single-issue motivation.

Arguably, the NL's failure to win over the Disarmament Movement was not only a key factor in the decline of the Movement but was also one of the greatest missed opportunities this century for the Left to create a mass movement outside the Labour Party. CND may have 'swallowed up' the NL, as Peggy Duff claims, but this was only possible because the NL itself had no clear idea of where it was going, or indeed, of why it existed.

The Campaign as 'Radical Extra-Parliamentary Movement'

THE DIRECT ACTION COMMITTEE

If the Movement was ultimately infertile ground for the Socialist Left—social democratic or Marxist—surely there was a greater potential for those who saw the Movement not as a pressure group—whether inside the Labour Party or out—but as the basis of a 'new style of politics' based on the extra-parliamentary, decentralised populism, typified by the diverse radicalism of the Aldermaston Marches and the Committee of 100 sit-downs of 1961?

This perspective begins, in the Disarmament Movement context, with the Direct Action Committee and its espousal of Gandhian ideas with their commitment to non-violent social revolution. The DAC grew directly out of the division within the British pacifist movement between the 'old guard' of the Peace Pledge Union, and the predominantly younger, more radically minded, Gandhians who came into the Peace Movement in the late 1940s and early 1950s. Whereas the PPU was based on the *individual's* refusal to countenance war and concentrated on the full pacifist case against war and the need to challenge the conscience, the 'new Pacifists' were centrally concerned with the attempt to plan for and create the concept, and ultimately the reality, of "a non-violent society . . . a politics based on non-violence" (Hugh Brock). The DAC was formed under the aegis of Hugh Brock, whose involvement with Gandhian ideas and opposition to the orthodoxy of the PPU dated back to the late 1940s. Brock, and the young people around him at the start of the DAC and before (Michael Randle, April Carter and, a little later, Pat Arrowsmith), came to nuclear disarmament as either long-standing, 'full' Pacifists, or as fellow travellers with the pacifist movement.[91] The conflict in the pacifist movement over whether to support nuclear disarmament arose in part as a result of the 'old guard's' contention that to emphasise *nuclear* disarmament and to campaign to this end with non-pacifists entailed a *de facto* acceptance of other forms of 'conventional' warfare; pacifists should, they argued, oppose war *per se*. However, just as important as this was their opposition to the politics of non-violent revolution which characterised the DAC: nothing short of a wholesale restructuring of society—non-violent in both ends and means—would, so the DAC argued, solve the real problems. Nuclear weapons, far from being an isolated aberration of an otherwise civilised society, were the logical product of a social system based on violence and injustice. The DAC was thus less than enthusiastic about the Labour Party and the argument that worthwhile progress could be obtained only through the established political channels.[92] In sharp contrast to the CND leadership DAC activists had no ties—political, ideological or social—with society's Establishment; indeed they had been socialised in an avowedly oppositional culture, in a movement that had always been outside the mainstream of British political life. Not that this meant that they were totally opposed to working through and with the Labour Party: despite the widespread views of those like Jacquetta Hawkes and Olive Gibbs (who believed that "those like Pat Arrowsmith were more anti-Labour Party than they were anti- the Bomb"), the DAC was happy to include Labour Party activity as one of many lines of approach, but was not interested in giving it exclusive or even major priority. As Pat Arrowsmith has pointed out: many of those in DAC "were anarcho-pacifists, and certainly saw that power lay with the people and one went to grass roots, to workers, and invited them to consider downing tools on moral issues like nuclear weapons. Whereas we didn't oppose constitutional action . . . we didn't see this as the prime importance." This again highlights one of the key differences in orientation between CND and DAC leaderships: the DAC activists were populist in their politics — they had no faith and consequently little interest in the political machines and the working of the central power structure. It would, however, be inaccurate to think of the DAC as having no appreciation of the importance of the Labour Party. As Alan Lovell has said of the DAC: "One of the most distinctive things about the DAC was that we were willing to break from the Labour Party . . . it did seem that if anything were to happen in British politics you would have to have a major restructuring of the Labour Party. . ." From the DAC activists' perspective the end to be aimed for was the creation of a non-violent society:[93] their central concern was thus different from that of more orthodox Left groups and their attitude to the Labour Movement at once more detached and in some respects more hardheaded. As they were not wedded to the ideological conviction that the working class was the sole agency of radical social change, their politics did not stand or fall on their relationship with the Labour Movement. They realised, as we have noted, the *strategic* importance of the Labour Movement in British politics in terms of the power structure, but they had no qualms about breaking where necessary with Labour Party policies (or in some cases actively campaigning against the Party);[94] and, as Lovell recalled, "this conviction and resolve was something that separated us off from the *NLR* (*New Left Review*). I always found the *NLR* rather ambiguous about the Labour Party".

To achieve what they wanted — the 'non-violent society' — there had to be a revolution, not only political but ideological: a change in the framework of thinking was necessary and this could be done only by direct contact with the people. This explains the importance attached by DAC to the Aldermaston March taking place *from* London *to* Aldermaston: the climax, and the logical end result, of the DAC march was the vigil/picket at the Aldermaston Establishment 'where the workers were'. CND, on the other hand, when they took over the March in 1959, felt equally strongly that the March must be *from* Aldermaston *to* London: this was partly for tactical reasons (i.e. more people would be attracted to the final day and the final rally), but also because "in effect they were marching on the *Government*".[95]

The orientations of the DAC and CND leaderships were thus *very* different on both specific Disarmament Movement issues and on general attitudes. But they were both motivated in their opposition to the Bomb by *moral* as opposed to political criteria. The DAC was not, save in the loosest sense, 'socialist', as April Carter confirmed: "none of us was Marxist . . . (nor were we) really linked into Anarchism . . . but we were very keen on the notion of people controlling their own lives . . . (there was) certainly a strong populist feeling". At the heart of the DAC campaign was the belief that nuclear weapons and the violent society that produced them were inherently evil and that only through convincing the ordinary people of this fact could they be abolished. For the Anarchist the State is the central institution and authority the central relationship of an alien modern society; for the Marxist the corresponding 'categories' are the capitalist mode of production and the ruling class. For the DAC Gandhian pacifist it was the military complex and the philosophy of violence that underlay it, which formed the central structure: the concepts and the actuality that had to be exposed and resisted. Although it had broken away from the old PPU tradition and had attempted to develop a philosophy and politics of non-violence on Gandhian lines, the DAC remained essentially a pacifist group whose justification for their activities and beliefs rested on the immorality of violence. The fact that nuclear weapons considerably magnified this immorality was important—as was the fact that many were led to pacifism by their anti-nuclear commitment (and not vice versa as was the case, for example, with Donald Soper).[96] Nevertheless the fact remains that the basis of their rejection of nuclear weapons and their advocacy of unilateralism, for *all* nuclear powers not just the UK, rested on the unequivocal pacifist contention that violence was wrong—and solved nothing. In this way they differed in degree from the CND leadership, who, rejecting pacifism, had to develop more complicated, diffuse and *ad hominem* arguments to justify their unilateralism. As we have seen, the profusion of arguments thus produced was confusing, and often contradictory. Whether or not the case was accepted, the DAC's perspective for the (admittedly long-term and uphill) struggle to create the non-violent society was, granted the basic pacifist assumptions about violence in general and nuclear weapons in particular, clear, consistent and in theoretical terms, unassailable.

The influence of American Direct Actionists, particularly in the Civil Rights field, was also influential, as Michael Randle, April Carter, Hugh Brock and Alan Lovell have testified. This latter connection was in part cause and in part effect of the DAC's international, and anti-imperialist stance.[97] Contrary to popular supposition, DAC was *not* concerned with symbolic protests—the 'witness' of a small number of committed individuals overtly laying themselves on the line as martyrs to the cause. DAC, according to both Hugh Brock and Pat Arrowsmith, was from the outset intent on establishing a large and militant Direct Action Movement modelled to some extent on the Civil Rights campaign in the USA. There were strong links in practice (if not always in theory) between DAC perspectives and Anarchist/Syndicalist ideology, and Pat Arrowsmith in particular spent a great deal of time and energy working with the TUs and workers trying to stimulate strike action in both armaments-linked industries, *and* in other unrelated TU groups which were geographically close to armaments factories or military bases. Although there were some relatively minor successes,[98] there was never the major breakthrough into mass strike action that Pat Arrowsmith was working for. Nevertheless there is no doubt that the objective of bringing about a 'massive General Strike' on the issue of unilateral nuclear disarmament was populist and quasi-Syndicalist in its assumptions and tactics. Such a strike, Pat Arrowsmith argued, would be "a more effective way of changing the Labour Party than marching, even in your millions, quietly from Aldermaston to London". The DAC was not concerned with trade unions at the bureaucratic, official level, but with rank-and-file trade unionists. This was the antithesis of the CND leadership's view—which was to negotiate at national level, to try to convince the TU leaders to deliver the bloc votes at the Labour Party Conference. The DAC was thus, as Hugh Brock has recalled, sceptical of "socialism and communism . . . somehow none of them seemed to be effective . . ." and its concerns were far wider and more ambitious than those of the more traditional CND leadership.

Its resources, theoretical as well as material, were not adequate for the huge tasks it set itself—as Hugh Brock admitted, the DAC was "never able to work out" the politics of the non-violent society, nor was it able to develop an adequate strategy of how to get there. In part this related, of course, to the nature of the society in which it was operating. Unlike its Civil Rights sister groups in the USA the DAC was working in a far more stable and less variegated political culture; the pacifist tradition in the UK has always been tangential to the mainstream political culture, with the possible exception of the pacifist wing of the Labour Party at various periods. There was, too, as April Carter has emphasised, considerable *urgency* in the DAC campaign, and "things were happening so fast . . . we didn't sit back and plan our long-term policy—it was more a sort of intuitive process". The DAC was, in fact, much more concerned in practice with developing a range of protest activities on the issue of unilateral disarmament, rather than with the wider task of transforming society.[99] As April Carter has pointed out, the DAC, unlike the Committee of 100 (see below), "never got itself involved in anything outside the general area of arms" although it saw the development of the philosophy of non-violence as being a logical extension of its agitation for nuclear disarmament.[100]

However, even given the inherent difficulties, both theoretical and practical, the DAC was never really true to its own self-image of populism. Although the DAC was interested in a different style of politics, and although it believed in the creation of a mass campaign, the DAC was, in Stuart Hall's view, "no more involved in a mass movement, nor prepared for a mass campaign than the CND leadership were!" There was a sense in which the DAC, for all its populism, remained elitist: radical pacifism, always a tiny minority movement, demanded high standards and a high degree of commitment. Those in the leadership of DAC were neither temperamentally, nor politically, prepared for the diversity and the political messiness of a real mass movement. From the outset the DAC was restrictive in terms of attracting potential supporters:

> We were trying to gather people together on the basis of stopping the tests, and ultimately stopping the manufacture of nuclear weapons . . . we gathered people together on that basis with the proviso that whatever activities we were involved in must be based on non-violence. . . . Those of us on the inner core were trying to find a political expression for this . . . we came up with the suggestion of not voting for any of the existing political parties—which of course meant a terrific rift with the whole CND field, who were for doing things through the Labour Party (Hugh Brock).

This was an attitude hardly likely to attract mass support, particularly when coupled with the DAC's ideological and moral opposition to the 'orthodox' Marxism of the non-Labour Left.[101] Again, it is important to emphasise in this context too the central part played by the concept of non-violence. Hugh Brock welcomed, for example, the New Left as "a *real, new* Left—with hopes of (our) influencing them towards a politics based on non-violence. . . ." The DAC rejected secrecy in the planning of its demonstrations (one of the major practical differences of opinion between DAC and Committee of 100) because the DAC considered secrecy to be "a military tool—and you would come into a head-on clash with other people. Whereas in our demonstrations we wanted everybody we were brought into touch with to understand exactly what we were doing and why we were doing it" (Hugh Brock). The DAC thus rejected Marxism not only from a moral point of view as a producer of human suffering, loss of freedom and so on, but also from the point of view of theory. The DAC rejected the fundamentals of Marxist thinking—that politics was at base a process of struggle between social classes whose social and economic interests were inherently different under capitalism, and that *conflict* was thus an indigenous part of the political process. The DAC's rejection of this perspective explains their relative lack of interest in enlisting the support of the organised Labour Movement.

> Hugh Brock: "I was never very much given to thinking about class distinctions. There are those people who were prepared to think through this thing — and it divided, for me, into people who would come along on the basis of our appeal and those who would not . . . (I did not) think of it in class terms."

As our findings have confirmed, the DAC supporters were predominantly either indifferent or hostile to Marxism. Their concern was to win the support of individuals, irrespective of class: even Pat Arrowsmith's persistent, energetic and diligent campaign to 'win over the workers' was couched in essentially individual and moral terms. Viewed in this light the DAC stood clearly in the tradition of radical, individualist, pacifism. Despite the increasingly 'revolutionary' language, and the collectivist, mass-movement ideological tone, the DAC remained essentially a Liberal movement,[102] basing its ideology on the individual and morality, rather than on the class and structural analysis.

In the final analysis the DAC was a single-issue pacifist campaign concerned in the first instance with unilateral nuclear disarmament and seeing itself as a ginger group to spur on the more timid and diluted CND; it also saw the unilateralist issue as "the thin end of the wedge towards a wholesale rethinking of defence policy" (April Carter). The central focus was thus the traditional pacifist concern with conflict and war. And the ideology underpinning this was the radical individualism of the ILP — a secularised Christianity: a politics based on the moral appeal and teaching of the 'Sermon on the Mount'[103] — partially impregnated with Gandhian ideas. The upshot was that the DAC never took its own propaganda for creating a mass movement seriously: it remained a small, dedicated, radical pacifist grouping — bubbling over with fresh ideas for protest, passionately committed to the cause, but lacking any clear ideological or strategic grasp, and destined to remain a small and exclusive group dedicated to the principles of non-violence.

THE COMMITTEE OF 100

The DAC was rapidly overshadowed, in the popular mind, by the Committee of 100 through the early months of 1961.[104] As the Committee of 100 grew and gained publicity, the DAC decided to disband and merge itself into the Committee's campaign, as Pat Arrowsmith recalled:

> After that Holy Loch demonstration (i.e. DAC demonstration at Holy Loch, 1961) we, the DAC, went into voluntary liquidation . . . some of our supporters were quite dewy-eyed but April and I were quite cold-blooded . . . although there was a certain difference in philosophy we were sensible enough to see that it drew on the same forces as the Committee of 100 and it was effectively the same sort of thing.

This is not the place to explore the strange story of the Committee of 100's formation; the issue here is rather to explore the perspective of the Committee of 100 and to compare its ideological formation with that of the DAC. In many ways there was a continuation of both theory and practice from the DAC to the Committee of 100; and there was, very significantly, a strong carry-over of personnel—most importantly of all Michael Randle, Chairman of DAC, became secretary of the Committee of 100. April Carter and Hugh Brock confirmed that Randle's appointment was seen as crucial:

> . . . the only reason we agreed to wind up the DAC and support the setting up of the Committee of 100 was that Michael Randle be brought home from Ghana to head it up as Secretary. If they did that, O.K., we went along, we wound up the DAC, and I think while Michael was maintaining the leadership of the Committee of 100 we thought it was O.K. (Hugh Brock).

Yet there was, as Pat Arrowsmith recalled, a very real mistrust and tension between the two organisations: "there was a certain amount of vituperation and, the sad thing was, it actually caused friction between DAC people. . . . I think the animosity was quite a bit between Ralph (Schoenman) and myself." This was, of course, due in part to the natural resentment of one organisation at being upstaged and taken over by a larger and more prestigious new organisation. But the *ideological* differences were more important and deep-rooted than these purely personal factors. To begin with, the Committee of 100 was, to a far greater extent than the DAC, a hybrid: it included Pacifists to be sure, but it also included Marxists, Anarchists, and a large number of people of no identifiable ideology who believed that the nuclear threat was of such gravity and urgency that Civil Disobedience was justifiable, despite its illegality. The DAC was 'pure' in the sense of being united around a wholly non-violent perspective: the Committee of 100 was not pure in that sense and, like CND, it contained wildly divergent ideological perspectives.[105]

It is impossible with the Committee of 100 to describe *the* ideology, *the* perspective: we can only isolate the major perspectives and discuss them. All perspectives, of course, envisaged extra-parliamentary action, primarily non-violent civil disobedience, as being the means of achieving the goal of unilateral disarmament (and, for many in the CND leadership, it was this avowed belief in *illegal* protest that formed the major, and unbridgeable barrier, between CND and the Committee of 100: as Jacquetta Hawkes recalled: "the basic thing was that most of us didn't want illegal action, that was quite definite".) The most straightforward motivation was to view the Committee of 100 as a vehicle for creating the necessary sense of urgency and public attention to bring home to the population as a whole the nuclear peril—and the case for unilateral nuclear disarmament. In other words, to see the Committee of 100 not as a separate ideological movement, nor even to see it as a radical movement in some senses 'to the Left' of CND, but to envisage it purely as a means of creating massive publicity and thereby popular support. It was the *urgency* and the need for *publicity* which underlay Russell's decision to give his backing to Schoenman's proposal to form the Committee of 100.[106] This was a pragmatic view: at this level ideology did not enter into it: Russell justified his espousal of Civil Disobedience in terms of the urgency of the issue.[107] And, had it not been for the personality clash between Russell and Collins, and the adamant opposition of the CND Executive to illegal action *per se*, there might, on the ideological level, have been a good chance of a coming together.[108]

Schoenman, on the other hand, had a very different perspective: in his view the military complex, the 'Warfare State', lay at the heart of a corrupt system. The objective of the Committee of 100 was to prevent the State operating by means of demonstrations of non-violent civil disobedience of ever-increasing size, filling the

jails and thus paralysing the system to the point of collapse. The flavour of Schoenman's apocalyptic political style was recalled by George Clark: after the enormously
successful 1960 Aldermaston March there was a meeting addressed by Michael Foot,
at the Marquee Club:

> (Michael Foot) was *particularly* bad, *particularly* bad! . . . he made an appalling
> speech, right out of time and touch, and this guy Schoenman . . . put forward
> this extraordinary proposition of surrounding the Houses of Parliament and not
> letting the legislators out until they gave way! That's how, publicly, the 100 was
> formed. . . .

Schoenman certainly had a syndicalist orientation and he viewed the function of the
Committee of 100 in straightforwardly insurrectionist, anti-political terms. Writing in
Peace News in the summer of 1961 he avowed that

> The model for our objective shall be, the General Strike . . . we are not a political
> party, we have no intention of providing a Civil Service or an alternative body of
> administrators. We have precise demands which must be pressed upon authority.
> They will acquiesce or face national disruption. There shall undoubtedly be a
> host of political consequences of our resistance. We must not be deluded by them.
> If we hand over our consciences to any political party we will be betrayed. There
> is no party, no bureaucracy, and no authority which may not outrage our most
> fundamental values.

Endeavouring to summarise and 'place' Schoenman ideologically, Stuart Hall observed:

> He was certainly not what I would call a 'pure fish' in terms of *English* political
> traditions. If he was an Anarchist he was an Anarchist of a different kind from
> English Anarchists; . . . he was an Anarchist certainly in the sense of really believ-
> ing in the capacity of the single individual will and the individual action to spark
> something off . . . on the other hand he did quite frequently make the connections
> between that kind of individualism of the will and the attempt to mobilise and
> bring off a kind of vanguardism among revolutionary forces, and there is a kind
> of Trotskyist element to that, although I never heard from Ralph anything that I
> would have thought identifiable as a developed Trotskyist analysis of the Cold
> War or the general situation etc.
>
>   So I would have said both of them with small letters: small 'a' anarchist and
> small 't' trotskyist in certain elements, but I think that it is only a rather feeble
> way of our saying he was a political animal we never quite understood.

As Hall went on to imply, Schoenman, despite his crucial importance to the Committee
of 100 and despite the strong emotions he aroused (e.g. from Jacquetta Hawkes and
Arthus Goss, who were quite outspoken in their hostility), was very much a man on his
own ideologically. It seemed reasonable to argue that if the jails *had* been filled it
would have presented the State with an *ideological* problem (i.e. to explain and justify
why this was happening). But, according to Stuart Hall, Schoenman believed that "if
you throw yourself time and again against the walls of the State, ultimately they will
crumble; very few people believed this in that full sense: and in some ways he, Schoenman, did — and in that sense his was a very extreme position". It was also in retrospect
a very *unrealistic* one: in George Clark's view it was pure adventurism to argue, as

Schoenman did, "that 10,000 or 100,000 people could swing the course of British politics". Michael Randle was perhaps nearer the mark: "The point at which you could actually bring Government to a standstill wouldn't be 50,000 it wouldn't be 100,000, it would be *millions*. So, if there was going to be that insurrectionary stage, we were a very long way from it."

In many ways, in fact, Michael Randle represents a more central perspective on the Committee of 100. In his view there was a much greater correspondence between DAC and the Committee of 100 than is usually assumed. The Committee of 100 marked, he thought, a shift "that one step further away from committed pacifism" where there was more diversity but also the possibility of a "coherent, radical politics evolving". The Committee of 100 was, really, an *extension* of the DAC, and did not mark a clear break. The problem, in Randle's view, was tactical: the Committee of 100 was committed to building, almost on a geometric progression, the size of its demonstrations. The demonstrations in London in 1961 were by and large successful, culminating in the huge September sit-down in Trafalgar Square. Again, Randle saw no difference of principle over whether demonstrations should be at bases or in large urban centres: "A lot of us favoured doing some of each! . . ." And there was a general agreement that the objective should be to build up to such a pitch that Government would, at some stage, be immobilised. How exactly this was to come about was an open question: and Randle and others were astute enough politically not to be carried away with the euphoria of the 1961 successes—they realised that it would be a long struggle. But, in the meantime, how could the Committee continue to build its strength? They argued that "the next stage of radical action" had to be a return to the bases: a determined effort to immobilise these prior to moving on in an attempt to immobilise the Government itself. The strategy of course failed: Wethersfield, Ruislip and the other demonstrations[109] marked the beginning of the fairly rapid decline of the Committee of 100. But it was a clear and coherent strategy, based on the quasi-anarchist, revolutionary populist ideology which developed out of the DAC and the Committee of 100, centring on the nuclear issue but broadening out into a wider critique of modern British society, and developing a programme for action.

Two final comments perhaps portray best the ideology underlying the Committee of 100. Stuart Hall pinpointed the composition, and thus the orientation, of the Committee of 100:

> I would have said that the new element (in the Committee of 100) was less a kind of pacifist philosophical rationale for Direct Action and more of a political one; people who may not have been committed philosophically to that way of going about it, nevertheless saw the *political* significance of stepping beyond the confines of traditional politics, traditional parliamentary-oriented politics . . . (Alongside the DAC Gandhians) there was a number of Committee of 100 people who weren't *philosphically* into that (i.e. DA and Civil Disobedience), but who were into it *politically* . . . into it as a *tactic* rather than a *principle*. . . .

And George Clark, talking of the nature of the Committee of 100 and of the radical wing of the movement generally, summed up the ethos of the radical perspective:

> . . . (1960) That's the first time they actually realised the power of the March you see . . . first and foremost it was a Campaign. Secondly, it was not so much a

Movement as a kind of political statement . . . we'd have three styles, that's what I wanted: the grass roots movement on the ground, in the towns, villages and so on throughout the year . . . we would apply the Civil Disobedience when the political thing wasn't working or responding; and the Easter March would represent the political statement of the *whole* movement. . . .

'Movement power'—that was what the Committee of 100 meant to George Clark and to most Committee of 100 campaigners. To take power from the bureaucracy of the CND leadership, from the Labourist tacticians, and place it in the hands of the Movement: a populist rather than a socialist motivation. The perspective did not, of course, come good. After Wethersfield the Committee of 100 suffered the same mortal blow as the CND leadership suffered after the defeat in 1961 at the Labour Conference. The failure of the Committee of 100 strategy belied its confused ideology: had it been clear on its ideological base it would have moulded its strategy accordingly. As it was, the grandiose schemes of Schoenman collapsed in disarray: the Committee of 100 which started with such drama and such success in 1960/1 was built on shifting ideological sand, and, from early 1962, all was confusion and decline.

The Campaign as a Single-issue Pressure Group

THE SCIENTISTS' 'ENVIRONMENTAL' PERSPECTIVE

There was, however, another significant strand of thinking in the Movement that was based neither on 'morality' in the sense we have discussed it earlier, nor on any form of 'political' motivation in the sense of an ideological or organisational commitment. There existed an influential group of eminent scientists who had been active in voicing their disquiet about A-Bombs and H-bombs from the time of Hiroshima and Nagasaki onwards. The key initiator of this Movement, certainly as far as the UK was concerned, was, of course, Bertrand Russell.[110] The emphasis of this group was always on the appalling effects of nuclear weapons, the overriding need to ensure that they were discarded and never used, and the consequent crucial importance of persuading both public opinion and governments of the need to implement nuclear disarmament as *the* priority.

All these motivations were there, of course, to a degree in all those involved with the Movement: none denied the importance of the issue of nuclear weapons itself. From the scientific/environmentalist point of view, however, there can be no doubt that the stark facts of the effects of nuclear weapons and the need to bring home to all sections of society the catastrophic implications of their existence, remained by far the most important part of the argument. Most scientists active in the Movement[111] were aware of both the moral and political connotations of the issue, but in their view the commitment to the issue of nuclear disarmament itself had to remain both paramount and exclusive. Thus, Professor Rotblat, among the most consistently active and committed of scientists in the CND Movement, has commented:

Whilst it was a moral campaign it was also a political campaign in that it arose from the anxieties about the continuing atmospheric tests, which despite Government disclaimers, people continued to be unhappy about, and they consequently sought to influence the Government's political decisions. . . .

But he also emphasised the long-standing and deep concern of the scientific community which centred on the issue itself:

> I, and others, who worked on the A-Bomb during the War knew just what nuclear weapons could do: we issued a manifesto . . . warning what the consequences of nuclear war would be and asking scientists to recognise the importance of their role in their own countries and to use their influence to try to affect Government policies. From this developed the Pugwash Movement. . . .

The text of this manifesto was as follows:

> We are speaking on this occasion not as members of this or that nation, continent or creed, but as human beings, members of the species of Man, whose continued existence is in doubt. . . .
>
> We have to learn to think in a new way: we have to learn to ask ourselves not what steps can be taken to give military victory to whatever group we prefer, for there are no longer such steps; the question we have to ask ourselves is: what steps can be taken to prevent a military contest of which the issue must be disastrous to all parties? . . . Shall we put an end to the human race; or shall mankind renounce war?[112]

The Manifesto (known subsequently as the Russell/Einstein Manifesto) was issued in 1955, and was signed by eleven prominent scientists, including nine Nobel prizewinners; apart from Russell and Einstein its signatories were: Max Born, Linus Pauling, J. F. Joliot-Curie, Joseph Rotblat, P. W. Bridgman, H. J. Muller, C. F. Powell, L. Infield and Hideki Yukawa.

As a result of this Manifesto, Russell was able to establish, with the help of the wealthy, liberally minded, Canadian-American industrialist Cyrus Eaton, the Pugwash Conference of Scientists. The first and major achievement of Pugwash was to attract scientists from both West *and East* who had in common not only their scientific expertise but a common commitment to the cause of disarmament. The ability to convince a sceptical outside world of the unbiased nature of the movement continued to be a major concern of both Pugwash and the subsequent 'scientist' strata in the CND. Professor Rotblat has testified to this:

> At first Pugwash was 'suspect', and in America we were openly called a communist organisation. . . . It took us several years to convince Western governments that we were genuine: then once they realised we were not pushing one ideological line they became very interested and tried to take us over. They wanted to tell us what we should discuss, who we should talk to, while I felt that if we accepted this it would be the kiss of death, even worse than being thought Communists. Therefore I always fought against us becoming aligned or a part of the Establishment.

In the early days of Pugwash, Russell, too, showed great concern with both the maintenance of this 'balance' and the attainment of international respectability. This was, as his biographer noted, "a tricky operation which only the aristocrat would have attempted with equanimity and which Russell almost alone among living men, had the background and the resolution to carry out with some chance of success".[113] Thanks in large part to Russell the Pugwash conferences established themselves as reputable and influential gatherings and, under the committed and expert guidance of Professor Joseph Rotblat, the Secretary General, they became a force to be taken very seriously by leading governments and their bureaucracies. This "pressure through expert and responsible scientific opinion" was a continuing theme not only in Pugwash but in the CND itself: a significant proportion of our sample was involved in CND from exactly this perspective. Paradoxically, however, Russell himself began to lose his close personal involvement with Pugwash just as it attained that credibility which he had been instrumental in achieving. As Pugwash "gained the confidence of governments, East and West, as it drew in for its annual conferences scientists who could influence events from inside rather than outside the Establishment" Russell's enthusiasm diminished.[114] In part this was, as Rotblat has recalled, because "he felt he had too little time left: he must try everything . . .", and in part it was a manifestation of Russell's lifelong, quasi-liberal, quasi-libertarian distrust of governments and bureaucracies *per se*.

Be this as it may, the Pugwash Movement, and the corresponding strata in the CND, continued to regard scientific influence at government level as the major means of accomplishing progress towards disarmament. The most politically aware scientists have, of course, recognised that both the elite pressure group and the mass-movement approach are needed: far from being exclusive it is argued that they are in fact complementary.[115] In his detailed study of the scientific background to nuclear weapons, Dr. John Cox (a former Chairman of the CND in the 1970s) comes to the conclusion that, horrific though the scientific capabilities and technology of nuclear weapons undoubtedly are, the problem is neither 'scientific' nor 'diplomatic': it is political: "There is, in fact, no difficulty in devising disarmament agreements: the difficulty is to force governments to implement them. In present circumstances the military-industrial complex have (*sic*) far greater power and influence than the ordinary people."[116] There is a clear distinction between this perception from the 'scientific left', and the perception of those, such as Professor Rotblat, who, although believing in political action, are to some extent non-aligned, and believe that so-called 'ideological' positions can only distort and cloud the issue.[117]

But, whatever the differences in political orientation, it was clearly the view of all those closely involved in the Movement from a scientific background, that *some* political pressure must be forthcoming if the desired end were to be achieved. However much they thought that the case must be argued in fundamentally scientific, environmental terms, there could be no denying that a political dimension to the Campaign was essential. Scientific evidence—and even scientific pressure—were acknowledged to be ultimately insufficient, on their own, to achieve the desired end of nuclear disarmament.

BERTRAND RUSSELL'S CAMPAIGN

It is within this context that Bertrand Russell's key role in the Movement—both the CND and the Committee of 100—should be seen. Inevitably, given his immense personal magnetism, fame, intellect, past involvement with all manner of radical campaigns, *and* his great age,[118] Russell is not readily classifiable. And he cannot be considered as 'merely' one of the group of scientists active in the Movement: in many ways he moved on a different plane from all others in the Movement and was the Head of

State in the Protesters' Republic. Yet, in terms of his *perspective* on the Movement he was initially very similar in orientation to the scientist/environmentalist group. His primary motivation from 1945 and the Hiroshima and Nagasaki bombings was to save the world from nuclear destruction. "There is no doubt", states Russell's biographer, "that the salvation of the human race from a nuclear holocaust was the last great attachment of Russell's life. . . ."[119] Far from viewing the development of nuclear weapons as indicative of a general malaise in society or the end product of an unworkable and/or immoral system, Russell originally (i.e. in the late 1940s) was urging the West to coerce the USSR into agreeing to a system of world government by using the threat of nuclear attack. (The USSR did not develop nuclear weapon capability until 1949 when she exploded her first A-Bomb.) Russell's advocacy of 'preventive war' with the USSR when the USA had the monopoly of nuclear weapons has often been held to be an aberration, an uncharacteristically warlike and aggressive bout of Western chauvinism which was incompatible with his later stance.[120] In reality the opposite was the case: not only was it quite in character for Russell to make shocking and outrageous statements, on political, as on other matters;[121] the fundamentals of the position he adopted in the 1940s were also consistent with his continued insistence in the 1950s and 1960s that nuclear weapons and the probability of the imminent destruction of mankind *must* be seen as the paramount issue overriding all other political questions. Once it is acknowledged that the prevention of nuclear war, and hence mankind's destruction, was the guiding aim of Russell's life and politics post-1945, then his advocacy of the need for world peace and disarmament via world government, to be achieved, if necessary, through coercion, became not only rational but necessary.[122]

Russell's attitudes were, of course, founded on the liberal assumptions of his own, lifelong, ideological framework: much else may have changed during Russell's life but, with the possible exception of his very last years,[123] he was consistent in his political philosophy. As one commentator has put it, he was "individualistic rather than state-centred, democratic rather than authoritarian, pragmatic rather than ideological, empirical rather than theoretical, rational rather than emotional, international rather than parochial".[124] He had the nineteenth-century Liberal's passion for internationalism — and he had a strong aversion for continental socialist theorising — an aversion that was, and is, so characteristic of the Anglo-American empiricist traditions of philosophy, social science and politics. Partly as a result of his unparalleled access to, and often friendship with, the whole range of the most eminent among international scientists, and partly as a result of his own grasp of the possible consequences of nuclear war, he became convinced that the rapid solution of the 'nuclear problem' was a *sine qua non* for the continued existence of mankind.

A number of factors arises from this period of Russell's involvement with the nuclear issue — which can be seen in some ways as a prologue to his main involvement. Most important is the overriding urgency and pre-eminent importance which Russell attached to the issue itself: this urgency and commitment continued unabated for the rest of Russell's life: as Clark has said: "From 1950 onwards Russell emerges as the world's most persistent propagandist for peace, devoting more and more time and effort to the cause. . . ."[125] As a corollary to this there was Russell's insistence that the issue must be brought to the attention of the world's leaders *and* the general public by any means appropriate: it was this conviction that underlay Russell's support for both

CND and Committee of 100 — and, in the earlier 1950s, for the Pugwash Movement of scientists. For Russell they were all part of the same generalised movement for nuclear disarmament, exerting pressure on opinion at different levels and in different ways but all having the unifying theme of the nuclear issue. A further important feature of Russell's attitude is apparent in this early phase: his non-socialist, non-structural, almost non-political, approach. And, despite Schoenman's attempt to persuade us otherwise it is clear that Russell was, and to a greater or lesser extent remained, a non-Marxist in ideological/theoretical terms.[126]

Russell's stance, however, was not merely non-socialist: in true nineteenth-century style he viewed politics as a process of imposing a set of clearly formulated utilitarian ideals emphasising the benefits of world order, rationality, international co-operation (*and,* of course, individual freedom and self-determination . . .) through a formal diplomatic and pragmatic political process.[127] It is worth noting here, too, that his implicit acceptance of the efficacy and desirability of the elite and formal processes of world politics and diplomacy were indicative of his own superlative aristocratic pedigree. There was, as Schoenman noted,[128] an ambivalence between Russell's support for democratic movements and his elitist belief that

> cultural excellence and unique achievement were the product of favoured circumstances. . . . He felt that excellence came from the special nurturing of individual talent and that meritocracy or cultural decline would follow the overthrow of privilege. He desired its overthrow but he mourned in advance some of the consequences as he saw them.

In all these aspects Russell differed from others in the leadership of the Movement: his perspective was closest to that of the scientists of the Pugwash group, particularly those who, like Rotblat, gave their support to the practical political activity of organisations like CND. But Russell's vast experience of political activity throughout the twentieth century, his intellectual dominance over an extraordinary number of fields,[129] and his aristocratic origins and attitudes, separate him from all other important individuals or groups in the Movement.

Consistent though his perspective was, his involvement with the nuclear issue does divide clearly into four periods: the Pugwash period of pressure via the international scientific community (1950 to 1958); the CND years (1958 to 1960); the Committee of 100 years (1960 to 1962); and the plethora of international campaigns and activities, principally of course the international campaign he mounted in opposition to the Vietnam war, between 1962 and 1970. It is to his involvement in the CND and the Committee of 100 that our attention must here be directed; but it must again be emphasised that he saw these campaigns as extensions of his other propagandist work to rid the world of nuclear weapons: there was no break in perspective between Pugwash, CND, and the Committee of 100, although there was a clearer distinction between all these activities on the one hand, and his increasingly leftist stance through the last years of his life.[130] Having been the moving force in establishing the Pugwash Conference, and subsequent pressure group, Russell was content to leave it to others to administer and develop.[131] Russell was concerned to open up other avenues for publicising the nuclear issue. As early as 1954 Russell had, in a memorable radio broadcast,[132] set the tone for his later passionate, all-or-nothing advocacy of the nuclear disarmament cause: "I appeal as a human being to human beings; remember your humanity, and forget the rest. If you can do so, the way lies open to a new Paradise; if you cannot, nothing lies before you but universal death." Although Russell had relatively little contact with either the NCANWT or the DAC,[133] there is no doubt that he was from the outset of the 'movement agitation' concerned to involve himself and lend his weight to the creation of a national organisation. It may be true that, as Clark has commented,[134] Russell's "real place in the Movement . . . (was) that of a figurehead giving academic respectability and white-headed publicity . . .", but Russell himself was never prepared to act merely as a figurehead, in either CND or the Committee of 100.[135] Russell was, of course, one of the original small group which gave birth to CND, and from the very beginning he favoured more militant measures to achieve the aims of CND than others in the leadership were prepared to countenance: as he himself has written:

> We both (i.e. Lord Simon of Wythenshawe and Russell) believed that the dangers must be called to the attention of the public in as many ways as possible and that if we stuck to merely meetings and even marches, no matter how admirable they might be, we should end by preaching only to the converted. The Chairman of CND did not approve of Civil Disobedience and so, though nominally the DAC was to be tolerated, it could not be openly aided by the CND.[136]

However, although Russell was, from the beginning, in favour of militant means to achieve the objective, he was by no means in the same ideological camp as the DAC. Although a Pacifist in World War I his pacifism had been of a very different tradition from that of the non-violent Gandhian Pacifists of DAC, and had been based more on the immediate, *ad hoc* issues at the time than on a political philosophy centring on non-violence. Thus, in the late 1950s immediately prior to the formation of the DAC, Russell was arguing that he was

> not in favour of its (the nuclear weapon's) abolition, as I've often been assumed to be. Fear is a great and effective force in human nature. The H-Bomb is a real deterrent in three ways *not* possessed by any previous weapons. It gives equal power to each side; the leaders are no safer than the rest of the population; and the devastation would be on such a scale as to make any victory very problematical indeed.[137]

Russell thus rejected the DAC's militant objectives of a 'non-violent society', and their specific policy commitment to *American* (and Russian) unilateral disarmament as well as British. In this very important sense Russell was arguing on the same ideological assumptions as the CND leadership of Collins *et al.*: that is, he accepted that nuclear weapons were an isolated evil of contemporary society, albeit an evil of unprecedented and hitherto unimaginable magnitude. The problem was thus to rid the world of these weapons, which could be achieved quite independently of social and political structural change. Unlike the DAC (and for that matter the Socialist Left) Russell saw no connection between the *form* of society and the development of nuclear weapons. For him nuclear disarmament was not only of paramount importance, it was also a genuinely 'single-issue campaign'. The reasons for Russell adopting this perspective are numerous and complex but the philosophical and ideological tradition to which he belonged led Russell to reject[138] the specifically socialist perspectives of the New Left and other Marxist groupings. But more importantly, in the Disarmament Movement context, it also led Russell to reject the Gandhian-inspired politics of non-violence advocated by the DAC (and the later espousal of this politics, linked to a quasi-anarchist perspective, adopted by many in the Committee of 100). Moreover, for all his immense erudition and incomparable intellectual ability, Russell had always tended to see politics in very 'black and white' terms. His humanist radicalism was outraged by the existence of nuclear weapons and he threw his immense influence and political tenacity and ingenuity behind the movement for disarmament. But he was always distanced to some extent from his radical supporters and their organisations partly because of this profound ideological gulf — and partly, of course, because of the immense differences in age, social milieu and intellectual interests and abilities that existed between himself and the Movement's 'rank and file'.

It is common knowledge that Russell's relationship, as President of CND, with the rest of the CND leadership, and in particular with Canon Collins, the Chairman, was somewhat strained from the beginning. It is less often acknowledged that Russell was also out of touch and to some degree out of sympathy with the Committee of 100 activists. Russell's motivation for giving his support to the foundation of the Committee of 100[139] was quite consistent with his previous activities in the cause of nuclear disarmament.

> "By the summer of 1960", Russell wrote, "it seemed to me as if Pugwash and CND and the other methods that we had tried of informing the public had reached the limit of their effectiveness. It might be possible to so move the general public that it would demand en masse, and therefore irresistibly, the remaking of present governmental policies, here in Britain first and then elsewhere in the world."[140]

Russell felt that CND "had shot its bolt and that no further success could reasonably be expected".[141] Russell thus welcomed the proposal to create a mass movement based on civil disobedience campaigns which would take the Movement out of what he saw as the political dead-end of conventional pressure-group activity within the confines of the Labour Party. This is not the place to look in any detail at the growing relationship, both personal and political, between Russell and Ralph Schoenman.[142] What is important in this context is to analyse Russell's perspective on the Committee of 100 and discuss how far his stance was consistent with his earlier activities. Russell's interest in an advocacy of Civil Disobedience was wholly consistent with his radical individualism. (As Clark has noted, the espousal of Civil Disobedience was "easy enough for those born into the aristocratic tradition but slightly shocking to the respectable middle classes who supplied the cannon-fodder of the Movement".)[143] As early as 1936 Russell had made his position on civil disobedience quite clear.

> I know well that this (Civil Disobedience) is a dangerous doctrine and that the claim to set up one's own individual judgement in defiance of legally constituted authority leads logically to anarchy. At the same time almost all great advances have involved illegality. The early Christians broke the law; Galileo broke the law; the French revolutionaries broke the law; early Trade Unionists broke the law. The instances are so numerous and so important that no-one can maintain as an absolute principle obedience to constituted authority.[144]

Civil disobedience was thus seen as a necessary means of achieving 'progressive' ends at certain critical times in man's history. In a rather different context Russell argued[145] that just as "the judges of Nuremburg believe that Germans should have committed civil disobedience in the name of decency and humanity" so should civil disobedience be justified in similarly extreme circumstances in the context of the H-Bomb. Whether civil disobedience was justifiable or not thus depended not on any abstract or theoretical consideration but on "the reasons for it being committed — the seriousness of the object for which it is committed and the profundity of the belief in its necessity".

Given this perspective it is not surprising that Russell advocated civil disobedience to further the nuclear disarmament cause. By the summer of 1960 "he was beginning to feel that the voice of the Church Militant, epitomised by Collins' chairmanship of CND, was becoming little more than a whisper in the parish magazine".[146] He thus gave enthusiastic backing to Schoenman's proposals: but there was a very wide division between them from the outset about the purpose of and justification for civil disobedience. Whereas Schoenman's intention was, as we have seen, openly insurrectionary and had the objective of bringing down the whole existing state system through a mounting movement of civil disobedience. Russell's viewpoint was characteristically pragmatic. Asked in an interview in 1963[147] why he had backed civil disobedience, Russell replied: "Purely to get attention. All the major organs of publicity are against us. . . . I have no views in principle either for or against Civil Disobedience . . . with me, it is purely a practical question of whether to do it or not, a method of propaganda." Russell's much-publicised dispute with Collins[148] was thus personal and tactical rather than ideological. To be sure, there were those within the CND leadership for whom the question of Civil Disobedience *per se* was a major ideological division,[149] but in reality it was a division over tactics — over the best way to secure the agreed end of British unilateral disarmament — although deeper divisions underlay the conflict, as we have argued earlier. Russell was no more in favour of 'Movement Power' than was Canon Collins — save in so far as the pressure of a mass civil disobedience movement would, in a tactical sense, in Russell's view, lead to the attainment of unilateral disarmament. Paradoxically, therefore, there was far more in common between Russell and the CND leadership in ultimate ideological terms than there was between Russell and the militant young activists of the Committee of 100 of which he was President.

Russell's charismatic presence was one of the Committee of 100's greatest assets during 1961 and the extraordinary blunder by the authorities in arresting and subsequently imprisoning Russell and his wife just before the September 1961 demonstration marked the height of Russell's impact and influence on the Committee. The sharply conflicting views within the Committee on its long-term purposes and functions were masked by the common concern with organising and promoting mass demonstrations, and, above all, by the spectacular success of the Committee both in terms of the mounting numbers of supporters and in terms of media coverage and attention.[150] In his most optimistic moments Russell could not have imagined greater 'publicity' successes than were achieved in the first year of the Committee's existence.[151] However, as both George Clark[152] and Russell,[153] from their different perspectives, realised the demonstrations of December 1961 were major tactical blunders and, by early 1962, Russell was beginning to become disillusioned with the Committee. In his autobiography he noted that

1. Aldermaston March 1958, first day, Turnham Green.

2. Aldermaston March 1958, first day, Turnham Green.

3. Aldermaston March 1958, second day, near London Airport.

4. Aldermaston March 1959, last day, entering Trafalgar Square.

5. Aldermaston March, 1959.

6. Aldermaston March, 1960.

7. Polaris Demonstration, February 1961, starting out from Speakers' Corner.

8. Polaris Demonstration, February 1961, Trafalgar Square.

The Committee had already begun to weaken itself in other ways. Long discussions were beginning to be held amongst its members as to whether the Committee should devote itself only to nuclear and disarmament matters or should begin to oppose all domestic, social and governmental injustice. This was a waste of time and a dispersal of energies.[154]

This was Russell the pragmatist, the political campaigner and political realist talking: he realised the organisational impossibility of mounting a full-scale assault on the established order via the Committee of 100. But it was also Russell the ideologue: Russell was concerned at this time with the single issue of nuclear disarmament and he had no sympathy with the wider (and admittedly confused and nebulous) social theorising of the anarchistic elements within the Committee. From this time onwards Russell's commitment to and involvement with the Committee of 100 began to decrease, not primarily because the Committee itself was losing impetus and direction — although this of course was important — but because the Committee was rapidly becoming a *generalised* social protest movement and drifting further and further away from the concerns of nuclear disarmament *per se*. It was, however, the Cuba crisis and its aftermath which finally led Russell to break formally with the Committee of 100. As his biographer has correctly surmised

> the world after the crisis differed in two subtle ways from the world before. Nuclear war had been avoided . . . however small the improvement might be, it did allow him to redeploy his forces and turn to other parts of the international scene where he felt he could set the world on the path he believed it should go. Quite as important, the balance of danger from the East and West appeared to have shifted. Russell despised the theory and detested the practice of Communism as much as ever; but after Cuba he believed that the US presented a greater threat to the peace of the world than did the USSR, a belief soon reinforced by the war in Vietnam.[155]

For Russell, then, as for George Clark, the immediacy and urgency had suddenly evaporated: the Bomb was still *the* problem but, because a nuclear holocaust had been avoided, it was clear that the prophecies of nuclear doom within the decade carried far less weight than before. For George Clark and others this meant diversifying activities into more community-based politics[156] — for Russell it entailed frenetic involvement on the 'conventional' international political stage for the remainder of his life. His concern broadened out into fields wider than the nuclear issue — and he became centrally concerned with the American war in Vietnam.[157] Schoenman has claimed that "every major political initiative that has borne the name of Bertrand Russell since 1960 has been my work in thought and deed", and, moreover, that the notion of Russell's being "taken over by a sinister young revolutionary . . . touched a partial truth".[158] There is, as Russell's biographer concluded, some basis of truth in both these claims, but it must be emphasised that, heavily influenced by Schoenman though he was, Russell's central perspective and his clear objectives as to specific actions did not, until after the Cuba crisis, deviate from his consistent and priority concern with nuclear disarmament. After Cuba his emphasis certainly shifted to a more generally anti-American stance, but, as argued above, this was due not only to Schoenman's influence but to a change in the objective situation *vis-à-vis* the prospects of nuclear war.

For Russell, as for others in the Pugwash movement, the overriding priority was for

nuclear disarmament to avoid the destruction of civilisation and possibly the total annihilation of humanity. Through the 1950s and up to Cuba, universal nuclear destruction was predicted by Russell as a short-term probability. Given this urgency, and
given Russell's own ideological perspective, it was quite natural for him to think of the
issue in global, 'human destiny' terms. Given his assumptions, *all* other political considerations appeared absurdly unimportant if not completely irrelevant. His consistency is undeniable: and his willingness to adopt relatively extreme methods of protest[159]
was not only justifiable but essential if his prognosis of the nuclear peril was accurate.
The problem remained, however, that "remember your humanity and forget the rest",
whilst admirable as a humanist slogan, did not solve the complex political and social
problems of mobilising support for the Movement. From all political perspectives
Russell's strategy and analysis were inadequate. Partly because of his sense of urgency,
which amounted almost to an obsession, partly because of his own patrician and intellectual arrogance and elitism,[160] and partly because of his dominant position on the
Liberal Left, Russell switched from one organisation and strategic platform to another
with bewildering rapidity.[161] The consistency of his concern with the nuclear issue
cannot be doubted; and the solid establishment of Pugwash must rank as a major
achievement. In the final analysis, however, despite Russell's (and the Pugwash movement's) passionate concern and commitment, it must be concluded that the nuclear
disarmament movement could not be treated as a simple single-issue campaign: the
political ramifications were both too important and too complex to be resolved by the
superficially attractive appeal to "Remember your humanity and forget the rest".

VIEWS FROM THE OTHER SIDE

As a postscript to these discussions of the various Disarmament Movement perspectives it is instructive to consider briefly the views of two of those politicians in power
during the 'CND years': Sir Harold Wilson and Lord Home.[162] Not surprisingly, Lord
Home was far more stridently critical of CND than was Sir Harold. There was general
agreement in CND leadership circles, however, that Sir Harold was consistently ambivalent in his attitude to the CND: Jacquetta Hawkes, for example, has recalled that
the CND leaders "did have meetings with Harold Wilson before he was leader and he
was rather shamelessly prevaricating—saying that we were doing splendid work but
ought not to get too much involved with the Labour Party—he meant that he didn't
want us in his hair! . . . we never really felt he was with us." According to Sir Harold
himself, however, there was considerable affinity on moral and 'cultural' grounds between the CND and himself: "I was never in the CND of course, but because of my
religious background I felt I understood their approach . . . they were a genuine,
sincere body who strongly believed in their moral campaign." There was no such sympathy from the Conservative side: Lord Home repudiated emphatically the suggestion
that CND was either important or influential:

> I would have thought that all of us were morally anxious to disarm in any way we
> could . . . (CND) didn't make very much impression . . . on the politicians of the
> day who were actually up to their necks in the business of disarmament anyhow
> . . . I don't think they had a major influence in affecting public opinion. . . .

Thus, although both leaders were opposed to the CND, the degree of animosity,
and the grounds for their opposition, were very sharply distinguished.

Sir Harold's major concern in relation to the issue was to avoid a split in the Labour Party over unilateralism[163] and he was far less concerned with the substantive arguments than Hugh Gaitskell had been. As Sir Harold recalled: "Hugh Gaitskell took a strong line against it, partly because he believed it played into the hands of the Russians, and he was always anti-Russian." But, as Sir Harold also noted, Gaitskell's opposition was also motivated by tactical and electoral considerations: "He believed, rightly in my view, (that) we would never become the Government purely on committed Labour votes, and what he would regard as 'defence irresponsibility', would be very damaging." From the outset of the "CND debate" in the Labour Party Sir Harold was concerned to avoid a split. His role in uniting Bevan with Gaitskell was central:

> The Executive was split from top to bottom (over the unilateralist issue in 1957), and I was very much involved in trying to urge Nye, not to get over-committed to the defence issue but rather seek to bring the Party together . . . Sam Watson came to me to talk about Nye, and I could speak to Nye, and in the end Sam Watson and Nye got together: it was Sam who did it. . . .[164]

Despite his assertions of moral affinity with the CND cause, Sir Harold's own role was consistently that of arbitrator between the CND Labour Left and the Party leadership. He agreed that Bevan's 1957 speech "killed it within terms of CND reaching the commanding heights of the Party". His decision to stand against Gaitskell for the Party Leadership was in no substantive sense based on a CND/Party leadership division: rather, his motivation was again based on party unity (and, no doubt, on personal ambition). "I stood against him in 1959 on Clause 4 because I began to realise that he couldn't unite the party, and to the extent that he wanted to 'rough-it-up' with the CND, while one might not agree with them, it takes all sorts to make a Party." Once in office Sir Harold Wilson became even more distanced from CND's perspective. Moving in the world of international realpolitik he could see no political or strategic justification for Britain unilaterally disarming. There were, from the Labour leadership's point of view, overwhelmingly strong political and economic reasons for Britain's rejecting any weakening of the economic, political and military ties with the USA. In Sir Harold's view, "the Americans were so powerful (that) we needed to have influence with them, not only on Foreign Policy issues but also on economic matters as well". This certainly formed the cornerstone of the Labour Government's Foreign and Defence Policy between 1964 and 1970 (see the steadfast support given by Wilson's governments to US policy in Vietnam despite mounting criticism within, and outside, the Party). The degree of influence which the UK was thereby able to exert on US foreign (or economic or political or military) policy was, arguably, negligible: and the implication of this sort of statement — that Labour was concerned to push US policy into more liberally-inclined channels — would also appear to be questionable, given the historical record of the 1964-70 governments. Be this as it may, it is clear that, from this perspective, there could be no question of Sir Harold giving any consideration to the political implications — leaving NATO, adopting 'neutralism' — of CND's moral case for unilateral nuclear disarmament. Similarly, there was, in his view, no strategic or defence justification for unilateral nuclear disarmament: "Proliferation was inevitable, particularly because of De Gaulle, and now Giscard; and certainly nothing CND could do or say could have stopped this . . . I would repudiate too the CND claim that they made possible the signing of the Test Ban Treaty." However, despite his firm dismissal of CND as a *political* force, Sir Harold emphasised the *moral* significance of the Movement: "This is a moral issue really not a political one." Indeed, Sir Harold echoed the opinions he attributed to Bevan: "Nye saw . . . that these were decent, fine, morally committed people"; and like Bevan, he was not prepared to initiate or to condone purges against CND supporters: "I was not looking for splits, for I would say they're all good chaps, essential to the Party, and it was my job to keep links around them all, which I did."

For Lord Home, CND supporters were far from being "all good chaps"! Indeed, although Lord Home affirmed that the CND "included good people . . . a great many good people", and although he described Canon Collins as "a very sincere man", he laid emphasis on the "riff-raff" who were active in the rank and file of the Movement. Even those whom Lord Home regarded as "respectable" and "sincere" he also regarded "as sincerely wrong. . . . And I'm not sure that that is not an even greater sin than anything else". In accordance with the views of the Conservative Party at the time, Lord Home not only expressed a generalised hostility to the CND's aims and methods, but also argued strongly against its having had any influence on government policy or actions.[165] Not only was the CND, in Lord Home's view, ineffective as a pressure group on government: he also claimed that those in power (principally the Prime Minister, Mr MacMillan, and Lord Home himself as Foreign Secretary) "were in Geneva trying to disarm. We were constantly talking to the Russians about the possibility of nuclear disarmament . . . we didn't want any kind of gingering up from the CND." Thus, the essential thrust of Lord Home's argument was that the CND was both ineffective and redundant: ineffective because of its methods and the inherent foolhardiness of its policies, and redundant because HM Government was already fully intent on disarmament. And, Lord Home argued, this could be achieved only through patient and persistent negotiation to achieve multilateral disarmament.[166] The Partial Test Ban Treaty of 1963 was achieved because "all of us, including the Russians, were afraid of the effect of the fall-out on unborn babies and so on . . . And they didn't need the CND to emphasise that . . .". Ultimately Lord Home's arguments were centred on the need to provide the UK with an adequate independent defence against the threat of Russian aggression in Europe.

> I think there are a good many reasons why we wanted one (an independent nuclear deterrent). First of all there was always the possibility that America in future years might not have backed up Europe. It was conceivable. Also, we did not think it would be desirable for the French to be the only nuclear power in Europe. (There would have been) all sorts of repercussions on Germany if that had happened.

The core problem lay, in Lord Home's view, in the USSR's aggressive intentions, and their willingness to employ duplicity to attain their ends. "I don't think they've left us with any option really but to stand on our guard." In Lord Home's view the CND's arguments were based on quite false assumptions — and its support consisted of the naïve coupled with the subversive. Finally, as a Parliamentarian, and as an aristocrat of impeccable lineage, Lord Home viewed with evident distaste the methods which the CND and its supporters employed. Had they concentrated their pressure, misguided though he considered their case to be, on the elite structures of government rather than on building a mass movement on the streets, they might well have had more impact: ". . . of course they (i.e. Canon Collins and Lord Russell) had access to the top table if they'd wanted to use it. No Prime Minister could have refused to see either of them or both of them together if they had wanted to use that pressure. They preferred the streets which personally I don't prefer, but that's their preference".

Although the opposition to CND and its policies was common to the established leadership of both the Conservative and Labour Parties, it can thus be seen that the reasons for this opposition, the degree of animosity, and the ultimate evaluation of CND, differed considerably. Sir Harold Wilson saw the CND Movement as expressive of a genuine and in many ways admirable moral concern with the perils of nuclear warfare, which, although politically misguided, was a bona fide component of the Labour coalition. If this was a somewhat patronising attitude it certainly was not dismissive of the CND as an organisation nor was it contemptuous of the CND's policies and perspectives. For Lord Home and the Conservative leadership, on the other hand, the CND was almost wholly to be deplored. Not only was it misguided in its policies, it was seriously misleading and gave a respectable cover to undesirable elements in society (Lord Home's "riff-raff"). Almost its only virtue, in Lord Home's view, was the manner in which it demonstrated the nature of British democracy— ". . . this is something to pride ourselves on, that the ordinary man could make his pro-test". However, as Lord Home went on to say, "the ordinary man, after a time, began to see that the protest was bound to misfire as long as the Russians didn't play along. And so the protest gradually petered out."

Perhaps the most important aspect of agreement between the two political leader-ships was their willingness to tolerate, and even, in Labour's case, to applaud some aspects of the CND's motivation, if not of its policy, as long as two conditions were fulfilled: first, that the protest should remain within the law; and second, and far more important, that the organisation should remain an unsuccessful minority move-ment and that its aims should remain unattained. The fact that these two conditions were fulfilled enabled both leaderships to adopt a tolerant and patronising attitude to the CND's aims and activities—and was a measure of the degree of the Movement's ultimate lack of success.

CONCLUSION

This Part has been concerned with a detailed analysis of the leadership views of the different ideological and organisational groupings within the Movement. We have suggested the various aspects in which each group's strategy was inadequate, in the long term, as a framework of thought and action for the Movement. It is of course considerably easier to analyse critically these strategies with the hindsight of 20 years than it was in the heat of the protest activity. But even after this passage of time the differences of perspective are still keenly felt by the participants, as we have demonstrated.

It thus remains, in the final Part of this study, to draw together the empirical and theoretical insights that have been gleaned from Parts II and III, and present a more positive analysis of what, in our view, were the major dilemmas facing the Movement's supporters at the level of both ideology and political practice. Finally, we shall attempt to assess the Movement's importance in the long-term perspective of Britain's political development.

References

All quotations attributed to leading Movement figures in the text of Parts III and IV are taken from the interviews conducted between January and September 1978, unless otherwise stated. (All interviews, except those with Lord Home, Msgr. Bruce Kent, Duncan Rees, Professor Rotblat, Lord Soper and Sir Harold Wilson, were conducted by Richard Taylor.)

1. For example, Pat Arrowsmith: "Oh! it was very bitter. When I think of the caucusing and caballing at CND conferences by DAC supporters and CND people who were sympathetic to DAC before the Committee of 100 was set up. . . ." Pat Arrowsmith, in conversation with Richard Taylor, January 1978.

    Michael Randle: ". . . in the *early* days of DAC it was a very tense relationship, lots of arguments and quarrels — it (the CND leadership) tried to stymie the March (March on London organised by DAC following the first Aldermaston March in 1958) that we'd organised and put us down . . . pretty crudely too, absolutely disgusting really!" Michael Randle, in conversation with Richard Taylor, May 1978.

2. For example, Alan Lovell: " . . . it is very difficult to separate out the DAC and CND. The Aldermaston March was after all key in that development — and Hugh Brock and Laurence Brown had the original idea. And the Aldermaston March was part of the politics of Direct Action . . . so there's not that kind of separation. It's only later on when the CND became much more formalised and the Committee of 100 was formed, that there seemed to be a real split between CND and the Committee of 100. At the time DAC thought of itself as, in a sense, the radical wing of CND." Alan Lovell, in conversation with Richard Taylor, September 1978.

3. Although some of those already involved and committed to Pacifism disputed this. Donald Soper, for instance, commented on the question of a difference in moral terms between conventional and nuclear weapons: "No, of course there is no moral difference: there aren't friendly and unfriendly bombs. There is an awful lot of nonsense talked about some nuclear weapons as if they are more immoral than others. . . ." Lord Soper, in conversation with Colin Pritchard, May 1978. For a graphic and detailed analysis of the effects of nuclear weapons see John Cox, *Overkill*, Penguin Books, 1977.

4. Walter Stein (ed.), *Nuclear Weapons and the Christian Conscience*, p. 23, Merlin Press, 1961.

5. Canon L. John Collins, *Faith Under Fire*, p. 308, Leslie Frewin, 1966.

6. Arthur Goss, in conversation with Richard Taylor, January 1978: "Two groups who took longest to come in were the Society of Friends and the Fellowship of Reconciliation. . . . The reason was that they were interested not just in abolishing *nuclear* war and *nuclear* weapons — they wanted to abolish *all* war, all weapons."

7. Even the New Left was by no means scornful of the moral perspective of the Campaign's leadership: Stuart Hall: "The combination of moral and political was never missing in anyone who got involved: I don't know anyone who would have said it was a purely political issue." Stuart Hall, in conversation with Richard Taylor, March 1978.

8. J. B. Priestley, "Britain and the Nuclear Bombs", *New Statesman*, 2 Nov. 1957.

9. *Ibid.*

10. *Ibid.*

11. *Ibid.*

12. For example, Canon Collins, *Faith Under Fire, op. cit.*, p. 326: " . . . one of our first aims should be to win a majority for CND policy within the Labour Party, and a second, so to put the case for nuclear disarmament to the British public as a whole that, at a general election, a Labour Party committed to our policy would be returned to power".

13. Arthur Goss, in the days of the NCANWT, for example, argued that to become an effective national campaign, respected and well-known national figures must be involved.

14. And this was not confined to ideological views of course. In terms of social background, social milieu, education, and, not least, *age*, Canon Collins and most of the Executive had almost everything in common with the Gaitskellite Hampstead group of Right-wing Labour leaders, and almost nothing in common with the young radicals of DAC (and CND).

15. See, for example, R. E. Dowse, *Left in the Centre*, Longmans, 1966.

16. The Labour H-Bomb Campaign Committee was formed in 1957 by Left Labour activists.

17. The famous references to a unilateralist policy driving "Britain into a diplomatic purdah" and resulting in sending "the Foreign Secretary naked into the Conference Chamber" deeply shocked many on the Labour Left as much for their *tone* as for the views they represented. (LPACR, 1957.)

18. Mainly, but not exclusively, on the Left of the Party. Sir Harold Wilson has confirmed this view: "Of course some non-Left supported CND, while some on the Left of the Party didn't support CND, indeed some of the Left hardliners would have thought CND a bit wet, though in general the majority of the Left would be CND. . . ." Sir Harold Wilson, in conversation with Colin Pritchard, June 1978.

19. Amongst leading Labour activists involved from early in the Campaign were Michael Foot, Sydney Silverman, Ian Mikardo and Frank Allaun (a substantial number of Labour Left MPs were CND supporters). There was also strong support from the 'Tribunite' Left in the Constituency Labour Parties.

20. As Frank Parkin, among others, has argued in *Middle Class Radicalism*, MUP, 1968.

21. i.e. Michael Foot, Frank Allaun, Ian Mikardo, Olive Gibbs and Lord Soper.

22. At one level the CND falls into the tradition of Foreign Policy-oriented, morally based single-issue pressure groups on the Labour Left, through the 1920s and 1930s.

23. Gaitskell's ideological position was clearly revisionist and very similar to that expounded by C. A. R. Crosland in *The Future of Socialism*, Jonathan Cape, 1956.

24. TGWU resolution: This Conference, believing that the great majority of the people of this country are earnestly seeking a lasting peace and recognising that the present state of world tension accentuates the great danger of an accidental drift into war, calls upon the Labour Party to make a clear declaration that the Labour Government will, when returned to office, establish our defence and foreign policies on:

    (a)   a complete rejection of any defence policy based on the threat of the use of strategic or tactical nuclear weapons;

    (b)   the permanent cessation of the manufacture or testing of nuclear and thermo-nuclear weapons;

    (c)   patrols of aircraft carrying nuclear weapons and operating from British bases ceasing forthwith;

    (d)   the continuation of the opposition to the establishment of missile bases in GB;

    (e)   a strengthening of the UN organisation, including the admission of representatives of the Chinese People's Republic, with a view to the creation of a new world order and the avoidance of a return to the methods of the cold war period;

    (f)   pressing for the reopening of discussion between nations at the earliest possible moment as the means by which world disarmament and peaceful coexistence can be most readily achieved.

    AEU resolution: This conference considers that world peace and nuclear disarmament are imperative. The only defence for Britain is for the settlement of international differences by negotiations and a spirit of toleration between the nations and an understanding that countries with different social systems can and must live with each other. Conference demands that the Government should press for an international agreement on complete disarmament, and in the meantime, demands the unilateral renunciation of the testing, manufacture, stockpiling and basing of all nuclear weapons in Great Britain. (LPACR, 1960, pp. 176-178.)

25. A battle which has to date always been won by the Right of course. See, for example, Tom Nairn, "The Nature of the Labour Party", in *Towards Socialism*, eds. P. Anderson and R. Blackburn, Fontana and New Left Books, 1965.

26. It is interesting to contrast Frank Allaun's view with the more bi-partisan approach of CND's current (1978) Chairman, Msgr. Bruce Kent: ". . . essentially it seems to me we need to capture those moderate Tories, and there are many of them, who would like a more rational and less disastrously expensive defence policy. If we convince them and have a bi-partisan approach this would be the ideal approach." Msgr. Bruce Kent, in conversation with Colin Pritchard, June 1978.

27. Both Jacquetta Hawkes and Canon Collins have emphasised that the early leadership of CND was firmly committed to its being first and foremost a *moral* campaign.

28. As our survey has shown, see Part II, very large numbers of people in CND were not, in their own estimation, political in orientation.

29. The crucial factor in Gaitskell's victory in 1961 was, of course, the winning over of major TU support. The Campaign for Democratic Socialism was an important propaganda arm for the Gaitskellite cause, and the appeal to 'loyalty' was as effective as ever. It should be noted, however, that the ease with which TUs were brought back into the fold testifies to the hollowness of the 1960 victory: the manipulation of huge bloc votes through the TU bureaucracies was, when it came to the

test in 1961, no substitute for work at the rank-and-file level. The need to work with TUs at this level is, according to Dick Nettleton, one of the major lessons that the modern CND has learnt: and, going with this, is the realisation that moral and political arguments must, in the TU context, be linked closely to pragmatic, economic issues of employment, investment and so on. Dick Nettleton, in conversation with Richard Taylor, January 1978. See *Postscript* for further discussion of this point.

30. See Nairn, *op. cit.:* Ralph Miliband, *Parliamentary Socialism,* 2nd edition, Merlin Press, 1973; David Coates, *The Labour Party and the Struggle for Socialism,* CUP, 1975.

31. Although Sir Harold Wilson recalled that Bevan "saw that these (CND) people were decent, fine, morally committed people" and he believed that "we must help them in the Movement" though he himself "couldn't be totally with them". Sir Harold Wilson, in conversation with Colin Pritchard, June 1978.

    Lord Soper believed that Bevan was far more committed to the CND than he appeared; "Bevan . . . believed that you must get Labour into power, even if it seems you have to relinquish CND, and then when Labour is in power, (Bevan would) be Foreign Secretary and then we can get going." Lord Soper, in conversation with Colin Pritchard, May 1978.

32. Allaun: "It is not true to say that there was little working-class support. I'd say it became more and more working-class as it went on."
    Nettleton: "By and large I always found that CND—and it was quite peculiar this—was, more or less accurately, a cross-section of the community. . . ."

33. Cousins' own position was undermined by the so-called compromise policy of R. H. S. Crossman/Walter Padley which attracted the support of the 'centre Left'. Having defeated Cousins' proposal at the NEC Gaitskell then carried his own policy, albeit narrowly at the NEC, through all the decision-making bodies of the party. For a full discussion of this, see Lewis Minkin, "The Labour Party Conference and Intra Party Democracy", PhD thesis, University of York, 1975.

34. Frank Cousins, in a letter to Richard Taylor, 7 Nov. 1977.

35. Although most of the early leaders were morally motivated they were, for the most part, convinced of the need to win over the Labour Party.

36. And this in itself had been the result, not of a move to the Left by the membership, but of the deaths in rapid succession of Deakin and Tiffin, leaving Cousins unexpectedly next in line.

37. Foot: ". . . I wasn't as antagonistic to some of them (i.e. the Committee of 100 supporters) as all that. And several of those who supported it were close friends of mine."
    Mikardo: "I felt it (the setting up of the Committee of 100) was almost inevitable. People tried their own ways. It's no good beefing about it."
    Allaun: "In a way I sympathised with the strength of their (the Committee of 100's) feelings—I admired, I helped to defend them, in certain cases. But I don't think it was the best tactic."

38. The Labour Left has very rarely won major victories within the Labour Party. For a further discussion of the reasons for this inherent weakness and its implications for future perspectives and action, see Part IV.

39. Nicolas Walter, "Damned Fools in Utopia", *New Left Review,* Nos. 13 and 14, January-April 1962.

40. One of the major thrusts in the creation of the New Left was the group of Communists who left the Party after the Russian invasion of Hungary in 1956. Both this group and the younger university radicals of *ULR* had major differences with the 'Old Left' of the CP. For a detailed discussion of the origins of the New Left see David R. Holden, "The First New Left in Britain (1956-62)", PhD thesis (unpublished), University of Wisconsin-Madison, 1976.

41. See the successive versions of the *British Road to Socialism,* the CP's policy statement first published in 1952. (The latest revision, in 1978, maintains the Parliamentarist stance as its central strategy.)

42. The CP's repeated attempts to affiliate to the Labour Party have always been completely unsuccessful.

43. Those involved in the radical extra-parliamentary groups in the Peace Movement were hostile to the Communist Party's politics—and they also viewed the CP as being both old fashioned and out of sympathy with the basic aims and attitudes of the Peace Movement. The CP never understood the ideology or the motivations of the DAC or the Committee of 100—although they dutifully publicised news of demonstrations, etc., in the *Daily Worker.*

44. For example, Olive Gibbs, a long-standing activist in Labour Politics in Oxford, as well as Chairman of CND following Canon Collins' resignation: "The CP wanted to get on the bandwaggon. (They decided to support CND) both to recruit members . . . and because they were losing members . . . they're opportunists. They're so damned respectable these days."

And, from the New Left and the DAC, Alan Lovell: "A lot of the impact of the politics of that time was the attempt to find a place between the US and the Soviet Union — a kind of Third Way. In that sense Marxism was always identified with the Soviet Union, with Stalin and so on. So we made a really big effort to detach ourselves from the politics of Stalinism and sectarianism . . . I think the issue of neutralism distinguished the CP from all other groups . . . the CP was always strongly pro-Soviet. . . . The only group that we in the DAC were really suspicious of was the CP. . . ."

45. This was confirmed by both Peggy Duff and Jacquetta Hawkes:

Duff: "(CP support) helped a bit in the 1960 Conference when we got the resolution through but we'd have got it through without the Communists. They never attempted to take it over because they obviously weren't strong enough. I don't think there was a single region, for instance, whose main officers were Communist. In fact they were a loyal body of men and always tremendously well-behaved on the March."
Hawkes: "We were all heartily sorry I think when we began to be supported by the Communist Party — it did drive out a lot of other people — on the other hand they always behaved extremely well, they were reliable in a way that many of the other groups were not — they always kept to what they said, they didn't break the law when they were working with organisations like ours. . . ."

In his book, *An Infantile Disorder? the Crisis and Decline of the New Left*, RKP, 1977, Nigel Young lays a great deal of the responsibility for CND's decline at the door of the CP: "After 1963, CND itself became year by year more steadily compromised by the CP . . . over the ensuing years this political embrace tightened, finally becoming fatal. . . . No other group had this kind of staying power; the libertarians had moved on into the Committee, into community action, or out of active politics. . . . CND's Labourists typically entered into tactical alliances with the CP. Dedicated, manoeuvering and repititious, the Party 'bored from within' in every sense. . . . (By the mid-1960s) CND was already in decline, but its destruction can be detected in the years of this stranglehold." p. 155. Contradicting these views, however, both Lord Soper and A. J. P. Taylor dismissed the Communists' role: "very unimportant" (Soper); "its the only movement I have known in all my experience from the '20s onwards where no Communists ever infiltrated: the Communists had no connection with CND and they never caused us trouble" (Taylor).

46. George Matthews, in conversation with Richard Taylor, January 1978.

47. Principally, the decision by the TGWU Annual Conference to support a quasi-unilateralist policy in the spring of 1959.

48. "The turning point, I think, was around the middle of 1959. . . . The situation had developed as far as public opinion, and opinion in the Labour Movement was concerned where the issue was combining the two (i.e. the long-standing CP demand for international agreement and a unilateralist policy for Britain)." George Matthews, in conversation with Richard Taylor, January 1978.

49. As exemplified in *The British Road to Socialism, op. cit.*

50. *New Reasoner*, editorial, Vol. 1, No. 4.

51. D. G. Arnott, "Campaign Notebook", *New Reasoner*, Spring 1959, p. 21.

52. Holden, *op. cit.*, pp. 91-2.

53. *Ibid.*, p. 92.

54. E. P. Thompson, "Socialist Humanism — an Epistle to the Philistines", *New Reasoner*, No. 1, p. 113.

55. Peter Sedgwick, "The Two New Lefts", p. 135, in D. Widgery (ed.), *The Left in Britain 1956-1968*, Penguin Books, 1976.

56. Holden, *op. cit.*, p. 115.

57. *Ibid.*, p. 114.

58. *New Reasoner*, editorial, Spring 1958.

59. However, it is important to note that, whereas the NL's main reason for supporting withdrawal from NATO was its position in favour of neutralism, the major reason for most CND and Committee of 100 supporters agreeing to such a policy was what they saw as the illogicality of a unilaterally disarmed Britain remaining within a nuclear alliance, NATO. The impact and importance of the NL on CND policy must thus be qualified, even in this central area of NATO and neutralism.

60. Although it is worth noting the NR's strong caveat on the rejection of the Communist society of the East: "we (do not) believe that advanced industrialism itself has given rise to a 'mass society' in which the antagonism between the power elite, or state bureaucracy, and the alienated individual has superseded, in importance, class antagonisms. The watershed of the October Revolution cannot be argued away; and we believe that in an atmosphere of relaxed international tension, the Soviet Union and Eastern Europe will prove to be the area of expanding liberty and human fulfilment,

whereas the West, unless transformed by a strong democratic and revolutionary socialist movement, will prove to be the area of encroaching authoritarianism." *New Reasoner,* editorial, Summer 1959, *loc. cit.* For a ringing denunciation of 'Natopolitan' culture and ideology, see E. P. Thompson (ed.), "Outside the Whale" in *Out of Apathy,* Stevens & Son, 1960.

61. *Ibid.*

62. Peter Worsley, "Imperialism in Retreat", in E. P. Thompson (ed.), *Out of Apathy, op. cit.*

63. *New Reasoner,* editorial, Spring 1958. See also E. P. Thompson, "NATO, Neutralism and Survival", *ULR,* 1958, Vol. 1, Part 4. This article spells out in more concrete detail the policy of active neutralism advocated by the *NR.*

64. E. P. Thompson, "Revolution", in *Out of Apathy, op. cit.*

65. Sedgwick, *op. cit.,* pp. 136-7.

66. Holden, *op. cit.,* p. 145.

67. Particularly evident in the work of Raymond Williams and Stuart Hall. As Holden (*op. cit.*) notes, the *ULR* was strongly influenced both by European existensialist writers (notably Jean Paul Sartre) and by non-Marxist writers in England (notably Richard Hoggart).

68. *New Reasoner,* editorial, Spring 1958. As Parkin, *op. cit.,* has shown, and we confirm, CND supporters were not at all 'alienated' from society. It was precisely because they were so 'integrated' that they were prepared to take such a major part in social and political protest on a moral issue of crucial importance to society at large.

69. In 1963, after disagreements within the NL, and the sale of the Journal, the personnel of the paper's editorial management was drastically changed. Henceforth, Anderson, Nairn *et al.,* took over the Journal—and changed its nature and its relationship to the Labour Movement; in effect it abandoned any *activist* commitment (see Widgery, *op. cit.,* pp. 510-12; also, for the bitterness which remains still, see E. P. Thompson, "Letter to Lesek Kolakowski", in *Socialist Register 1973,* eds. Miliband and Saville, Merlin Press, 1974.)

70. Peter Worsley, *NLR,* No. 12, Nov./Dec. 1961, quoted in Sedgwick, *op. cit.,* p. 143. Sedgwick himself, however, was highly critical of the "incongruity of the proposed coalition" and argued that this was "indeed the diplomacy-in-exile of an ideal Republic: fantasies of Statecraft, hallucinated expediences, clouded the social vision of the NL and inflated its self-importance" (pp. 143-4).

71. John Rex, "Britain without the Bomb", NL pamphlet, 1960; see also Stuart Hall, "NATO and the Alliances", pamphlet (n.d., probably 1960).

72. See, for example, the interviews previously cited with Jacquetta Hawkes, Canon Collins, Arthur Goss *et al.* See also Collins, *op. cit.*

73. Young, *op. cit.,* describes the realignment of the NL after 1960, as being "with the traditional Left, at times supporting the CP against the Trotskyites, in the main pursuing a traditional and fellow travelling tactic within or alongside the Labour Party." p. 147.

74. Young, *op. cit.,* p. 146, quoting Peggy Duff.

75. *'Sanity',* May 1964 (quoted in Sedgwick, *op. cit.*).

76. Young, *op. cit.,* p. 146.

77. Sedgwick, *op. cit.,* p. 145.

78. Peggy Duff, *op. cit.,* p. 128.

79. Quoted in Sedgwick, *op. cit.,* p. 140.

80. *Ibid.,* pp. 140-1.

81. *Ibid.,* p. 142.

82. Sedgwick, *op. cit.,* pp. 144-53 and Young, *op. cit.,* pp. 144-53.

83. Sedgwick, *op. cit.,* p. 151.

84. Michael Barratt Brown, "Do We Need a New Political Basis?", *Peace News,* 20 Oct. 1961 (quoted in Holden, *op. cit.,* p. 320).

85. Holden, *op. cit.,* p. 19.

86. Duff, *op. cit.,* p. 195.

87. Young, *op. cit.,* p. 74.

88. Quoted in *ibid.,* p. 74.

89. There is of course a voluminous literature on Marxist attitudes to the Labour Party. The classic modern analysis of the problems is Ralph Miliband, *op. cit.*

90. Duff, *loc. cit.*

91. Pat Arrowsmith recalled that at the time of her first involvement she was not a pacifist but "a nuclear pacifist. . . . I was one of those who came into pacifism by thinking that if the end product of war in this day and age is the nuclear bomb then I must oppose war, period; so I became a pacifist and joined the PPU."

92. April Carter, for example, emphasised that "we all (in the DAC), either through long experience or through 'instinct', agreed that the way forward was not through the Labour Party: we didn't want to get stuck in party politics — what we were trying to do was mobilise a much wider movement."

93. "All the time we were talking around this concept of a non-violent society, a non-violent politics. But we were never able to work it out . . ." (Brock).

94. "In the DAC we certainly felt that the Labour Party was crucial: it had to be changed and changed in a radical way. That led us into direct campaigns against the Party . . ." (Lovell).

95. Quote from Pat Arrowsmith. This was confirmed by both Jacquetta Hawkes and Canon Collins.

96. "I came into CND because I'm a pacifist and a socialist. . . . I took the CND in my stride: as a Pacifist, I must seize every opportunity to advance the cause as I see it to be" (Soper).

97. Hugh Brock, the editor of *Peace News* from 1955 to 1964, recalled that the paper had given support to numerous Movements for African freedom at the time of the Mau-Mau troubles and that there were references in the minutes of the PPU to *Peace News* "becoming the Journal of the Movement for Colonial Freedom!"

98. For example: the half-day strike, at Stevenage, of building workers; the one-day strike at Carrington's Petro-Chemical site between Liverpool and Manchester; a token dinner hour stoppage at Bristol Siddeley Engines, etc. (These and other similar events were recalled by Pat Arrowsmith in conversation with Richard Taylor.)

99. Although Michael Randle, April Carter and Pat Arrowsmith all emphasised that, whilst they saw nuclear weapons as the central and immediate issue, they never regarded it as an isolated single issue, unrelated to wider socio-political questions.

100. Hence the DAC's interest in Sir Stephen King-Hall's proposal for a Royal Commission to investigate the possibilities of non-violent defence and the DAC's attempt in 1961 "to push through CND the idea of non-violent defence" (Carter).

101. There was some ambivalence over the DAC's attitude to Marxism. April Carter stated quite categorically that "None of us was Marxist. For a number of reasons we were very hostile to the CP . . ."; but later, in the same conversation, she emphasised the "generally sympathetic" attitude of the DAC towards the New Left. Similarly, Michael Randle: ". . . we did turn away from Marxism to some extent, partly because of its association with pro-Soviet Peace groups. But it wasn't a *complete* break . . . there was a *strong* Marxist influence there, even if it was a *critical* Marxist influence! . . . it was a Socialist and a broad Marxist position. . . ." This 'sympathy' to Marxism by non-Marxists mirrors the idealistic response noted amongst large numbers of the rank-and-file activists of the Movement in Part II.

102. i.e. Liberal in the sense both of having an essentially *individualist* perspective, and basing its ideological assumptions on a non-socialist position.

103. For a discussion of ILP ideology see Nairn, *op. cit.*; and C. Pritchard and R. Taylor, *Social Work: Reform or Revolution?*, chap. 4, pp. 48-50, Routledge & Kegan Paul, 1978.

104. Although not formally inaugurated until October 1960 (following the premature leak to the Press on 28 September 1960 of the plans to establish the Committee), the idea of establishing such an organisation had been under intensive discussion in the Movement since the spring of 1960 (as both George Clark and Michael Randle have recalled).

105. Canon Collins in particular saw the political and organisational threat of the Committee of 100. Unlike the DAC, the Committee of 100 represented a very real threat to CND's dominance of the Movement.

106. Russell made this clear in several public pronouncements, including his statement at the Official Secrets trial of February 1962. The detailed history of Russell's involvement in the creation of the Committee of 100 and his motivations and perspective are well described in Ronald Clark's biography, *Russell*, pp. 576 ff., Jonathan Cape and Weidenfeld & Nicolson, 1975. See below, pp. 85-92, for a fuller discussion of Russell's perspective.

107. See Clark, *op. cit.*, chaps. 22 and 23; see also Bertrand Russell's *Autobiography*, Vol. 3, Allen & Unwin, 1969.

108. Schoenman approached Donald Soper at one stage and asked him if he "would be interested in standing for the leadership against Collins: of course I refused" (Soper). With hindsight it is interesting to speculate what might have ensued had Soper become Chairman of CND: he was certainly more acceptable to both wings of the Movement than Collins.

109. i.e. Brize Norton, York, Manchester, Bristol and Cardiff. For a brief discussion of these demonstrations see Part I.

110. Russell, along with the Priestleys, Kingsley Martin and Kennan, was the initiator, in the immediate sense, of CND itself. He was CND President from its formation in 1958 to October 1960 when he resigned over the Committee of 100 issue. He was the President of the Committee of 100 from its formation in October 1960 to January 1963. See Biographies, Appendix III for further details.

111. Although it is important to note the reluctance on the part of the scientific Establishment to become involved: ". . . the scientific case, which is mixed up with morality but is rational as well, was very strong—although unlike both Germany and the USA we never got strong support from physicists. . . . I had very many friends among physicists and they all evaded the issue in one way or another . . ." (A. J. P. Taylor).

112. Quoted in Cox, *op. cit.*, p. 26.

113. Clark, *op. cit.*, pp. 545-6.

114. *Ibid.*, p. 547.

115. This point was emphasised by Rotblat. "There is room and need for both (i.e. Pugwash and a CND type of mass movement). You need the individual approach and the mass movement, one doesn't contradict the other and this is one reason why I have been involved in both Pugwash and CND."

116. Cox, *op. cit.*, p. 179.

117. Rotblat, for example, said that he "would like to see the Liberals take up the nuclear issue as they are in a position which does not appear to be doctrinaire . . .".

118. For a brief review of Russell's life and political activities see Appendix III. See also Russell's *Autobiography, op. cit.*, and Ronald Clark, *The Life of Bertrand Russell, op. cit.*

119. Clark, *op. cit.*, p. 517.

120. Not unsurprisingly the Communist Party never really forgave Russell for this period of his political life. George Matthews, for example, commented that: "We used not to take it up very often but we did remember that Bertrand Russell himself advocated the dropping of the A-Bomb on Moscow in the late '40s. . . ."

121. To take just two examples from the political sphere to illustrate Russell's propensity for outrageous or extravagant remarks: in a letter to Dr. Walter Marseille, 5 May 1948: ". . . Communism must be wiped out, and world government must be established . . . I do not think the Russians will yield without war. I think all (including Stalin) are fatuous and ignorant. But I hope I am wrong about this." Quoted in Clark, *op. cit.*, p. 524.

   And, an oft-quoted passage from Russell's address to the First Annual Conference of the Midlands Region Youth Campaign for Nuclear Disarmament in Birmingham on 15 April 1961: "(Kennedy and MacMillan) are much more wicked than Hitler . . . we cannot obey these murderers. They are wicked and abominable. They are the wickedest people that ever lived in the history of man. . . ." Quoted in Russell, *op. cit.*, Vol. 3, p. 144.

122. Russell's views at this time are well summarised in an address, "The International Bearings of Atomic Warfare" given to the Royal Empire Society on 3 December 1947, quoted in Clark, *op. cit.*, p. 522. "I should like to see as soon as possible as close a union as possible of those countries who think it worthwhile to avoid atomic war. I think you could get so powerful an alliance that you could turn to Russia and say 'it is open to you to join this alliance if you will agree to the terms; if you will not join us we shall go to war with you!' I am inclined to think Russia would acquiesce; if not, provided this is done soon, the world might survive the resulting war and emerge with a single government such as the world needs."

   Russell confirmed his attitude at this time in an interview in 1959 on BBC TV's 'Face to Face' with John Freeman quoted in Clark, p. 528: "What I thought all along was that a nuclear war in which both sides had nuclear weapons would be an utter and absolute disaster . . . not that I advocated a nuclear war, but I did think that great pressure should be put upon Russia to accept the Baruch proposal, and I did think that if they continued to refuse it might be necessary actually to go to war."

123. Ralph Schoenman argues forcefully that, during his last years, "his attitude towards Capitalism and American imperialism . . . bears a decidedly Marxist character. . . ." Ralph Schoenman, "Bertrand Russell and the Peace Movement", in G. Nakhnikian (ed.), *Bertrand Russell's Philosophy*, Duckworth, 1974, pp. 227-8. But Schoenman's argument here is not convincing, Russell un-

doubtedly came to see American aggression, in Vietnam and elsewhere, as a greater threat to world peace than Soviet expansionism, following the Cuba crisis. He also came to be far more sympathetic to some aspects of Communism as a social and governmental system than he had been previously, but he did not change his long-standing individualist Liberal stance on ideological questions — and never became even remotely convinced of Marxism as an ideological framework of analysis.

124. Edward F. Sherman, "Bertrand Russell and the Peace Movement: Liberal Consistency or Radical Change?", in G. Nakhnikian (ed.), *op. cit.*, p. 256.

125. Clark, *op. cit.*, p. 532.

126. See Schoenman, *op. cit.*; see also, Russell, Vol. 3, *op. cit.*; Clark, *op. cit.* Although as noted earlier, he became considerably more sympathetic to Communism as a world system during the 1960s, and particularly at the height of the Vietnam War.

127. This belief was there in his 'CND years' — see the *New Statesman* correspondence between Russell, Kruschev and Dulles, November 1957 to 1958, but became considerably more marked during his intervention in the Cuban Crisis of 1962 and the subsequent and very wide-ranging attempts at international direct diplomacy through the later 1960s (see Clark, *op. cit.*).

128. Schoenman, *op. cit.*, p. 233.

129. Not only was Russell one of the great twentieth-century philosophers and mathematicians, he also wrote extensively on education, politics, aspects of sociology, morality, sex and education. He was also a Nobel Prize winner for Literature!

130. There is a strong case for arguing that this Leftist stance was due primarily to the influence of Ralph Schoenman. It is also important to note that Russell eventually severed his connection with Schoenman and, in Clark's words, became "once more his own man". Clark, *op. cit.*; Russell, *op. cit.*, Vol. 3.

131. See Clark, *op. cit.*, chap. 20, for details of the Pugwash Conference development and Russell's and Rotblat's involvement.

132. Russell's 'Man's Peril' broadcast on BBC Radio, 23 Dec. 1954. Quoted in *ibid.*, p. 538.

133. Although Russell was a sponsor of both the NCANWT and the DAC, and gave frequent verbal support.

134. Clark, *op. cit.*, p. 553 (although Clark adds that he was "also . . . a tactician making common-sense policy amendments which often prevented demonstrators making fools of themselves . . .").

135. Peggy Duff recalled that Russell "was . . . not exactly dictatorial, but he liked laying down the law. And I think the Canon (Collins) made a mistake . . . in the first year or so, 1958/9. He saw Russell as a sort of figurehead to be trotted out on occasions whereas Russell really wanted to be in charge. . . ."

136. Russell, *op. cit.*, Vol. 3, p. 103.

137. Russell, in an interview in the *Daily Mail,* 15 May 1957, quoted in Clark, *op. cit.*, p. 554.

138. It might be more accurate to say that Russell ignored and failed to comprehend the analyses of the Left (both 'Marxist' and 'Libertarian') which linked the Bomb to wider social and political questions. It is certainly true that Russell never wrote or spoke publicly, at any length, of his reasons for rejecting these views.

139. The initial idea for the Committee of 100, in so far as it can be said to emanate from an individual rather than a general mood, came not from Russell but from Ralph Schoenman, who then persuaded Russell to give his support to the venture (see Russell, *op. cit.*, p. 110).

140. Russell, *op. cit.*, p. 109.

141. Clark, *op. cit.*, p. 569.

142. See Russell, *op. cit.*, Vol. 3, chap. III: Clark, *op. cit.*, chap. 21; C. Driver, *The Disarmers,* Hodder & Stoughton, 1964, chap. 5; G. Clark, "Remember Your Humanity and Forget the Rest", in Benewick and Smith (eds.), *Direct Action and Democratic Politics,* Allen & Unwin, 1972.

143. Clark, *op. cit.*, p. 560.

144. Russell, "Which Way to Peace?", 1936, quoted in *ibid.*, p. 574.

145. Russell, *Autobiography, op. cit.*, p. 25.

146. Clark, *op. cit.*, p. 575.

147. Russell, interview with *Playboy* magazine, March 1963, quoted in Clark, *op. cit.*, p. 574.

148. See *ibid.*, pp. 572-85; Driver, *op. cit.*, pp. 112 ff.; Canon John Collins, *op. cit.*, pp. 319-24; Russell, *Autobiography, op. cit.*, pp. 110 ff.

149. For example, Jacquetta Hawkes: "There just was, from that moment (i.e. the creation of the Committee of 100) the division between those who wished to break the law and felt that things must be done very quickly . . . the basic thing was that most of us didn't want illegal action, that was quite definite."

150. As Michael Randle has recalled: ". . . we (the Committee of 100) had committed ourselves to 2000 people (for the February 1961 demonstration): we'd never had a DAC demonstration with more than 100 people! . . . I was very sceptical as to whether we'd get our 2000 . . . the actual demonstration turned out to be bigger than we had anticipated: about 5000 took part." By the time of the September 1961 demonstration the numbers had grown to about 17,000.

151. Not only was the formation of the Committee of 100 and the subsequent disagreement between Russell and Collins given maximum press coverage, the spectacle of the internationally known octogenarian philosopher being sentenced to jail (prior to the Semptember 1961 demonstration) gave the Movement its biggest possible publicity boost both nationally and internationally.

152. George Clark has written: ". . . the government began to take a more sensible line in dealing with us, and the Committee over-reached itself . . . (i.e. in organising the Wethersfield/Ruislip demonstrations, etc.) . . . it saddened me to see the Committee walk so easily into a trap. The search for sensations in order to keep in the public eye, and the aim of bringing the whole war machine to a standstill by filling the gaols was romantic and pure adventurism." G. Clark, *Remember Your Humanity and Forget the Rest, op. cit.*, p. 184.

153. Russell wrote of the Wethersfield, etc., demonstrations: ". . . the Committee, in its inexperience of holding large demonstrations not in London but in the country, were too optimistic, especially in matters relating to transportation. . . . The Committee had made a mistake . . . in announcing beforehand that it would make a better showing than it could possibly hope to do and in not planning thoroughly for alternatives in foreseeable difficulties." Russell, *Autobiography, op. cit.*, p. 120.

154. *Ibid.*, p. 120.

155. Clark, *op. cit.*, pp.602-3.

156. George Clark: "I reached the conclusion that it would be necessary to move away from 'national demonstrations' and search for a basis of a movement which was prepared to go beyond moral gestures and symbolic actions . . . so in the summer of 1962 I organised a journey around Britain which was to last for five months and to take us over a distance of more than 5000 miles. The object was to carry the message of Aldermaston to every village-green, form CND groups where none had existed and strengthen those already in existence. . . . During 1963 our conceptions about ourselves began to change, and (we) moved steadily away from CND." G. Clark, *Remember Your Humanity and Forget the Rest, op. cit.*

157. See Clark, *op. cit.*, chaps. 22, 23 and 24; Russell, *Autobiography, op. cit.*

158. Schoenman, in Nakhnikian, *op. cit.*, quoted in Clark, *op. cit.*, p. 583.

159. Russell certainly regarded civil disobedience as an extreme tactic. For example, he wrote, in 1961, that civil disobedience as a method of propaganda is "difficult to justify except in extreme cases, but I cannot imagine any issue more extreme or more overwhelmingly important than that of the prevention of nuclear war". Text of Russell's address on 5 April 1961 to the first Annual Conference of the Midlands Region Youth Campaign for Nuclear Disarmament in Birmingham, subsequently printed as a leaflet "On Civil Disobedience".

160. Peggy Duff has commented that she regarded Russell as "a throwback to the 18th century where you had eccentric nobles, where they got away with doing eccentric things because of their noble families, etc. And Russell was a bit like that."

161. Jacquetta Hawkes' outraged reaction to Russell's behaviour was typical of the CND leadership: ". . . the way the Committee of 100 was set up was almost incredible. When you think that Russell was the President and my husband (J. B. Priestley) the Vice-President and that he was supposed to be absolutely part of us — and then the invitations and so on were done in *dead secret*. . . . It seemed such an extraordinarily irresponsible thing to do, in secret, by our President. . . ."

162. Hugh Gaitskell was leader of the Labour Party during the most stormy period of CND's life. Mr. Wilson, as he then was, succeeded as leader following Gaitskell's death in early 1963, when he won the leadership ballot in the PLP against George Brown and James Callaghan. Sir Alec Douglas Home, as he then was, became leader of the Conservative Party and Prime Minister in succession to Harold MacMillan in 1963; he had been Foreign Secretary during MacMillan's 1959 Government.

163. "I could see that this issue could develop into a potential major split with unilateralist motions being put forward and the resultant opposition creating problems and disruptions . . ." (Sir Harold Wilson). It might well be argued that the desire to preserve party unity was the major motivating factor for Sir Harold throughout his long tenure of the Party leadership.

164. Ian Mikardo has corroborated the role played by Sam Watson, the Durham Miner's leader, in persuading Bevan to ally himself with the leadership's policy.

165. He was not, of course, alone in this. Such a veteran and persistent Peace Campaigner as April Carter has been similarly dismissive of CND's long-term influence in governmental policy.

166. Lord Home emphasised the difficulties caused by the Russians' refusal to countenance inspection of their territory: this insistence "stymied (the negotiations) at every point because you had to verify any disarmament that took place".

PART IV

Twenty Years On — the Achievements and the Failures: An Evaluation

IN PARTS II and III we have reviewed and examined the Movement both empirically and theoretically by means of the survey material available from the activists and the interviews conducted with the leadership. Here, we shall draw together some of the main themes emerging from these examinations and try to evaluate the Movement — having the great advantage, of course, of 20 years' hindsight.

The overall orientation of our study has been towards the analysis of the importance and political significance of the Movement *as* a Movement, rather than with the detailed and often intricate discussion of the policy goals of the Campaign. There is no doubt that the issue of nuclear disarmament itself was the central mobilising cause for the Movement; equally, there is no doubt that virtually all of the major groupings in the Movement defined their involvement primarily, though not exclusively, in terms of the central issue. However, crucial though the issue was, and is,[1] the major significance politically and historically of the Movement between 1958 and 1965 lay in its character as a mass movement unparalleled in twentieth-century Britain, rather than in its achievements on the specific issue of nuclear disarmament itself. It was the mass movement aspect that made CND *et al.* very different from and far more important than other superficially similar single-issue campaigns.[2]

The Campaign and the Nuclear Issue

Nevertheless there is a range of important questions relating to the specific achievements and failures of the Movement and it is with a consideration of these that we must begin this evaluation. A large proportion of Movement activists, 25%, believed that the Movement did *not* fail in its primary objectives, that its successes far outnumbered its failures, and that its impact on the national and international nuclear scene was profound. Such feelings are natural enough from 'core activists' who have invested so much emotional and political capital in the promulgation of the cause. However, it is our view that any serious consideration of the Movement must begin from the no doubt unpalatable fact that the Movement failed to achieve its central policy objectives. Interestingly, this is a view shared by a number of leaders of the Movement: April Carter, for example, was "rather pessimistic . . . I suppose we awakened people's awareness of the dangers; but you can't measure this, can you? I don't think we had much if any effect on governments and politicians — I don't think the Test Ban Treaty was due to our efforts." Ironically, as we have seen, this evaluation was very similar to that of Lord Home.

Reduced to essentials there were three major objectives of CND policy. The first and most fiercely held proposal was that Britain should take the moral lead and, as the third nuclear power, unilaterally renounce nuclear weapons; the second, that there should be no nuclear bases in the UK and that no aeroplanes carrying nuclear weapons should be permitted to fly over UK territory; and the third — held by the political Left to be absolutely central to the Movement's objectives, but rejected or given low priority by some of the other sections of the Movement[3] — that Britain should leave NATO and work for the creation of a neutral, third force in the world. There is no escaping the stark fact that none of these proposals was accepted by the Labour Party (let alone by the then Conservative Government). Indeed, more than 20 years after the formation of CND — a period which has included 11 years of Labour Government — none of these proposals has made any further advance towards acceptance.[4] It is, however, beyond dispute that the Movement did attain massive support: not only were there demonstrations of unparalleled size, the opinion polls showed a consistently high percentage support for the CND's unilateralist policy through 1959 and 1960, and this was particularly remarkable bearing in mind the opposition of both major party leaderships and the majority of the media. The inability of the CND leadership to capitalise upon this support constituted a major failure — and was, as we shall argue, related to the ideological and strategic limitations of its outlook. The net result of this failure was the decline and eventual disintegration of the mass movement, leaving behind a much reduced and very different organisation pursuing a more orthodox pressure group role.

Thus, even when concentrating on the specific policy failures of the Movement it is impossible to ignore the wider ideological and political issues. In terms of achieving the specific objectives of the Campaign it seems likely that a conventional pressure group approach, utilising the establishment contacts of the very prominent public figures in CND's leadership, would have been more likely to lead to success than the mass movement approach which developed from the outset in 1958. Such diverse observers as Stuart Hall and Lord Home have concurred with this view. Be this as it may, there was no holding back the great tide of popular protest: there were deeper and more diverse roots to the Movement than the specific protest against nuclear weapons. The issue of nuclear weapons in fact symbolised a whole range of social and political discontents and only a mass movement of popular protest, quite separate from established political interests, could have given them expression.

There was a clear and central commitment, both strategic and ideological, to working in and through the Labour Party. Up until the Conference victory in 1960 this strategy appeared to be successful: when it became apparent, during 1961, that the Labour Party, having failed to abide by the Conference decision of 1960, would decisively reject unilateralism at its Conference in 1961, the leadership had no alternative policy to offer. CND continued, through 1961-1964/5 and beyond, to press for the adoption of its policies by the Labour Party. With the approach of the 1964 Election, the replacement of Gaitskell by Wilson as leader of the Labour Party, and the changed international and defence situation post-Cuba, the adoption of CND policy by the Party became increasingly unlikely. The vicious spiral of decline thus began to take effect: as the attainment of CND's goals through the Labour Party became increasingly unlikely so the mass support for the Movement and the enthusiasm of both leaders[5] and rank and file began slowly but surely to diminish — which itself reduced further the influence and impact of the Campaign within the Labour Party, and so on.

All in all the Movement failed to achieve its objectives and the leadership of CND failed to adapt its ideology and its strategy to the existence of the mass movement. (The failure of the more radical sections of the Movement to capitalise on this mass support was, we shall argue, of equal or even greater importance in the long term.)

Despite this rather bleak summary of the Movement's failures on its specific policy objectives, there were some notable successes relating to the nuclear issue itself. The Movement certainly "achieved a *massive* piece of political education" (Ian Mikardo) and "awakened the world—not just this country—to the threat of a war" (Frank Allaun). These may be achievements that are hard to quantify but they are nevertheless very *real* and *valuable* achievements. The public awareness of the nuclear threat and the appalling dangers of nuclear war were in large part due to the propaganda and activities of CND and related organisations. This was a major step forward and has resulted in the long-term heightening of public consciousness on a whole range of related environmental questions—the contemporary debate on nuclear energy for example.

Even more directly linked to the Movement's policy concerns, there can be little doubt that CND, and related movements both in the UK and abroad, played an important part in persuading the politicians to agree to the Partial Test Ban Treaty of 1963 (and subsequent Disarmament agreements such as the Non-Proliferation Treaty of 1968). President Eisenhower put the point simply and succinctly: "I think people want peace so much that one of these days governments had better get out of their way and let them have it."[6]

It must never be forgotten that it was the direct hazards of *nuclear testing* that began the agitation which led to the formation of CND. Throughout the early years of the Campaign the urgent and emotional issue of the *effects* of nuclear testing was a key motivating factor in attracting support. And exercising popular pressure on politicians to come to some agreement to end such horrifically destructive (and unnecessary) activities as nuclear testing was an extremely important, worthwhile and beneficial aspect of the Movement's agitation. As Dick Nettleton has said: "It is true to say, at a very minimum, that the world would have been considerably more radioactive had it not been for CND. And that's a *very* materially important thing. What the incidence of cancer would be now is anybody's guess. . . ."

However, just as the 1960 Labour Conference victory and the peaceful resolution of the Cuba crisis both, in their very different ways, heralded an immediate 'victory' for the CND cause, but a rapid subsequent fall-off in CND's support and influence, so the 'achievement' of the Partial Test Ban Treaty of 1963 marked the end of an era. As Jacquetta Hawkes has said:

> We did contribute to the nuclear Test Ban—and I'm afraid that's another factor that encouraged the break-up, we felt 'we've done something'—and perhaps we had more direct participation in that than we realised even at the time. So that made a sort of excuse for those of us who were apolitical to wander off!

Thus, although the Movement undeniably had its successes and these were important, in terms of its specific objectives it was on balance a failure: its central objectives were not achieved and have not been achieved since, and its partial successes had the paradoxical effect of further weakening its own central campaign.

The Wider Importance of the Movement

An obvious and very important question thus arises: how and why did such a well-supported Movement achieve so little — in policy terms — in a society whose politics is supposedly responsive to the popular will? Although this *is* a central question it can be answered only by reference to the wider political context in which the Movement operated: an examination of this context will also enable us to demonstrate the areas in which the Movement's fundamental importance lies. This is not of course an entirely original contention. Stuart Hall, for example, whilst stressing that the influence of the Movement was "ENORMOUS! . . . politically it was *very, very* influential", argued that, paradoxically, the Bomb was "the *one* thing we couldn't do anything about!"

In general terms this is the view that we ourselves take. The explanation of precisely where this significance lies is intimately connected with the analysis of the reasons for the Movement's failure. It is to an examination of these interrelated issues, and their implications for future advance on the Left, that the remainder of this Part of our study is devoted.

'SPIN-OFF' EFFECTS

To begin with there was a range of 'spin-off' effects of the Movement which, while directly related neither to the specific policy objectives of the various organisations nor to 'politics' *per se,* were of considerable social significance. Perhaps foremost amongst these was the explosion of 'youth culture' which began its rapid growth in the late 1950s. Whilst the causes of this development were undoubtedly economic in origin, the Disarmament Movement certainly marked one of the major manifestations of this newly-found autonomy and self-confidence on the part of the middle-class youth of the nation. There were, of course, many, many others; nevertheless the Movement marked a watershed in the establishment of an identifiable, and culturally rebellious, youth lifestyle. As Parkin has noted,

> much of the Movement's appeal for the young did derive from (its) anti-adult, anti-authoritarian character. . . . The Bomb could be, and was easily held up as a symbol of the older generation's moral and political bankruptcy, the supreme example of adult wickedness and folly.[7]

Moreover, the street demonstration tactics of the Movement — so alien to the elite leadership who found this sort of politics distasteful, undoubtedly added to the attraction for many young people.

> The excitement of a four-day march, with its attendant personal sacrifices and discomforts suffered for the sake of a cause, the fellowship and the conviviality . . . combined to create an appeal which could not be matched by the daily round of routinised politics.[8]

This potent combination was a significant feature of the Movement, particularly for young people, as our survey has demonstrated. Yet it is also important to re-emphasise that this was not a case of a radical younger generation confronting a reactionary older generation: only a relatively small minority of young people in the UK became involved in the Movement, and, as both Parkin's and our study have shown, these were largely middle class. Equally important, most of those young people involved were in fact from relatively radical families and had a large measure of parental sympathy, if not always approval.

Our survey has shown, not unexpectedly, that there was a high proportion of younger activists in the more militant organisations of the Movement (e.g. the Committee of 100 and the various 'far-left' groups). Significantly, it showed too that these activists had gone on to a variety of other single issue and/or community action campaigns rather than into 'orthodox' politics.

This leads on to two more political themes which would seem to run through our study. There is, as we have seen, clear evidence that a considerable number (37%) of core Movement activists have become involved in the rapidly growing environmental movements of various sorts.

The second important feature to arise from the 'youth culture' aspect of the Movement was the growing hostility and lack of common ground between the elite, conventional (and older) leadership, and the radical, predominantly non-party political (and younger) rank and file. There is thus an overlap — indeed a mutual reinforcement — of two separate tendencies in the Movement which existed from the beginning but were exacerbated by various factors as time passed. There was, first, the sharp distinction in terms of age (our survey has shown that it was a Movement predominantly of 'the old' and 'the young' — the 'middle-aged' being relatively under-represented); and, although the rank and file of the Movement of course included a substantial proportion of older people, the leadership, *of CND,* was exclusively of the older generation. The discrepancy in age between the leaderships of CND and the Committee of 100[9] was not the least of the factors making for conflict between the two organisations. Second, there was the sharp and growing distinction between the elite leadership and the rank and file.[10] As Stuart Hall has emphasised, these cultural factors all came together within the Movement in a highly significant manner and many of the important aspects of the Movement were connected with this cultural ethos: "the arguments between young people and old, between the Front of the March and the Back, the cultural ambience of being in it . . . (the Movement) was a way of talking about a hell of a lot of those things".

THE POLITICAL DIMENSION

The other major effects of the Movement also involved this cultural ambience but move us into the directly political areas of concern which are the main focus of this section and indeed of the study as a whole. In a very central and important sense the experience of the 1958/65 years, in particular the years from 1959 to 1961, changed British politics fundamentally and for the foreseeable future. The Movement was, as we have emphasised throughout, not a single-issue pressure group along traditional lines, but a *mass movement* characterised by *mass* action. By 1960 the Aldermaston March had become a massive demonstration of disparate groups[11] and individuals and from this time onward, the different parts of the Movement increased their own autonomy and there was a marked growth of 'movement power'.

This was of course an extremely important development from the point of view of the Movement itself: CND (as well as the DAC and the Committee of 100) was henceforth committed willy-nilly to a strategy of bringing extra-parliamentary mass pressure to bear upon the Government.[12] But it was even more important in the long-term context of British politics: the Movement was the forerunner of many similar extra-parliamentary and demonstration oriented campaigns in the next two decades.

Although the CND leadership never abandoned its Labour Party contacts and strategy—of which more later—the Movement did mark a clean and clear break with Parliamentary and conventional politics. What is clear, both from the history of the post-war years and from the empirical evidence, is the profound influence of the Movement upon the creation of a widespread style of populist politics. The notion that people, collectively, can exercise some control through Direct Action (whether legal or illegal) undertaken by themselves on either a parochial or a national level, has become a dominant aspect of the British political scene since the early 1960s.[13] The Movement was not of course the only precursor of populist politics—there was also, most obviously, the interrelationship between the Movement and the Civil Rights Movement in the USA—but there can be no doubt that the very widespread development of such political action in the UK has been greatly influenced by the Movement. In part, this was again due to the sheer *scale* of the demonstrations, which showed that this type of politics was both practicable and impressive: but it was also attributable to the mood, the ethos, difficult to quantify but strongly apparent, created by the Movement. It became evident that something *could* be done by 'ordinary people' about major issues, that there *were* things to protest about, and that a questioning of authority and of received opinion was not only desirable but possible and potentially effective.

The massive public support for the Movement was in considerable part attributable to this new mood in politics and society. As our survey has shown, one of the major effects of the Movement has been to produce activists in a wide range of campaigns and movements[14] generally characterised by their specificity and their single issue objectives. However, subsequent political activity *on the Left* amongst Movement supporters was relatively low: support for the 'Liberal Left' showed general decline, whilst commitment to the Marxist Left among our respondents had remained virtually unchanged over the 20 years (despite the relatively large growth of the Marxist Left during the late 1960s and early 1970s). The originally small group of Anarchists had further declined, although it can reasonably be argued that many of the 'community politics' activities of movement supporters have strongly anarchistic overtones.

These facts constitute a crucial and somewhat unexpected aspect of our study. One of the central hypotheses that we wished to test empirically was the extent to which the Movement had 'radicalised a generation'. Several of our respondents claimed that the Movement had in fact had this effect; and, in some senses, such as those discussed above, this was of course true. But, on the level of hard, committed political radicalisation, the effect of the Movement over the 20-year period has been minimal: there was no evidence to support the hypothesis that Movement activists became the core of the new far-left groups which emerged in the late 1960s.[15] Indeed, the effect would seem to have been rather to alienate and disillusion a substantial section of a generation from orthodox politics of both the traditional Liberal Left *and* the Marxist Left. The mass movement for nuclear disarmament was not converted to the mass movement for socialist change which so many had hoped for. The Movement led neither to the radicalisation of the Labour Party nor to the creation of a new socialist force in British politics. Yet there were a great many political radicals in the Movement who had one or other of these objectives in view, and there was certainly the potential and the enthusiasm, in terms of numbers and commitment, to make some long-term radicalisation of British politics seem possible, even likely.

There were, in our view, four basic alternative strategies through which the Movement could have pursued its aims: and our survey has shown that these alternatives were apparent too to Movement activists. A substantial number of Movement supporters were of course 'apolitical' moral protesters — and in general believed that the campaign must and would succeed by mobilising such enormous and widespread moral pressure that 'the Government' would have to accede to the mounting outrage of the general population.[16] From this perspective there was no link between the cause of nuclear disarmament and radical politics — indeed, little consideration was given to 'strategic' questions of how to attain the Movement's objectives. The leadership of CND came, to some extent, as we have argued, under this heading.

However, there can be no doubt that, if the aims of the Movement were to stand any chance of gaining acceptance, a political strategy *had* to be formulated and acted upon. The more astute members of the leadership realised this from the outset and were determined to add their considerable weight to the second strategy for advance: to convert the Labour Party to CND policies. There was, too, a very substantial section of the Movement which was firmly committed to the Labourist perspective, and for those who, whatever their reasons, believed that the Labour Party and the Labour Movement constituted the only method of advance — in nuclear and foreign policy as in all else — then the task was quite straightforward: to convert the Movement wholly to operating within and on the Labour Party and Labour Movement.[17]

The third and fourth strategies were less conventional. On the New Left there was a strong conviction that the Movement marked the crucial break with the discredited and sterile politics of the 'Old Left' — both Labour and Communist. The New Left saw the Movement as the basis and the core of a new, democratic and humanistic socialist movement which would revitalise and change fundamentally British society and politics. Whether this would or should come through the Labour Party or through a new and separate organisation was a problem which the New Left never satisfactorily resolved.

The final alternative, envisaged by some of the radicals in the DAC and the Committee of 100,[18] was the creation of a quasi-anarchistic, populist, direct action movement concerned initially with the nuclear issue but seen ultimately as an important stage in the creation of a mass, extra-parliamentary movement committed to Direct Action as a means, and the non-violent, decentralised, directly democratic society as the end.[19]

These then were the essentials of the four strategies: the moral/apolitical; the Labourist; the New Left; and the Direct Actionist. The ideological and political struggle between these perspectives for control of the Movement was crucial for the directions and decisions that were taken. Moreover, the inability of any one of the three political alternatives to take hold of the Movement resulted in the inevitable failure, not only of the specific Campaign, but, more importantly, in the long-term absence of a mass radicalising force in British politics.

The Strategies for Advance and their Wider Relevance

Many movement activists (about a third according to our sample) rejected any political context for the Movement's aims. And there can be no doubt that much of the Movement's appeal rested on entirely moral and humanistic motivations. Those in the CND leadership (and to some extent in the DAC and the Committee of 100) who accepted the need for political action did so only on the assumption that the essentials of CND's case remained on the moral plane. Moreover, for many, like Canon Collins, the task facing CND was confined to the single, central issue of unilateral nuclear disarmament. Wider questions of socio-economic structure and the achievement of a society operating on different assumptions and with different objectives were seen as either irrelevant or tangential to CND. For the 'moral protester' the Movement's strategy was, like the issue itself, a straightforward, simple matter. Protest should be on the moral plane, because the objections to nuclear weapons were fundamentally moral in character, not political. Inasmuch as 'strategy' was important it was assumed that CND policies could be put into effect via the existing political parties with no major implications for other political developments. In summary then the 'moral strategy' was simple and direct — and assumed a single-issue orientation.[20] Faced with the enormity of nuclear weapons and their effects, the emotive response was to call for a moral campaign couched in apolitical absolutes.

It is our contention that this was a wholly mistaken perspective and that the dominance of this 'moral' approach, whilst admirable in its fundamentally humane motivations, was a major contributory factor to the Movement's failure. There are several reasons for this categoric dismissal of the 'moral' perspective. At the practical level it has to be realised that *political* change of this radical type can come only through *political* action: there can be no hope of success for any Movement which does not tap some source of potential political power, as Canon Collins and others in the leadership, and many other of our interviewees, realised both at the time and subsequently.[21] A political strategy was thus essential if the Movement was to become more than what Ian Mikardo described as "an annual orgasm every Easter". More fundamentally, however, there was, as those on the New Left and in International Socialism argued,[22] a very strong and intrinsic political dimension to the whole debate over nuclear weapons. At its most extreme this found expression in the Permanent Arms Economy theory which attempted to demonstrate the structural necessity for the existence and accumulation of nuclear weapons within capitalism, from within the traditional Marxist categories of economic analysis.[23] More plausible, and more widespread, was the contention of those in the New Left (and some of those in the Labour Party) that 'unilateralism' was a call to a new way of politics over and above the specific 'moral lead' argument involved in the central CND case. If Britain had renounced nuclear weapons unilaterally but remained within NATO and firmly committed to the values and defence of western capitalism (as many in CND believed should have been the policy of the Movement), then the effect of unilateralism would have been negligible. For the policy to have any real meaning and importance it had to be allied to a *political* programme of commitment: withdrawal from NATO, a commitment *against* both major power blocks and the ideological systems which underpinned them, and a commitment *to* non-aligned politics and a new humanistic socialism. Further, the Movement was intimately involved in the attempt to create a new force for a democratic, humanistic and radical politics in the UK, whether inclining to the socialist New Left or the anarchistic Direct Actionists of the DAC and Committee of 100.[24]

It is within this context that the true significance of the Movement lies. The purely 'moral' protesters were not involved in the real struggle: their strategy had no chance of achieving the specific policy objectives of the Movement — and their orientation had no point of contact with the long-term political realities of the Movement's central concerns.

It is thus within the context of the directly political strategies that the Movement must be analysed. Not only did these strategies offer the only potentially viable mode of advance for the Movement *per se:* they also represented the long-term alternatives for achieving a general change of political direction in the UK. In post-war Britain[25] the alternatives for advance on the Left, for a qualitative change in the political environment, have been for the most part circumscribed. However, the Disarmament Movement of the late 1950s and early 1960s provided a real opportunity for such advance and the alternatives posed for the Movement represented in microcosm the dilemma facing all those on the Left in the unique, and alien, political culture of the UK.

In the context of our study therefore it is necessary to look again in some detail at the three political strategies which were possible for the Movement and analyse the implications for British political culture as a whole.

THE LABOURIST STRATEGY

The most pervasive and orthodox perspective held to the view that the Disarmament Movement was ultimately a pressure group on the Labour Movement. As the earlier quotations from Ian Mikardo have made abundantly clear the dominant Labour Left view of CND *et al.* was that, whilst the various non-Labour strands of the Movement may have been eminently worthy, the only thing that mattered in the end was how far the Movement could exert pressure on the Labour Party. The Labour Left was dismissive of what it regarded as the soft emotionalism of the moral protesters. Mikardo summed up this view accurately, though a little too harshly perhaps:

> . . . the real question is do you want a united Movement that doesn't get you any action or do you want one that has its divisions but does have a bit of cutting edge — Jacquetta Hawkes would have loved a CND which drew much more on religious and moral support and which carried on a mixed emotional and moral campaign . . . that would have appealed to many members of CND, probably a majority, but it would never have got anywhere!

This Labour Left stance is in many ways a very strong one (the same logic is used too by the Communist Party). Given the assumption that the Labour Movement is the genuine, democratic mass movement of the British working class, then, so the argument goes, any move towards socialist transformation, whether on the local, national or international scale, must be channelled through that Movement. In political terms this means the Labour Party, and in industrial, the TU Movement. Thus, for the Labour Left, on grounds of general ideology, action for progress began and ended, in the Disarmament Movement context, as in all others, with the Labour Party and the Labour Movement: without involvement with the organised working-class movement no campaign can be socialist in the long term — it will tend towards bourgeois dilettantism or it will fade away. Moreover, in terms of *power* there is, on this argument, no alternative to working in and through the Labour Movement. To pretend that some Movement outside this framework can be effective is quite illusory — and thoroughly unsocialist. Thus whilst we found no evidence, in either our survey of core activists or in our discussions with leading figures, to substantiate the familiar claim that Labour Left supporters entered the Movement in order to pursue their campaign to change the Labour Party leadership, it is true that from this viewpoint the two objectives merged into one another. The Movement was seen very much as one of a number of pressure groups on a right-wing leadership; the fact that the Movement was a *mass* movement tended not to impress the Labour Left leadership over much. As Mikardo has observed: "Another 10,000 or 20,000 or 50,000 non-political people don't compensate for the loss of those who can exert *political* pressure at the point of *action*". To achieve the Movement's objectives, it was argued, was part of the overall strategy of winning over the Labour Party to socialism, and thus of replacing the Gaitskellite leadership. How was this change to be achieved? As all Labour Left-wingers know, the Left in the PLP has always been a relatively powerless minority;[26] and, thanks to the dominance of Right-wing TU leaders, the Labour Movement outside Parliament has also been characterised by its hostility to the Left. Whilst the pressure of organisations like CND would have helped the Left to reverse this trend, this was seen as essentially secondary, supportive action: the real battleground had, by definition, to be the Labour Party and the Labour Movement. By the same process of reasoning, the Direct Action activities of the DAC and Committee of 100 were seen, with some irritation, by Labour Left-wingers as irrelevant and/or counterproductive.

There were and are two ways in which the Labour Left saw the struggle for Left power in the Labour Movement being pushed forward, both in general terms and in the specific case of CND: through winning over major TUs to Left policies, and through building a strong alternative leadership in the PLP. On the TU front there was, superficially, considerable early success—culminating of course in the 1960 Labour Conference victory. But this victory was, as already stated, both misleading and short lived and reflected more the views of Frank Cousins, general secretary of the largest union in Britain, the TGWU, who waged his own highly personal campaign for both nuclear disarmament and the removal of Gaitskell from the leadership of the Party. The TU support for 'CND style' motions in the 1960s was not the result of a deep understanding of and commitment to the policies of unilateralism and neutralism; still less was it a commitment to CND as an organisation. Moreover, the mass of the TU Movement, the rank-and-file members, was not on the whole sympathetic to unilateralism.[27] The unreality of the bloc voting system at Labour Conferences whereby a handful of major TU leaders control the outcome of the debates has never been so clearly or forcefully demonstrated as it was in 1960 and 1961.[28] The 1960 victory did not result in closer liaison between TUs and CND: Gaitskell's notorious smear, that CND consisted of Pacifists and fellow-travellers,[29] touched the TU leaders, always sensitive to accusations of fellow-travelling, on a raw nerve. Given these circumstances, and the ambivalence of CND itself about its involvement in Labour politics, it was not surprising that Gaitskell and the Campaign for Democratic Socialism found it so comparatively easy to reverse the decision at the 1961 Conference. The involvement of the higher reaches of the TU Movement in the unilateralist movement had been a very transitory and almost artificial affair.

Even more important, however, was the inability of the Movement to attract significant working-class support. Several of our interviewees drew attention to the considerable involvement of working-class activists[30] and it is true that both demonstrations and local branches contained a proportion of working-class, TU activists. (And it is certainly true, as Frank Allaun reminded us, that the CND today has maintained and extended its TU and working-class support amongst activists.) However, there can be no doubt that the Movement never managed to attract the support of ordinary, working-class, Labour supporters, let alone the apolitical or Tory sections of the working class. There was never any serious possibility of mobilising mass working-class support, either for the mainstream activities of marches and demonstrations or for the localised industrial action envisaged by Pat Arrowsmith and others.

It is important here to note the wide gulf between the working class and the radicals of the youth culture in Britain, the USA and the West generally. This applied — and indeed still applies — at a number of levels. Politically, the organised Labour Movement, both TUs and Labour Party, has been extremely suspicious of, if not hostile towards, any grouping or Movement pursuing extreme or unorthodox political objectives. This has been particularly true if the Movement has been predominantly middle class in composition. Although we would not agree with the stark dichotomy that Parkin[31] draws between working-class and middle-class protest movements, there is, historically, considerable evidence to support the contention that the British Labour Movement has often had a highly critical (not to say conservative) attitude towards single-issue, reformist campaigns.[32] It was on the social and psychological plane, however, that the working class[33] took the greatest exception to the Disarmament Movement. The adoption of the highly unorthodox methods of protest was of course one area of tension: for most of those in the Labour Movement, Direct Action of any sort was anathema. Even more important though was the alternative culture that the Movement stood for. Although this had a considerable basis in reality — not least in the political contexts that we have discussed — it was the sensationalist aspects that were blown up and distorted by the media. The common conception of the Movement, in an era far less permissive and tolerant than our own, fostered by the popular press and the broadcasting media, centred on alleged promiscuity, drugs and irresponsibility. Attention was drawn always to the so-called 'beatnik' element and to the minority outbreaks of violence. However much this may have been a caricature of the Movement, it was a powerful psychological barrier between the working class and the Movement, and one which was, and is, continually reinforced by a hostile media.

It is important to note, however, that this lack of working-class support was not something that concerned many of the leaders of CND or DAC/Committee of 100. Leaders with orientations as different as Jacquetta Hawkes and Hugh Brock were equally dismissive of the importance of working-class support and other leading figures expressed similar views.[34] The absence of working-class support — a *crucial* weakness from a socialist point of view — was thus not seen as much of a problem by most movement activists:[35] a further demonstration that the central orientation of the Movement was not in fact socialist — the central categories and concepts of the Movement were not those of a socialist movement. And despite the importance of a Labourist perspective within the Movement the protagonists of this view did not succeed in persuading the activists to alter their ideological stance.

Before continuing the analysis of the Labour Movement perspective it is important to note here a related and very significant point. One of the major failures of the Disarmament Movement between 1958 and 1965 was its relative disregard of the economic implications of disarmament — particularly in terms of trade unionists' concern over jobs. The concentration on the moral and political dimensions, to the virtual exclusion of the economic, was a measure of the degree to which the Movement was dominated by middle-class attitudes and priorities. And, of course, it tended to alienate TU support. This case was made strongly by Dick Nettleton who argued that

> when unemployment and slump came, as they did, then CND had to face up to this issue and do battle on it in real hard terms . . . while I feel its OK for Union Annual Conference to be passing resolutions saying nuclear weapons are a bad thing, get rid of them, it was a different thing for Union Conferences to be discussing in detail the actual future of their industry: 'what are we going to do—do we want these arms contracts?'.

To secure serious discussion of its arguments within the industrial Labour Movement, CND would have had to develop along the lines suggested by Nettleton (and indeed they have since done so). The fact that CND signally failed to do this in the early years was an important factor in its failure to win over the Labour Movement.

To return to the main theme of analysis: there seems to us, as we have argued, to be a number of central reasons why the industrial Labour Movement was not won over to the Movement. But what of the political Labour Left—ground on which CND was far more at home and had firm allies? Surely a mass movement led by a predominantly Labourist clique would provide exactly the vehicle for the Labour Left to pursue, legitimately, its desire for a change in the leadership and the direction of the Party. And, looking at it in reverse, surely the Labour Left offered the Movement the ideal opportunity to translate its tremendous mass power into political action. Here was a situation where both the interests and the commitment to the single central issue of the two groups coincided.

The prospects of this alliance were, of course, immeasurably enhanced by the Labour Party's third successive General Election Defeat in 1959, under Hugh Gaitskell's aggressively Right-wing leadership: the unity of the Party was, by late 1959, looking very precarious indeed. Given all this, how was it that the CND/Labour Left alliance failed to take the Labour Party by storm and sweep away the Gaitskellite leadership?

We need here to look both at the Disarmament Movement and the Labour Left and analyse their strengths and weaknesses. Although the Movement was led by a group that had predominantly Labour sympathies this was by no means true of the whole Executive.[36] They did not see the Movement as *political* in this conventional Labour sense and did not wish to compromise the moral drive and 'purity' of the Movement by entanglement in Party politics. There was also the disquiet expressed by many, in both leadership and rank and file, about close association with what was seen as the committed Socialist Left of the Labour Party. Construing their Movement as a moral crusade they were anxious that it should not be diverted (and perverted) by the 'politically motivated' men of the Left. There was thus a substantial section of the Movement that was hostile to, or at best wary of, the 'Labour connection'.[37]

However, even for those in the leadership who realised that the only practical way to achieve the objectives of the Movement was to work through the Labour Party, there was a less than wholehearted commitment to the Labour Left. The key person here was Canon Collins. There were those on the Executive who were wholly committed to the Labour Left argument—principally Kingsley Martin and Michael Foot—but it was

Collins who led the Movement and who represented the dominant view of the Executive during the crucial 1959/61 years. Collins believed that "a real Christian can never be a good party man", and that, although "the bulk of the Executive . . . were left of Toryism (their support for CND was based) on moral principles uncompromisingly . . .". Commitment to the Labour Left was thus not central to Collins' view of the Movement, and even after the 1960 Conference victory, many CND activists were unwilling to devote their campaigning energies to securing their position within the Labour Party. Many of them were not politically committed at all whilst some, like Jacquetta Hawkes, hardly realised the significance of the 1960 Conference. Of those who *were* politically committed, many feared, with good reason, that an abrupt move to bring the whole Movement into the Labour Party would have alienated a large degree of support. Even for those who were ready to undertake this agitation within the Labour Party, the tactics and procedures to adopt were far from clear. In Stuart Hall's view, as we have noted earlier, the Movement was "bizarrely unprepared" for its success — or rather for the success of unilateralist policies — at the 1960 Conference. No strategic plan was ready for building on that success — no bridges had been built between the Movement and the Labour Party and no organizational contact existed. This stood in marked contrast to the experienced, determined, and well-organised and successful Gaitskellite campaign through 1961 to ensure the reversal of the decision.

From that time on the CND leadership was, strategically speaking, floundering. Their strategy of winning over the Labour Party via Labour Left and TU backing had, most unexpectedly, come good in 1960. But the reversal in 1961 and the subsequent burying of the issue in 1962 and the years following, leading up to the election-induced unity under Wilson in 1963/4, left the Movement high and dry. Popular support grew dramatically through 1961 and continued strong through 1962 and 1963, but the leadership had nothing else to offer except the now discredited, and increasingly unrealistic, Labour Party strategy. As the years passed so disillusionment with this perspective deepened, and the divisions and cynicism within the Movement grew.[38]

If there was some ambivalence about the *CND* leadership's commitment to the Labour Left, there was no such ambivalence in the case of the DAC and Committee of 100. Leaders and activists (a much less sharp distinction than was the case in CND) categorically rejected the Labourist perspective. Their central concern was with the issue itself and with the creation of a direct action, non-violent, extra-parliamentary politics to achieve this objective, and also, ultimately, to supersede the conventional party political system. To subsume the Movement in the orthodox party political struggle, to equate the objectives and tactics of the Movement with those of the Labour Left would have been complete anathema to the Direct Actionists, and they rejected this alliance as firmly after the 1960 Conference decision (which they regarded with some justification as an artificial vote by the various bureaucracies) as they had done before.

It was thus unlikely that the leadership of CND could have brought the whole of CND (let alone the DAC and the Committee of 100) into the Labour Movement struggle. However, as many realised at the time, as this was the strategy adopted for good or ill by the leadership, it was essential to try to implement it at the most favourable opportunity — that is, following the 1960 Conference victory. The failure to do this was in part the responsibility of the CND leadership, as we have indicated. But it was also due to the inherent weakness of the Labour Left.

To clarify the argument let us suppose that the Labour Party had, historically, had a balance between Right and Left, and that it had been led sometimes by socialists of the Left and sometimes by social democrats or revisionists of the Right. Suppose further that in the late 1950s the authority and strength of the Left in the Party (Parliamentary as well as national) was equal to that of the Right. In this hypothetical situation, the explosion of a mass movement like CND on to the political scene, backed by several of the large TUs, might well have presented the perfect—and the perfectly genuine—opportunity for the Left to challenge and defeat the Right and lead the Party, and the Movement, along a unilateralist and neutralist road. The Movement's reluctance to be drawn into 'Labourism' would, in these circumstances, have been overcome, perhaps, by a powerful and *authoritative* Labour Left.

That this hypothesis did not correspond to political reality hardly needs emphasis. One of the most long-standing and important facts about the British Labour Movement—and one which differentiates it sharply from most of its European counterparts—is its persistently and peculiarly weak Left.[39] This weakness has been both organisational and ideological and has its roots in the framework of British political culture.[40] Given these unpropitious antecedents there was in reality only one hope of the Labour Left's achieving power, and thus, from this perspective, of translating CND's campaign slogans into political action. This was, of course, for an individual or group of individuals of ability, attraction and authority to emerge on the Left of the Party and, at a time of critical weakness, wrest power from the Right and thus reverse the pattern of previous Labour Movement politics. In many ways the late 1950s did seem a time when this might prove possible: having lost the 1951 election, the Labour Party proceeded to lose both the 1955 and 1959 Elections, *and* they were under the leadership of probably the most doctrinaire Right-wing leader in the history of the Party—Hugh Gaitskell. All through the middle 1950s the power and influence of the 'Bevanites'—the organised Labour Left grouping under the leadership of Aneurin Bevan—was growing.[41] The Bevanites included some of the most able politicians of twentieth-century Britain: Crossman, Wilson, Freeman, Foot and many more. Above all, of course, they had, in Bevan himself, one of the outstanding politicians of the age. A superb orator, a great House of Commons figure, a socialist bred in the unique traditions of the Welsh mining community with an unshakeable attachment to that peculiarly British ideological stance of 'democratic socialism', Bevan towered above all his colleagues, Gaitskell not excepted.[42] As George Clark has recalled, Bevan at his peak, as he was during the Suez crisis of 1956, made a very considerable impact on ordinary people because of the moral strength and commitment of his politics: "There's no doubt he did cut across the politics of Gaitskell and the Government and he reduced Trafalgar Square to a drawing room and moved people to think that Britain could actually behave differently. A *fantastic* speech!"

Yet despite all these extremely favourable circumstances there was little likelihood of Bevan taking power from the Left. Attlee had long ago decided that Bevan should succeed him as leader of the Party when the time came,[43] but, in the event, it was Gaitskell and not Bevan who won the contest in the PLP. The forces of the Right of the Party were too strong for a proclaimed, indeed a vociferous, Left-winger ever to triumph.[44]

Bevan was thus faced with the classic dilemma of all Left politicians in Britain: should he remain true to the socialism he had passionately believed in, and to whose attainment he had devoted his life, with the sure and certain result that he would be denied access to political power? or should he compromise his principles, at least in the short term, in order to achieve some degree of acceptability to the rest of the Party, reach an understanding with the leadership, and thus attain power? There has not been, in the history of the British Labour Party to date, any prominent Left-winger who has successfully risen to a position of power in the Party, retained his Left ideological stance in practice as well as in theory, and managed to translate this into political action for the advancement of socialism. (Some may, however, wish to argue that George Lansbury marked a partial exception to this rule; others, rather less credibly, that Tony Benn has the potential so to do.) The problem is intractable; and it seems likely to remain so whilst the balance of forces, both 'physically' and ideologically, remain as they are at present in the Labour Party.

Be this as it may, there is no doubt that Bevan, following his defeat in the leadership contest by Gaitskell, chose the second alternative and opted for power with compromise. This was by no means necessarily a selfish or ignoble decision. Bevan had come to the conclusion that he was most unlikely to achieve high office (and therefore political power) in the next Labour Government unless he reached some *modus viven-di* with the Gaitskellite leadership. Moreover, he was also well aware that the continued Left/Right split severely reduced the Party's chances of winning power at the next Election. In the opinions of most of our interviewees (i.e. Michael Foot, Sir Harold Wilson, Lord Home and Ian Mikardo), however, Bevan's motivation was not one of personal power-seeking (as Mikardo put it: "If Nye had been interested in office . . . he could have had office years and years before . . . he was very unambitious. . . .") Rather, his abrupt change of line on the unilateralist issue, which marked his overt reconciliation with the leadership, was due, in Mikardo's view, to his "passionate desire to end the era of confrontation and he saw himself as a possible architect of a new international pact . . . and he swallowed some of his convictions in order to move forward to achieving that". Also it must be remembered that Bevan's international reputation with both the Third World and the Communist bloc was unique and therefore he, more than any Western politician, had perhaps the chance to achieve a real breakthrough to *détente* and disarmament. Lord Soper's view was similar, though perhaps a little less flattering to Bevan:

> Aneurin Bevan believed that the primary task was to get Labour into power, even if it seemed at the time that you had to relinquish CND. When Labour came into power and Bevan was Foreign Secretary, *then* we could have got going . . . I think Bevan was a political animal from first to last, and he believed that what he was doing was the right approach to gain our ends.

Michael Foot, whilst agreeing broadly with these analyses, also emphasised that, in his view, Bevan genuinely disagreed that unilateralism was the best policy, in the immediate situation, for the Labour Party to adopt to bring about international nuclear disarmament and world peace, and that his opposition to unilateralism stemmed from principled, as well as strategic, motivations.

Whatever the motivations, the fact remains that Bevan did change his mind on unilateral nuclear disarmament, and that this change in 1957 marked a break with his erstwhile colleagues and followers on the Left, and a corresponding coming together of Bevan and Gaitskell in an apparently unified Party Leadership.[45]

This was a quite crucial occurrence in the context of our discussion of the Labour strategy *vis-à-vis* CND. For the historical and political reasons already given it was unlikely[46] that the Labour Left would in any circumstances have been able to win control of the Labour Party, and thus bring about the political action which would lead to CND policy being implemented. Once Bevan had 'defected' — for whatever reasons and however temporary that defection might be held to have been — any hope of the CND policy becoming accepted as part of a generally Leftward move in the Party virtually disappeared. His decision to ally himself with the leadership on the defence issue was crucial both for CND and for his own political future. By rejecting CND he had, in a bitter parody of his own words, surrendered 'the commanding heights' of the Labour Party not only for unilateralism but for his own vision of democratic socialism. There was no remotely comparable figure on the Labour Left to take up the CND cause — or indeed to take up the cause of the Left in the Party. Bevan's action paved the way for a reunited Party. Despite the traumas of 1959 and 1960 the Left had little chance of toppling Gaitskell and the Right, and Bevan's 'unity move', in 1957, can be seen in retrospect to have laid the foundations for the Party unity achieved by Gaitskell in 1962 and brought to triumphant electoral victory in 1964 by Harold Wilson. Paradoxically, therefore, the CND *leadership's 'Labour strategy' was outdated even before CND was formally inaugurated:* Bevan had in effect dealt a death-blow to the chances of converting the Labour Party when 'CND' was merely a mood, an ethos, and had not progressed to an organisational form with firm policy objectives and so on.

Sir Harold Wilson and Ian Mikardo, by no means always of a mind, were agreed on this. In Sir Harold's view Bevan's 1957 speech "killed any chance of CND reaching the commanding heights of the Party, as it meant that they would never be able to get a CND manifesto accepted and they would never have a majority either in the Executive or in the Parliamentary Party . . ..". If the assumptions of the 'Labour strategy' perspective are accepted then we would in the final analysis agree, as so often, with Ian Mikardo's blunt verdict that "There wasn't really much hope once Nye had gone".

However crucial Bevan's role may have been in the specific context, the basic structural weakness of the Left in Britain was, in our view, the underlying cause of its inability to move the CND case forward in the Labour Party. Moreover, the Labour Left's own peculiar brand of emotive Leftism[47] served to confuse and obscure the political potential of CND as a socialist movement. The inherent inability and unwillingness to think and act 'structurally',[48] and the reflex Parliamentarist assumptions,[49] once again resulted in the Labour Left's being unable to realise the potential of a mass movement whose roots and being were essentially *extra*-parliamentary.

What would have happened had Bevan lived, and retained his commitment to the Left, is one of the most interesting 'ifs' in British politics. It is, of course, arguable that, with his unique brand of 'ILP' socialism, Bevan could have liberated the dormant, crusading radicalism of the Labour Party, and that this in turn might have led to real socialist advance. Whether this would have resulted, or whether the structural and ideological constraints would have proved too great, must remain an open question.

THE 'NEW LEFT' STRATEGY

If the Labour Left was, arguably irrespective of the 'Bevan case', not a viable long-term channel for CND either in specific policy or wider 'movement' terms, many socialists and 'progressives' saw the New Left as the way forward. Unlike the Labour Left the New Left was (potentially if not always actually) linked neither to conventional party politics in Parliament nor to the ideological precepts of Labourism. In many ways it represented precisely the catalyst that could have brought together a radical, humanistic socialism and the moral fervour of the Movement. Its politics and its style were, certainly in the case of the *ULR* (*Universities and Left Review* group), far closer to the Movement than to any of the established, conventional political organisations. As we have argued earlier, the roots of the NL lay in the dramatic events of 1956 — and the consequent disillusionment of many CP members with orthodox Communism; and the coming to political consciousness of a whole new generation of radical Leftists deeply critical of both capitalism *and* Communism, unattached but committed. The coming together of these two strands, encompassing some of the very best intellectual talents of the post-war period,[50] presented in many ways a much more viable strategy for a Left/Movement alliance and advance than did the Labour Left road. Here was a *genuinely* New Left — many of those in the DAC, not in any normal sense socialists and certainly not Marxists,[51] believed that the NL offered a coherent and desirable alternative to conventional Left politics. This was a socialist politics that came nearer to the heart and soul of the Movement: the NL, like CND, was outraged and appalled by the existence of nuclear weapons; both were characterised by youthful enthusiasm, idealism and commitment; and both were committed to an eclectic, relatively tolerant, and extra-parliamentary movement style of politics.

Most crucially of all the NL had a range of well worked-out and coherent policy demands which, whilst linking in to Movement objectives, were also couched within a wider conception of a NL socialist politics. The NL had a clear conception of how it wanted to 'move CND on': it realised clearly that unilateralism *per se* was, from a socialist viewpoint, of little value in the long term. Moral gestures do not get you very far along the hard, realpolitik road of Socialism. To achieve serious, structural advance and harness the power of the Movement to this end, the NL pushed hard for the adoption of 'positive neutralism', and, as we have seen, succeeded in having this, and the commitment to withdrawal from NATO formally accepted by the Movement in 1960/1. For the NL, socialism meant not only the rejection of nuclear weapons on moral grounds, and principled opposition to American capitalism and American alliances, it meant too a positive, optimistic and ambitious espousal of a Third Way — a *positive neutralist* road which would unite all non-totalitarian, non-capitalist, but potentially socialist societies into one loosely organised but united movement for humanistic socialism, inspired, as it were, by the 'early' rather than the 'late' Marx.

This was the objective — and ambitious though it was, and far too optimistic and in some ways naive as it may now seem with 20 years' hindsight (20/20 hindsight is a great gift, as Ralph Miliband once observed), it had a coherence and a socialist logic to it that was enormously appealing. And, in the British context, it can be argued that it had the potential to by-pass the whole impasse of the Labour Left.[52]

However, it is here that, as we saw earlier, the problems with this perspective begin to emerge. The New Left flirted with extra-parliamentary politics and was at different stages variously attracted to Voters' Veto, INDEC, DAC, revolutionary politics and the rest, but it always remained essentially wedded to *Labourist* politics and *Labourist* assumptions. Despite its many *New* Left tendencies it was, ultimately, always firmly anchored in an '*Old* Left' concept of socialist politics. Thus its very attractiveness and strength as a new alternative for those on the Left was compromised and diluted from its earliest stages. From one point of view it can be argued that the NL represented a necessary stage along the road to the growth of a mature, extra-parliamentary, Marxist Left, which had the ideological and organisational strength to separate itself from the Labour Party. On this model the NL was merely a temporary, and somewhat confused, staging post on the road to real socialist advance. Alternatively, and we would argue more realistically, the NL can be seen as probably the last determined attempt to radicalise and revivify the Labour Party, to inject some socialist purpose into an otherwise essentially barren and demoralised Social Democratic Party. As our study has shown a large proportion of intellectual leftists have, since their Movement involvement, opted out of political activism and become disillusioned with politics.[53] From almost any socialist point of view the subsequent history of the Labour Party has been a sad and sorry story — and the Party can ill-afford the absence of this generation of socialist and creative intellectuals.

The main point remains, however, that the NL was, in practice, inextricably committed to Labourist politics and ideology (and increasingly so as the 1960s wore on),[54] and that the subsequent disillusionment with politics was the perhaps inevitable result.

Yet it was not only in terms of its attachment to Labourism that the NL failed to fulfil 'its early promise'. Without reiterating all the arguments, we must emphasise again the importance of its almost complete lack of a working-class base, and its equally important inability to communicate with and activate the Disarmament Movement. These were quite crucial failures. No socialist movement can hope to advance, or even maintain a credible existence, without establishing a real presence in the working class (something which the IS/SWP for all its manifest faults as a socialist organisation did realise, and attempt to act upon, in the late 1960s and early 1970s.)[55] The NL had no such presence — and showed little sign of working to acquire it.

Equally, no movement basing its existence on its place in CND (and the other disarmament organisations) could hope to convince that Movement of the need to analyse the structure of the society that had produced nuclear weapons and the consequent necessity of embracing a new socialist perspective, unless it had the ability to communicate its programme *and* its ideology effectively: this the NL manifestly failed to do, not least because the language and arguments of its over-academic Marxism were so foreign to British political culture.

The NL had many advantages as a potential catalyst for breaking the log jam of British politics — it was a new and vibrant grouping with enormous talent and energy, a logical, coherent and attractive interpretation of socialism rooted firmly in the Marxist tradition but having also strong cultural and intellectual links with the British Labour Movement experience; *and* above all, it had a strong base in the Disarmament Movement. Despite the fatalistic assumptions of the Labour Left view, the Labour Party is not a static, immovable monolith: there *are*, potentially, other avenues to both power and socialism. And one of the most attractive and potentially realisable of these, in the UK, is a new alliance, on a NL basis of some description. There is thus nothing inherently foolish or ridiculous in the notion of a NL regrouping leading to a re-formation of the organised working-class movement around a socialistically oriented party, or grouping.[56] However, for this strategy to achieve credibility, at least four crucial requirements must be fulfilled: the grouping in question must be serious and united in its desire to create a new formation; there must be strong and close links with the organised working-class movement (including the trade unions); there must be sufficient division and disillusionment within the existing social democratic organisation to make a 'split' feasible; the ideological basis and the specific policy objectives of the grouping in question must be clear and coherent, *and* must have an intrinsic appeal to a substantial number of people who are potential recruits. It will be obvious from our previous discussion that, in our view, the NL failed to qualify to a greater or lesser extent on all these counts.

THE 'DIRECT ACTION' STRATEGY

With all its faults and weaknesses the New Left did present an exciting, serious and potentially viable way forward, not only for the attainment of the specific movement objectives but also for the revitalising of the British Left. The same cannot, in our view, be said for the third political strategy of the Movement—the strategy which undoubtedly commanded the greatest support amongst the Movement's radical wing.

The non-violent Direct Action wing of the Movement contained four major orientations (as well as numerous subdivisions). There were those who believed, with Ralph Schoenman, that the Movement marked the beginning of a period of outright confrontation between 'the people' and the 'oppressive State', and that by mass Direct Action in the streets the State machine could be paralysed and eventually overthrown. This quasi-syndicalist, populist view was far closer to Anarchism than it was to Socialism, and Schoenman himself specifically rejected working within the confines of any 'party', socialist or otherwise. The commitment to non-violence, as both a strategy and a principle, which was so central to the DAC tradition, was tangential to, if not altogether absent from, this perspective.

The second and more 'mainstream' orientation can be characterised as broadly libertarian socialist. These activists, like George Clark and Michael Randle, put the nuclear issue at the centre of their politics but increasingly broadened out from this to develop a theory and a strategy of radical politics which incorporated, as we have seen, populist notions of decentralisation, community power, and a radical moralism as the basis of political action. These activists, too, were enthusiastic about the potential of the Movement but realised the enormous difficulties and barriers that any radical force would encounter.[57] Although considerably further removed from Anarchism in any 'formal' sense, activists of this orientation rejected any form of communist or social democratic socialism: as we have seen, their relationship with and attitude towards Marxism was complex and ambivalent, but their antipathy towards the major 'socialist' *organisations* of the time was clear and deeply held.

The 'purist' Direct Actionists of the DAC, who form our third major orientation, overlappped to a considerable degree with the latter grouping but they were distinct and separate. The central reference point of their political ideology was of course the nuclear issue: but, over and above that, their objective was the creation of a society based upon non-violence. The young activists of the DAC were indeed a new, radical and socially oriented group within the pacifist movement, striving for radical social change—but their commitment to *pacifism* was no less strong than their commitment to radicalism. For these activists — April Carter and Pat Arrowsmith for example — the *ideology of violence* was at the heart of existing society and their key objective was to replace this with a 'politics of non-violence'.

The fourth and final orientation within the Direct Action wing of the movement was that which regarded Direct Action as a *tactic* pure and simple. The supreme exponent of this view was Bertrand Russell, who held that the issue was so important and so urgent that Direct Action tactics were justifiable. There was thus no 'ideology' in which Direct Action played a major part, underlying this approach, as was the case with the others. For Russell and those of similar outlook the Committee of 100 was conceived entirely in terms of the tactical manoeuvres necessary to bring about the specific aims of the Movement.

The Direct Actionists thus differed considerably over their orientations, but they had a number of things in common. Most obviously, they were agreed, from whatever motives, that non-violent civil disobedience was a justifiable and necessary tactic to achieve the ends of the Movement. They were all agreed, too, that the CND leadership was not fulfilling its role satisfactorily and that some more overt and striking lead was necessary. Most important of all, in the long-term ideological context, was their rejection, to a greater or lesser extent, of socialism as an ideology, and their equally vehement rejection of the various organisations of the Left as vehicles for achieving either the objectives of the Movement or the wider radicalisation which most of them were seeking. There was a unanimous and fierce dismissal of the Communist Party which was seen as Stalinist, and cold-war oriented with no genuine interest in either the Movement or the cause of nuclear disarmament. (Ironically, and typically, the media portrayed these Direct Actionists as Red extremists!)

More importantly, there was a general cynicism and lack of interest in the potential of the Labour Party (or, for that matter, the Labour Movement) as an agency for the sort of changes that were desired. Many of the activists who supported the DAC and the Committee of 100 voted Labour, but, as our interviews bore out, there was no real involvement or conviction.[58] Moreover, the repeated attempts at mounting alternative electoral outlets — Voters' Veto, INDEC — testified to the continuing desire to create an alternative formation to the Labour Party, and probably to Parliamentary politics *per se*.

The other important unifying characteristic of the various tendencies within this orientation was a negative one. None of them had a clear and coherent programme of objectives over and above the central demands of unilateralism and the rest of the CND official policy package. The DAC, to be sure, had a highly ambitious (and highly unrealistic) policy programme which included unilateralism for the West as a whole; but there was no attempt to come to terms with the real nature of the power structure, national or international, or the real possibilities for political change. The DAC's programme was, for all its radicalism, still couched in the traditions of the somewhat esoteric, if not positively eccentric, British pacifist movement. Apart from its strong links with a small section of the Labour Left (far weaker post-World War II than pre-war) this Movement had never had any remotely 'powerful connections' and had never had any realistic chance of gaining majority support for its policies. Its underlying conceptions had been individualist, almost salvationist, and much opposed to collectivist socialism. The DAC 'purists' did try to change this — and certainly its Gandhian-influenced, socially oriented pacifism *was* very different. But it produced no central conceptions — in either theoretical or organisational terms — to replace the old individualist creed of pacifism. It centred its whole ideology on the concept of the 'nonviolent society', and yet it produced precious little definition of this society and even less about how it intended to bring about this monumental change. Moreover, in organisational terms, it discounted to a large extent the traditional alliance with the pacifist Labour Left (anyway a declining force) and concentrated on populist tactics on a quasi-syndicalist model, and on the creation of a new and militant movement of Direct Actionists who had no political purpose other than to attain the specific policy objectives of the DAC. In this latter case there was no clear notion of whether this should consist entirely of 'popular pressure' at the extra-parliamentary level, or whether it should involve attempts at electoral politics outside the conventional party system.

The programme, if such it can be called, of the Schoenman militants was far vaguer. The objective was the traditional anarchistic, voluntarist society where power resided in the hands of the people, and the exploitative, bureaucratic and repressive State had been crushed by the popular will. However, the Anarchism professed by the militants of the Committee of 100 was not for the most part based on a mature conviction that an anarchist analysis and prescription were the correct and desirable way forward for the Movement and for society generally in the UK. A leading Anarchist[59] has confirmed our contention that whilst many in the Movement may have been acting on anarchistic assumptions and principles, this was an unconscious adoption of tactics and attitudes that seemed appropriate in the immediate context, rather than a long-term and principled commitment to Anarchism *per se*. The fact that this was so much a hybrid and 'gut reaction' Anarchism perhaps explains the relatively high drop-out rate amongst the Anarchists in our study over the 20-year period.[60] At all events, although the prospects for such a militant upsurge of insurrectionary fervour may briefly have looked rosy, in 1961,[61] there was never much doubt that the forces of the State were more than adequate to cope with the demonstrators. The police, the Government and the politicians showed their usual sure grasp of both tactics and psychology in isolating and eventually crushing the militant wing of the Movement.[62] Despite the grandiose protestations of Schoenman and the militants of the Committee of 100, this was not serious politics at any level: George Clark was surely correct when he dismissed this particular brand of secular Messianism as 'pure adventurism'.

The strategy of the libertarian socialists — the community-oriented decentralists — was in most cases more realistic. Whilst they placed great emphasis on 'Movement power', and the need for control to be firmly in the hands of the Movement, they had for the most part no illusions about the enormous problems facing the Movement in both its 'immediate' and its long-term objectives. Rejecting both the orthodox anarchist and the (various) orthodox socialist conceptions, assumptions and models, most activists of this tendency concentrated their attention on the immediate task of building a bigger and more radically oriented peace movement. From this involvement in radical peace politics, would emerge, they hoped, a more politically conscious and aware movement. Their more long-term objectives and strategies were, however, vague and undefined. Most, in the end, opted for variants of George Clark's 'Community Politics' — populist, decentralised and radical, with an individualist and 'small group', rather than collectivist, orientation. The extent to which this tendency has in fact dominated all ex-DAC, ex-Committee of 100 activists, can be seen from the subsequent involvements of the 'Direct Action' respondents in our study.

Overall, this Direct Action perspective commanded considerable support in its various guises, within the Movement. It appears to us, however, that such a perspective contained insuperable problems. These were fundamentally twofold: the Direct Actionists had no coherent and realistic strategy for attaining their objectives (either short or long term); equally important, and intimately linked to this, they had no worked-through ideological analysis within which to interpret their Movement involvement and objectives. The appeal of Direct Action — particularly in the high-tension atmosphere pre-Cuba — was of course tremendous, particularly to young people inexperienced in both political action and life itself. As E. P. Thompson and others remarked at the time, this was a new generation, radical, but not socialist in the conventional sense. They had grown up with a healthy scepticism of Russian communism as well as Western capitalism. The Direct Action response to conventional politics should always be seen in this context: 'a plague on both your houses' was the dominant attitude and it spread from the rejection of the broad ideological positions, as perceived, of communism and capitalism, to a dismissal of all orthodox methods of protest and political action. If the commitment was to be to a new politics, a new, nuclear-free society, then that commitment must be all-embracing and total — and it must mark a break with hitherto accepted political practices. There must be no compromises, no prevarication, no half-measures: the Movement must retain its dynamism and its purity. Such was the message.

There was, and perhaps is, much to applaud in such sentiments. The history of the British Left is, after all, and despite its achievements, an illustration of the problems following compromise, involvement with 'the system', and eventual absorption. The problem was, however, that the Direct Actionists had no even remotely viable alternative. Unlike either of the other two political perspectives we have discussed there was no conceivable way that their politics could have brought about either the short-term policy objectives they were aiming for, or the long-term radicalisation which was implicit in their actions. Such a key figure as Michael Randle has, to all intents and purposes, confirmed this; looking back 20 years to the Direct Action campaign of the Committee of 100 in 1961, he recalled that even at its height, the civil disobedience Movement was not within sight of creating a 'revolutionary situation': to achieve this would have required *millions,* rather than *thousands* of active supporters. The most that could be hoped for, even at this high point in 1961, was, realistically, to involve Direct Actionists in ways "which directly affected the (Government's) ability to carry out the programme of preparation for nuclear war . . .".

To claim even that for the Direct Actionists proved, in the long term, far too optimistic. As far as the more ambitious long-term aims and objectives were concerned it must be concluded that, attractive and understandable though Direct Action politics was for many at the time, it represented ultimately the politics of immaturity: the desire and the belief that dramatic and immediate anti-authority political action would secure the objectives. The testimony to the fallacy of this view lies in the short-lived existence of the Committee of 100 as a mass movement.

Why Did the Movement Fail?

We are now in a position to return to the question of why the Movement 'failed'. To some extent, as we have shown, the answer lies within the Movement itself: it was so divided — at all levels and in all senses — that its potential power was severely reduced. Its consequent inability to decide upon one single, coherent strategy — or, come to that, a single agreed programme of long-term objectives — led to confusion and eventually disillusionment. There was also a number of quite extraneous factors which were crucial: in particular the Cuba crisis and its resolution demonstrated both the irrelevance of the UK when it came to a real crisis between the 'Super Powers', and the ability of the American and Soviet leadership to pull back from the nuclear brink. Added to this was the impact of the Partial Test Ban Treaty of 1963, which dispelled the psychological atmosphere of tension. Given the closing of the Labour ranks under Harold Wilson, who was intent on unifying the party prior to the imminent General Election, the Movement was, to all intents and purposes, declining by 1963/4. The Campaign had been in existence for five exhausting years by this time and many of the early supporters — rank and file as well as leaders — were becoming tired and perhaps disillusioned.

In reality, of course, nothing significant had changed: nuclear weapons continued to be stockpiled in both the East and the West, nuclear technology progressed to even more frightening levels of sophistication, and Britain, under a 'socialist' government continued the conservative policy of independent deterrence and staunch membership of NATO (as well as subsequently giving support to the USA in Vietnam). Moreover, the critical need for a fresh radicalising force in British politics had become painfully evident after a year or two of the Labour administration. By that time, however, the Movement, as a mass movement, was virtually finished, and was increasingly overshadowed by the mounting international agitation against the American war in Vietnam. This is not to say that the *need* for the Movement had disappeared: the contemporary CND has a vital role to play in pressurising government, but it is a very different type of organisation and there is little indication that it will again have the ability to mobilise mass support.

The Movement of 1958/65 was very much an expression of a whole range of concerns prevalent at the time, all of which found representation (often symbolic) in the campaign against nuclear weapons. The Movement was very much 'of its time' therefore: it gave expression to a whole new mood of questioning and frustration with the materialistic society of post-war Britain. Sparked off by the Suez and Hungary crises of 1956, the Movement was characterised by a deep and passionate conviction that morality must be brought back into politics.

At one level, the inability of the Movement to translate this moral drive into effective political action lay at the heart of the Movement's failure. Most supporters did not want, psychologically or morally, to have to deviate from their total, simple call for unilateral nuclear disarmament. The political implications and ramifications of the Movement were a distraction, at best a side issue, for most supporters (viz. the high percentage in our study who put loyalty to the Movement before any other ideological or organisational commitments).[63] A movement of moral purity and no political action, however, would, as Ian Mikardo and others drily reminded us, be very good for the soul and for the spiritual improvement of those taking part, but it would achieve nothing. The simple, practical point that to achieve major (or even minor) changes in policy, politics and ideology one has to indulge in *political* planning, *political* organisation, and *political* action, seems to have been ignored by a large number of Movement supporters. Because they did not want to compromise their moral fervour and resolve by entering into the complex and messy world of politics, the Movement on the whole tended to remain aloof from any realistic political action. Those strategies, discussed at some length above, which involved a long-term political perspective for action, neither commanded sufficient support, nor had sufficient coherence to shake the Movement's firmly apolitical ethos.

Even more important than these grave internal weaknesses, however, was the nature of the political culture in which the Movement had to operate. The failure of the Movement — and the inability of any of its strategies to make a serious political impact in anything other than the short-term — is indicative of the deeply conservative political culture of modern Britain.[64] That the Movement represented an attempt at all levels — policy, ideology, style — to *radicalise* British politics, cannot be doubted. And this is, precisely, the central reason that the organised Labour Movement and the working class rejected the Movement's policies and politics. The *structural* hold of the Right in Britain is well documented[65] — what has become evident only in the last decade or so is the Right's equally important *ideological* hegemony.[66] In this context the Movement must be seen primarily as a brave but unsuccessful attempt to break this stranglehold and introduce a whole new approach and political orientation to the UK. This stranglehold cannot, of course, be total — and it cannot remain 'watertight' in the long term. Indeed it would have been by no means impossible for a *politicised* Disarmament Movement to have acted as the catalyst for the generation of a new, radicalised Movement committed to humanistic socialism: a New Left, in fact, as envisaged by E. P. Thompson, Stuart Hall and the other New Left activists. This would have required major shifts not only by Movement supporters, but by the Left of the Labour Movement (Labour Party *and* Trade Unions), and by the New Left itself.

All this is, however, conjecture. All we can say with any degree of confidence is that the only Movement strategy with any reasonable chance of success — that of the New Left — foundered and virtually disappeared. That there was the potential within the Movement for support for some such new initiative seems to us evident from our study of core activists: the degree of support for radical, humanistic, morally based socialism — as exemplified in the general ideological orientations of our activists in 1978 — contrasts starkly with their lack of enthusiasm for any of the political organisations of the Left, both then (i.e. 1958/65) and now. That the New Left failed to capitalise upon this potential, and that it failed to make a decisive transformation of Labourism, and thus take substantial sections of the Labour Movement into a new socialist era, must mark a very significant watershed in the history, not only of the Disarmament Movement, but of modern British politics generally.

The Achievements

This leads us on, finally, to the question of how significant the whole episode — that is, the whole growth and decline of the Disarmament Movement between 1958/65 — has been in the broad sweep of modern British and Western political development. To begin with it must be emphasised again that there was a whole range of extremely important social effects of the Movement that we have referred to earlier in this section. These alone would justify a prominent place for the Movement in the history of post-war Britain with undoubted reverberations in the USA and the West generally. Many of the developments in the 1960s and beyond would have been unthinkable without the Movement's influence, as several of our interviewees and respondents have pointed out.[67] Important though these effects were, however, they must be seen as essentially tangential to the central concerns of the Movement.

What *political* impact did the Movement make? At one level, the Movement failed completely to achieve its objectives. The point need not be laboured here but it must be noted that, in terms both of destructive power and proliferation, if not in terms of international tension, the nuclear peril is considerably *greater* today than it was at the height of the mass-movement agitation. For that reason alone it may be argued that the case for putting every effort into the contemporary CND is a very strong one. But there are wider and, in our view, crucially important respects in which the Movement had a very profound political impact. In the context of the Labour Party it showed yet again the fundamental weakness of the Labour Left; more than this, however, the whole 1960/61 conflict over unilateralism and the authority of Conference demonstrated, as April Carter has argued, "that the Labour Conference no longer, if it ever had, controlled Party policy". Indeed it might be said to have given the lie once and for all to the notion of party democracy in Labour politics. Henceforth there could be little doubt that the PLP, even in opposition, acted as a virtually autonomous agency and was not subject to the control of the Labour Movement outside Parliament.[68] It might be thought, too, that the experiences of 1960/1 would have served to alienate the Left of the Movement from involvement in the Labour Party (and to some extent this has been the case, as our study has shown).[69] However, the virtual absorption of the New Left into the Labour machine prior to the 1964 election, and the continuing struggles of the Labour Left to assert its policies and its strength, have shown that many on the Left still cherish hopes of a radicalised, socialist Labour Party—democratically controlled by the mass Labour Movement and committed to socialist politics. Despite the Disarmament Movement experience—and subsequent activist Left movements such as the Anti-Vietnam war groups and the quasi-Trotskyist groupings which expanded so dramatically post-1968[70]—there has not as yet been any significant break in the hold of the Labour Party on the Left in the UK.[71] Indeed, following the Labour Party's heavy defeat at the 1979 election, the struggle for power between Left and Right in the Party has resurrected the hope, on the Left, that the Party may yet be 'won for socialism'.

Somewhat contrary to our expectations our study showed quite conclusively that Movement involvement did not, to any significant degree, lead core activists into the Far Left. And yet a large number of our respondents (and, for that matter, a number of our interviewees) disillusioned with Labourism, were sympathetic to, and eager to become involved in, a genuinely humanistic and radical socialist movement. The high degree of agreement with 'Marxism' (compared to the very small number of activists involved in the CP or any other contemporary Marxist grouping) testifies to the vacuum that has existed on the Left for many years now. Perhaps that vacuum will continue to exist, as the Labour Left and the sectarian Left between them continue to neutralise and divide the potential forces for socialism in the UK. Alternatively, the 1980s may see the coming together of various Left groupings (including a substantial section of the industrial and political Labour Movement) to form a genuinely socialist New Left. Whether or not this latter alternative comes to fruition there are many on the Left who see the creation of such an alliance as the major task for socialists in the 1980s.[72]

The Disarmament Movement played a crucial part in this long, slow, tortuous, process of 'opening up' the alternatives on the Left, and it is in this that its ultimate political significance as a Movement lay. For the first time since before the war a mass movement arose which offered to activists and to society at large a range of possibilities for radicalising activity both within and outside the confines of conventional Parliamentary politics. The Movement may not have led to the formation of a viable New Left in the UK, but it demonstrated very graphically the political alternatives open to those who desired to see such radical change in society. Equally emphatically, of course, it showed in clear relief the major obstacles to be encountered by any serious radicalising force in British society, and exposed the solidly conservative infrastructure of the British social and political system.

The great moral and emotive spasm which gave rise to the Movement in 1958 did not find adequate political expression. In a sense, the Movement remained, in Mervyn Jones' words, "a therapy",[73] an opportunity for people to express their fear and horror at the vast enormity of nuclear weapons. To *achieve* any change, however, the Movement had to move beyond this into single-issue politics. To some extent this important step *was* taken,[74] but here again we return to the basic problem. No single-issue campaign can be effective, except within very narrow limits, unless its agitation is linked into and complements a wider organisational and analytical political movement. The various political strands within the Movement agreed that 'the Bomb' was not an isolated aberration of an otherwise acceptable society[75] — but they differed sharply in their analysis and their prescription, and more importantly they failed to convince the mass Movement of the need for long-term political restructuring if the ultimate aims of the Movement were to be achieved.

At one level then the Movement was the precursor of a whole range of very important protests against the growth of an uncontrolled, super-technological society, and has its true heirs in a variety of local and national movements — from tenants' associations to the Ecology Movement — which are concerned with decentralising and humanising society, curbing the unbridled growth of the technological society at the expense of the world's resources, and putting power into the hands of ordinary people. This struggle — in terms of consciousness as much as political organisation — has progressed dramatically since CND was founded in 1958. This will undoubtedly be one of the key areas nationally and internationally for political debate and decision in the last decades of the twentieth century. To the extent that CND gave birth to this new movement, its importance was very great indeed.

An equally significant, but far less positive, aspect of the Movement's importance, however, was its failure to transform its mass support into the basis of a new radicalising force in British politics. The strength of the conservative political cultures of all Western societies has been graphically demonstrated since the 1950s. The inability of the Disarmament Movement to transform the political scene in the UK has been paralleled by the even more dramatic events in France (the May events of 1968) and the Anti-Vietnam War Movement in the USA. Both of these had far-reaching effects and importance but failed to achieve any fundamental restructuring of the level of political consciousness, let alone political *events*. Despite their massive potential power there appears as yet to be no prospect of such 'spontaneous', issue-oriented movements achieving the fundamental change for which many on the Left in Western societies have been striving since the 1950s (and, indeed, for long before then).

Whether or not the descendants of the CND protesters in the Ecology Movement can combine with the disaffected socialists of the social democratic parties and Left groups to form a genuinely new and more coherent New Left, may well provide the answer to Bertrand Russell's question: 'Has Man a Future?'[76] The nuclear peril has *not* diminished but increased, and the urgent need for a *political* solution to this and related problems is greater today than it was at the height of the mass nuclear Disarmament Movement. The work of that Movement, far from being over, has in reality only just begun.

References

1. The dangers of nuclear war are convincingly argued by the contemporary CND organisation to have *increased* rather than decreased in recent years. See Postscript.

2. DAC and the Committee of 100 had wider and more radical objectives but agreed in large part with CND about the desirability of the initial proposals.

3. The Direct Actionists in particular, whilst accepting the desirability of the UK leaving NATO, did not see this as an issue of paramount importance. Pat Arrowsmith, for example, in answer to a question about her views on NATO and neutralism, said: "I could never get very worked up about this. As a Pacifist I could never see it as a problem really. I was opposed to NATO of course, because it was equipped with nuclear weapons. I could see no argument whatever for being in: the argument for getting out seemed a part of the argument for getting rid of the Bomb really. But I never wanted to emphasise it particularly—after all, the Bomb itself was the issue, the central issue—NATO was/is all bound up with nuclear strategy."

4. It is, however, important to note the commitment to unilateralist policies by Labour Conferences in the early 1970s, and the marked resurgence of unilateralist feeling in the Party in 1980, as exemplified by the adoption of the 'Peace, Jobs, and Freedom' statement.

5. This was particularly true of Labour MPs who had been active in the leadership of the Movement. By 1963 all had disappeared from the CND Executive and distanced themselves from CND in preparation for 'Labour unity' under Harold Wilson at the forthcoming General Election.

6. President Eisenhower, quoted in J. Cox, *Overkill*, Penguin, 1977, p. 179.

7. Frank Parkin, *Middle Class Radicalism: The Social Bases of the British Campaign for Nuclear Disarmament*, MUP, 1968, p. 157.

8. *Ibid.*, p. 159.

9. Always excepting Bertrand Russell, of course!

10. This division applied almost exclusively to the CND: the leadership and rank and file of the DAC and Committee of 100 were far less sharply differentiated.

11. Indeed this disparity displeased a proportion of the original nuclear protesters: 10% of our sample believed that the Movement had been damaged by association with the various 'fellow-travelling' organisations.

12. Although it continued with a whole range of other activities, campaigns and pressure tactics.

13. This has ranged from localised campaigns, on just about every conceivable issue, to extremist and violent political action in the UK, the USA, Europe and Japan. As Arnold Wesker has commented, there is a sense in which the Movement was the precursor of most undesirable developments: "I felt that the Angry Brigade and the other acts of violent protest were a spin-off. I suppose the CND led to the smaller and more extreme Committee of 100, which led to smaller and even more extreme movements as a result of social, political and psychological frustration."
    Although this was undoubtedly one strand of development—and is interestingly paralleled elsewhere (e.g. the Baader-Meinhoff group in West Germany)—it must be seen as atypical.

14. Fifty-seven per cent of the sample was involved in either single-issue campaigns or local community politics.

15. Only 2% of activists in the Movement *went on* to membership of, or strong support for, any of the Marxist or Far Left groups. See Part II, p. 33.

16. Our survey found that 39% were classifiable as primarily moral protesters and a further 48% had equally moral and political objections to the Bomb. Only 13% were *primarily* 'anti' for political reasons.

17. Although one of the most forceful protagonists of the Labour strategy, Ian Mikardo, was adamantly opposed to pressurising others to follow this line, as the following interchange demonstrates:

"Q. In your activity in the Campaign were you trying to push the line pretty forcefully that everyone should work through the Labour Party?

A. No, absolutely not. Quite the contrary in fact. Everybody had their own role, everybody must do their own thing. And there was a role for people outside the Party. . . . There was no chance of persuading the whole Campaign — and, anyway, I think you have to allow people to make up their own minds as to how they fulfil their political role . . . none of my business. . . ."

18. Some, but not all. The DAC and Committee of 100 were themselves complicated coalitions of different ideological groupings — although, as we argued in Part III, the DAC was considerably more homogenous ideologically than either CND or the Committee of 100.

19. The extent to which this notion was allied to either a wider socialist perspective or a more anarchistic view, varied considerably.

20. The key implication of this orientation being that the issue in question marked an aberration in an otherwise acceptable social and economic system. This is discussed in more detail in Part III. This is not *necessarily* the case with a single-issue perspective, of course. Dick Nettleton combines this orientation with a wider political analysis of the long-term structural changes needed: "I really do think there is a place for, and always will be, single-issue bodies — and my attitude, as far as the Left is concerned, is that they should accept and welcome them . . . but not be seeking to pull them off the issue to do some more generalised thing. . . . There were people around who thought CND was the Revolution, and would storm the barricades and bring (capitalism) down. I don't think it ever was that; I think it always was, and still is, a single-issue organisation which will, in some form or other, go on until its objective is achieved . . . historically those things do take a long, long time. . . . You can easily stand on the soapbox on the street corner and condemn capitalism *in general*, in vague terms, until you're blue in the face; and that's not a *bad* thing to do . . . but you have *got* to, at the same time, be fighting capitalism whenever you happen to meet it: that can be anywhere — in industry, on issues of peace, foreign policy: it can be, I suppose, in the campaign against killing the whale."

21. Among the interviewees who made this point in various ways were Ian Mikardo, Michael Randle, Stuart Hall, Lord Soper and Peggy Duff.

22. For the New Left arguments see Part III. International Socialism, although a very small grouping at this time, was very active in both discussion and action in formulating a campaign based on a theoretical Marxist analysis to justify their 'neither Washington nor Moscow' stand.

23. For a full and clear statement of this theory see Michael Kidron, *Western Capitalism Since the War*, Penguin, 1970. See also Kidron, "Capitalism — the Latest Stage", in Harris and Palmer (eds.), *World Crisis*, Hutchinson, 1971. Kidron has since modified his theoretical position considerably in the light of detailed attacks from, among others, D. Yaffé, "The Marxist Theory of Crisis, Capital and the State", *Revolutionary Communist Journal*, Vol. 2, 1973.

24. Principally as found in the politics of the New Left, see Part III. However, in this broad sense, there was a determination to seek out and define a new politics in the DAC, the Committee of 100 and other sections of the Movement. Despite the very real divergences — which are discussed below — there was considerable ideological and strategic common ground.

25. And to some extent in twentieth-century Britain generally. The contexts are different but the problems remain basically similar. The lessons of the Disarmament Movement experience in terms of the overall development of British political culture are discussed below.

26. See R. Miliband, *Parliamentary Socialism*, 2nd edition, Merlin Press, 1973; see also T. Nairn, "The Nature of the Labour Party" in Anderson and Blackburn (eds.), *Towards Socialism*, Fontana and New Left Books, 1965, and D. Coates, *The Labour Party and the Struggle for Socialism*, CUP, 1974.

27. This was generally admitted by TUs. The relative ease with which Gaitskell and the Campaign for Democratic Socialism managed to persuade the major TUs (excepting the TGWU of course) to reverse their stand and back the leadership's policy in 1961, testified to the lack of genuine concern over unilateralism in the rank and file of the industrial Labour Movement. For a detailed and convincing account of the trade unions' attitudes, see Parkin, *op. cit.*, chap. 6.

28. The control by the big TUs of the Labour Party is well established. The extent to which this by-passes

the supposedly democratic process by undermining the power of the leadership (and thus of the Right Wing) is a matter of debate. The classic work on this subject is R. T. McKenzie, *British Political Parties*, Mercury Books, 1959, but a recent work has challenged some of McKenzie's central theses: Lewis Minkin, *The Labour Party Conference*, Allen Lane, 1978.

29. Gaitskell's final aggressive speech at the Labour Party Conference Defence debate in 1960 is justly one of the most famous in the Party's history. The relevant passage in this context was: "What sort of people do you think we are? Do you think we (i.e. PLP) can simply accept a decision of this kind? Do you think we can become overnight the Pacifists, Unilateralists and Fellow-travellers that other people are? . . . There are some of us . . . who will fight and fight and fight again to save the Party we love." LCAPR, 1960.

30. For example, Michael Foot, Dick Nettleton, Frank Allaun, George Matthews, among others.

31. Parkin, *op. cit.*, chap. 3.

32. To select, almost at random, examples from any period of the Labour Movement's history is not difficult: e.g. the No Conscription Fellowship, the Suffragette Movement, the various unemployed workers' movements of the 1930s, and the campaigns to reform the law on capital punishment, abortion and homosexuality in more recent times. None of these has received majority support from the Labour Movement.

33. Olive Gibbs, for example, made this point explicit. See Part III, p. 61.

34. "We did in fact have a lot of contact with the organised (Labour) Movement when we went to meetings, and on the March we would be entertained by the Labour Mayor and Councillors which for most of us seemed all right, seemed enough. . . . I don't remember it was a thing we discussed very much" (Jacquetta Hawkes).
"I was never very much aware of this 'middle-class' thing at the time . . . I was never very much given to thinking about class distinctions" (Hugh Brock).

35. Only 9% of our sample believed that one of CND's weaknesses was its middle-class nature.

36. For example, Jacquetta Hawkes, Arthur Goss, A. J. P. Taylor.

37. Sixty-two per cent of our sample firmly disagreed with the suggestion that the Movement declined because it 'became too political'; while factor analysis showed clearly that many core activists believed that the public perception of the Movement as 'too political' was a major factor in the Movement's decline.

38. And disillusionment with the Labour Party remained: over the 20-year period the Labour Party has lost more support than any other group amongst our sample.

39. See Miliband, *op. cit.*; Nairn, *op. cit.*; Coates, *op. cit.*; also C. Pritchard and R. Taylor, *Social Work, Reform or Revolution?*, chaps. 4 and 7, RKP, 1978.

40. The unique and fundamentally flawed ideology of the Labour Left is still in need of detailed political and historical analysis. For useful introductory analyses see Nairn, *op. cit.*; R. Barker, *Political Ideas in Modern Britain*, Methuen, 1979; J. M. Winter, *Socialism and the Challenge of War*, RKP, 1974.

41. See M. Foot, *Aneurin Bevan, 1945-60*, Vol. 2, MacGibbon & Kee, 1973; L. Hunter, *The Road to Brighton Pier*, Barker, 1959; Peggy Duff, *Left, Left, Left*, Allison & Busby, 1971.

42. See Foot, *op. cit.*, for an excellent, if somewhat uncritical, biographical and political study.

43. See Hunter, *op. cit.*, p. 123.

44. For a development of the argument of why there has been, continues to be, and will be, a Right-wing dominance of the Labour Party, see the key 'Postscript' to the second edition of Miliband, *op. cit.*

45. Both Ian Mikardo and Sir Harold Wilson confirmed that it had been Sam Watson, the Miners' leader, who was instrumental in persuading Bevan to alter his stance on unilateralism prior to the 1957 Conference debate.

46. Although, arguably, the emergence of a 'charismatic' Left figure combined with a real crisis in the Party's fortunes might have produced such a dramatic change.

47. For further discussion of this 'emotive Leftism' see C. Pritchard and R. Taylor, *op. cit.*, chap. 4; also Nairn, *op. cit.*, and Miliband, *op. cit.*

48. For an evaluation of the lack of Marxist influence either ideologically or politically in the UK, see Nairn, *op. cit.*, and S. Pierson, *Marxism and the Origins of British Socialism: the Struggle for a New Consciousness*, Cornell University Press, 1973.

49. The classic analysis of Labour's 'Parliamentarism' is Miliband, *op. cit.*; see also D. Coates, *op. cit.*

50. For example: E. P. Thompson, Raymond Williams, Stuart Hall, John Saville and Ralph Miliband.

51. As we emphasised above, leading DAC activists were very hostile to the CP and to what they regarded as 'Stalinism'.

52. Naïve and exuberant the New Left may have been but, in these days of apparent 'party rigidities', it is too easily forgotten that the Labour Party itself rose from virtually nothing at the beginning of the century to become the party of government in 1923/4. The recent meteoric (and perhaps short-lived) rise of the SNP demonstrates the ability of a party with an appealing 'single-issue' base to achieve dominance. Similarly, in the USA, the adoption in recent years by the Democratic Party of two 'unknowns'—Eugene McCarthy and Jimmy Carter—as Presidential candidates shows that political systems are never 'closed' to new forces.

53. For instance, 37% of the New Left members are either apolitical or support 'other' parties (mainly the Ecology Party). Only 10% of them are Marxist linked, with 3% supporting the Conservatives!

54. By the 1964 election the New Left was solidly Labourist in orientation (as we noted above). It was of course a different story once the Wilsonian brand of Labourism had become apparent.

55. See Peter Shipley, *Revolutionaires in Modern Britain,* Bodley Head, 1976; D. Widgery, *The Left in Britain, 1956-68,* Penguin, 1976; Harris and Palmer (eds.), *op. cit.*

56. For arguments to this effect see, for example, Ralph Miliband, "Moving On" in Miliband and Saville (eds.), *Socialist Register 1976,* Merlin Press, 1976.

57. Not least from the organised, sophisticated forces of the State (see above, Part III, for Randle's and others' views).

58. i.e. there being an increasing 'no-vote' or 'would-not-vote' response from the two groups.

59. Our source was unwilling to be named here but was strongly of this opinion in conversation with Richard Taylor.

60. i.e. 'support' dropped by a half from 1958/65 to 1978.

61. i.e. following the September 1961 demonstration and prior to the Wethersfield *et al.* demonstrations.

62. Principally by means of very heavy jail sentences following the Official Secrets trial in early 1962.

63. i.e. in 1958/65, 31% of the respondents had no political allegiances, by 1978 this had risen to 34% —so much for the campaign as a 'radicalising' force!

64. There has yet to be a comprehensive study on either the political culture of Modern Britain or the ideology of the Labour Movement, but for various aspects see: R. Barker, *op. cit.;* Miliband, *op. cit.;* and *The State in Capitalist Society,* Weidenfeld & Nicolson, 1969; Coates, *op. cit.;* Pierson, *op. cit.;* McKenzie, *op. cit.;* Minkin, *op. cit.;* S. H. Beer, *Modern British Politics,* Allen & Unwin, 1959; Pritchard and Taylor, *op. cit.,* chaps 3 and 4; R. E. Dowse and J. Hughes, *Political Sociology,* Wiley, 1972.

65. See, for example, J. Urry and J. Wakeford (eds.), *Power in Britain,* Heinemann, 1973; J. Westergaard and H. Resler, *Class in a Capitalist Society,* Penguin, 1978.

66. Principally in the work of Ralph Miliband, *The State in Capitalist Society, op. cit.;* see also the numerous translations and commentaries on the work of Antonio Gramsci, and the work of Poulantzas and others published by New Left Books in the 1970s.

67. For example, Stuart Hall, Dick Nettleton, George Clark.

68. For the implications of this see Miliband, *Parliamentary Socialism, op. cit.* (Postscript), and Coates, *op. cit.*

69. Over 50% of the respondents were active Labour Party supporters in 1958/65; bearing in mind the 31% not then eligible to vote in 1959, the present 40% of support is a significant withdrawal from the Labour Party.

70. See Shipley, *op. cit.;* and Widgery, *op. cit.*

71. None of the sectarian Left groups (i.e. SSL/WRP, IS/SWP, IMG *et al.*) managed to break through to 'credibility'; although in the late 1960s and early 1970s they grew rapidly it seems unlikely that any of them ever exceeded 4000 in membership. The CP has, of course, had this problem for considerably longer! Its membership through the 1960s and 1970s has fluctuated between *c.* 22,000 and 29,000, currently (1979) being just over 20,000. See Shipley, *op. cit.*

    'Marxist' candidates in the 1979 election averaged only 320 per seat; the new Ecology Party averaged 730 and the neo-fascist National Front 680 votes per seat.

    All these derisively small percentages of the poll are in part the result of the notoriously unfair British electoral system; but they also indicate, again, the firm ideological hold that the established political parties and their ideologies have on the British political scene.

72. See, for example, Miliband, *op. cit.* ("Moving On"); also see article in the *Guardian,* 30 April 1979, entitled "Labour Party: a house but not a home".

73. Mervyn Jones, *Today The Struggle,* Quartet Books, 1978, p. 357.

74. i.e. the majority accepted the need for pursuing their *moral* campaign through the *political* vehicle of the Labour Party.

75. Although as Stuart Hall has remarked CND did "fetishise (the Bomb) in terms of 'megatons' and 'destruction' and 'human lives' . . ."

76. Title of Penguin Special by Bertrand Russell, 1961.

Postscript
CND Lives: The Last Campaign?

WITH the election of the first Wilson Government in 1964 CND rapidly disappeared from the public scene: the Aldermaston March, and other mass rallies, continued to be organised through the late 1960s—and CND became one of the constituent organisations of the Anti-Vietnam War Movement—but its days as a *mass movement* had ended by 1964/5. Since that time CND has changed its nature from a broadly based mass movement to a relatively small, issue-oriented pressure group. It is something of a paradox that today's CND resembles much more closely the pressure group originally envisaged by the campaign's early leaders. The current Chairman of CND, Msgr. Bruce Kent, has acknowledged that the days of CND as a mass movement are over unless, somewhat prophetically, a major nuclear disaster occurs. CND now has strong links with the Left of the Labour Party, particularly at PLP level,[1] but unilateralism is not a 'key issue' in the Left/Right struggle in the Party, nor is it a rallying call for those who want to reassert socialist values within the Labour Movement. Despite the continuing and very real dangers of the nuclear threat the whole ethos of the debate in the Labour Movement has become far more pragmatic, less emotional, and more concerned with the detailed strategic and scientific arguments.

The specific policy demands of CND have changed relatively little since the early days, although the political and strategic context within which these demands are put has altered dramatically. Thus, as Diana Collins has pointed out, any decision by the UK to disarm unilaterally (in nuclear terms) in the 1970s/1980s would not have the same impact as it would have had when the UK was one of only three nuclear powers. The 'moral example' argument, so important to the early Campaign, has thus been severely weakened and made more complex by the decline of the UK as a world power and by the proliferation of nuclear powers, both actual and potential.

Nevertheless CND retains, as the core of its policy, the demand that the UK should abandon its nuclear weapons, unilaterally if necessary. The emphasis has changed somewhat, however: this is now seen much more as a first step to other, international objectives—to world-wide nuclear disarmament, of course, and also to British withdrawal from NATO and subsequently a winding-up of both NATO and the Warsaw Pact.[2] Unlike the early CND, today the campaign recognises clearly the importance of the economic dimension of the issue: in conjunction with TU sympathisers CND has developed impressive programmes detailing ways in which productive capacity, at present used for military purposes, could be redeployed on non-military work. The Lucas aerospace project, for example, testifies to the practicality of such proposals—and shows how concerned and aware the CND has been over profits and jobs when putting forward alternative, economic 'anti-nuclear' proposals.[3]

The *dis*advantages of the absence of mass support are obvious, but there are, too, important advantages for CND in its present situation. There are no ideological schisms (the present (1979) Chairman of CND is a Roman Catholic priest and the secretary a member of the Communist Party, for example), and the Campaign is united in its approach in a way that the mass movement never was. CND has important alliances with a number of sympathetic groups: the Campaign Against the Arms Trade (CAAT),[4] Friends of the Earth, the Ecology Party,[5] some trade unions,[6] the new Anti-Nuclear Campaign[7] and, of course, various pacifist organisations.[8]

One of the major differences in policy between the early CND and the contemporary Campaign lies in the attitude taken to the peaceful use of nuclear technology. In the early Movement, as a number of our interviewees have recalled,[9] there was a widespread belief that nuclear technology was, potentially, an enormously beneficial development for mankind. Since that time CND, in common with the whole Environmental Movement, has come to realise the terrifying dangers surrounding the nuclear energy programme and has joined with a range of organisations in opposing the powerful economic and industrial interests which are involved in the promotion of the nuclear energy industry. This has involved direct conflict with powerful multinational companies and major branches of the bureaucratic State apparatus.[10] Apart from the intrinsic dangers of the nuclear energy programme there is little doubt that the development of nuclear energy has considerably increased the threat of the proliferation, and therefore the use, of nuclear weapons. To take but one example, the rapid increase in the amount of fissionable material in the world has rendered the dangers of a terrorist-inspired nuclear catastrophe a real and terrifying possibility. As Dr. Kissinger, the former US Secretary of State for Foreign Affairs, has observed, the "nuclear catastrophe looms more plausible".[11]

In this Postscript we will very briefly review and speculate upon some of the activities of the 'heirs and successors' of the earlier nuclear disarmers who, as William Greaves has said, "seem likely to set a trend for the 1980s equally virile to that launched by their mothers and fathers of the CND".[12]

From the earlier protesters there has emerged six groups of people. There are, first, those who have, because of political failures and/or disillusionment, occasioned not least by the passage of time, opted out of political activity with an attitude of 'there's nothing the individual can do'.[13] Second, there are those, albeit a minority, who have gone on into Marxist politics—via the Anti-Vietnam War Movement and the emergent groupings of the late 1960s and 1970s.[14] Third, are those involved in ecological and environmental pressure groups of various types. The fourth group comprises those who have worked in and through the Labour Party, and devote their energies to achieving a more radically inclined Labour Movement, and the fifth, those who have become involved in community politics and other single-issue, localised campaigns. Finally, there are those who have continued to devote their main energies to CND itself.

The Anti-Vietnam War Movement, dramatic though it was in Europe as in the USA,[15] failed to produce an effective New Left in the UK, although in the late 1960s this did seem to be a possibility. The relatively small proportion of our sample who have gone on into 'Left politics' testifies to this failure, as does the whole phenomenon of the mass movement's dispersal. The tragedy of Vietnam has, of course, had profound consequences for American society and politics which have as yet by no means worked their way through in institutional and ideological form. (In terms of individual suffering there is considerable evidence to show that post-Vietnam traumas continue to haunt both civilians and former members of the US forces.)[16]

In the UK the impact was naturally less fundamental — and the radical potential unleashed by the protests,[17] culminating in the huge march through London in 1968,[18] foundered on the familiar inability of the Left to gather its forces together and unite to break through the ideological and political barriers. As a radicalising agency, the anti-Vietnam war organisations (BCPV and VSC)[19] must, like the Disarmament Movement, be adjudged in the final analysis a failure. The second New Left (of the late 1960s) failed for much the same complex of reasons as had its predecessor a few years earlier.

Among the most obvious and direct inheritors of the early CND are those involved in what can be broadly described as the Environmentalist Movement.[20] Not only are the issues involved related directly to the Nuclear Disarmament Movement, the style, tactics and, to some extent, the problems to be faced in the Environmentalist Movement are reminiscent of the early CND. There is, indeed, an almost *déjà vu* feeling — should these 'Green' protesters develop their campaigns as an informed pressure group, or should they seek mass support? Should they use extra-parliamentary methods of popular protest to bring the issues home to the people and thereby raise public consciousness, or should they create their own political party (the Ecology Party) and try to attain power through the conventional electoral process? The debate follows uncannily similar lines to the previous CND/DAC/Committee of 100 disputes over tactics, strategy, objectives and ideology. Whatever the outcome there can be little doubt that the issues brought to the fore by the Environmentalists will continue to be matters of urgent debate in Western and Third World countries in the 1980s and 1990s.[21]

Undoubtedly the nuclear energy issue, with its problems of waste, possible pollution, and dangers of abuse, has come to symbolise a number of global ecological threats which Higgins has placed into six categories — the problems of: population explosion, food, non-renewable resources, pollution, science and technology, and nuclear abuse.[22] On the other hand, critics of the anti-nuclear lobby (or what Lord Rothschild has termed 'eco-nuts')[23] have argued that most of the environmentalist protests, while sincere, are over-simplifications: pseudo-scientific and dangerous to the future welfare of industrial society. The industrialist's view was concisely put by the Chairman of Shell, Mr. C. Pocock, who argued that "the creation of wealth in a world of want is a moral duty. I suggest that that morality is just as valid as the morality of the environmentalists."[24]

Is it just a question of differing perceptions of morality? Cotgrove and Duff[25] have found that attitudes towards nuclear power are complex and cut across party boundaries, though apparently a majority of people has the severest reservations about nuclear energy. However, it seems that the *action* they would be prepared to take depends upon their socio-ideological position: the issue is not at present strong enough to alter deeply-rooted political, moral and psychological values and attitudes.

What does seem clear is that the appealing original concept of 'atoms for peace' is now being seriously questioned, even by some of the ardent early enthusiasts.[26] There can be no doubt that the contemporary movement has brought to the fore these crucial questions of the environmental future — and, similarly, the links between this problem area and the continuing nuclear weapons threat is brought into focus by such organisations as CND.[27]

There remains, however, the central and unresolved political problem. How relevant is the history of the earlier Movement to today's protesters? This brings us back to our last three groups of CND 'heirs'. There are many who, disillusioned and cynical about conventional politics, in large part because of their Disarmament Movement experience, have moved into community politics of various types. There is an idealistic and populist motivation here, not altogether dissimilar from that of the DAC. If the power of the Movement cannot shift the existing political machines to support for these crucial objectives, then, so the argument goes, activists must go back to the grass roots, build from the bottom, engage in direct, local issues which people really care about. In this way a decentralised, genuinely participatory democracy can be established which will by-pass the traditional, corrupt, undemocratic, machine politics of the established system.[28]

In stark contrast to this group are those who have channelled their activism into the Labour Movement and pin their hopes for both a solution of the specific issues of nuclear policy *and* an overall radicalisation of British politics on a change in the power balance of Labourism.[29] Although this latter orientation still commands majority support amongst Movement activists it has, according to our study, slowly but surely lost ground over the intervening 20 years. With the return of a Conservative Government in 1979 strongly committed to Right Wing policies including a clear adherence to the nuclear deterrent,[30] the future prospects for a more radically-oriented Labour Government, committed to socialist policies including unilateral nuclear disarmament, look bleak indeed.

The political problems encountered by the early Movement thus remain—and, if anything, are writ larger. The failure of the early Disarmament Movement to achieve its objectives stands in sharp contrast to both the Black Power/Civil Rights Movement and the Anti-Vietnam War Protest Movement in the USA which achieved considerable successes despite public hostility. Why has the Disarmament Movement failed where the others have, at least to an extent, succeeded? The answer must surely lie, as the contemporary CND in the UK has at least partially realised, in both the *political* and the *economic* dimensions of the Movement and its policies. Whereas the Disarmament Movement relied in the last analysis upon morality, reason and dramatic protest, the American movements had some economic muscle—and they had a highly militant, determined and largely united political stance. Long term, the American movements have disintegrated and have not brought into being that 'radical America' which their leaders had hoped for. But they *have* achieved a large part of their initial objectives. Because the Movement in the UK was one of middle-class radicalism *par excellence* and was therefore largely unconcerned with basic economic issues of jobs, investment alternatives and so on, it failed to make the crucial breakthrough to the working class. It thus failed to build up sufficiently powerful forces to confront the massive vested interests of the military/industrial/State complex.[31] Modern Western society operates to a large extent on the principle proclaimed, despairingly, by Schumacher: "call a thing immoral, soul-destroying, a peril to peace—so long as you have not shown it to be 'uneconomic' you have not really questioned its right to exist, grow and prosper".[32]

Unless and until some means can be found to bring together the economic and the political into a new and powerful movement the problems will remain and the Orwellian 'double-think' of senior politicians on nuclear as on other issues will continue to be the norm.[33] The anti-nuclear lobby has to try to convince the rest of the population that conventional wisdom and science are wrong; that the established, powerful and knowledgeable have asked the wrong questions or given the wrong answers (and often both!). It is a sad but salutary fact that humanity in the mass often appears to be 'afraid of freedom'.[34] The ethos of our contemporary state capitalist, bureaucratic society encourages the view that complex matters should be 'left to the experts' and that ordinary people should concern themselves only with their own immediate problems and development. To change this is a major ideological task which can be accomplished only by a fundamental political breakthrough — or, indeed, by a massive environmental and/or nuclear crisis.

The issue for the 1960s protester was stark and urgent — 'the Bomb' overshadowed everything. That threat is with us still and has indeed increased: it has been added to by the realisation that industrial society, unless rationally planned and controlled, is potentially self-destructing. To achieve a major change in priorities, direction and ideology has become a task of overwhelming and immediate importance. The early Nuclear Disarmament Movement, for all its manifest faults and confusions, pointed the way — and the new combination of forces in society, of which CND is one of many — is continuing the struggle.

However, just as the early Movement failed primarily because it could find no solution to the *political* problem of achieving radical change in the UK, so the new and growing movement must face similar frustration unless it is able to act as the focus and the catalyst for a reorientation of progressive political forces in the UK and the West in general.

Unless this crucial battle can be won mankind may well, with final insanity, self-destruct through nuclear confrontation. The heirs of CND are, perhaps, engaged in the last campaign of protest: upon the success of this and related campaigns will depend the continued existence of industrial civilisation.

References

1. Many prominent Left-wingers have in their various ways been actively pursuing the goal of a unilateralist Labour Party: e.g. Ian Mikardo, Frank Allaun, Stan Newens. See, for example, D. Griffiths, *Labour and Disarmament: a Time for Decision*, Labour CND, 1977.

2. D. Griffiths and D. Smith, *How Many More — the Spread of Nuclear Weapons*, CND, 1978.

3. See the CND pamphlet *Arms, Jobs and the Crisis*. This gives details of two conferences of TU delegates and CND members called to discuss the jobs/arms equation.

4. See the range of material published by the CAAT, e.g. "British Arms Sales and Human Rights", Factsheet 17. Sponsors of CAAT include the UNA of Great Britain, Pax Christi, and London Greenpeace.

5. The Ecology Party, which fielded 52 candidates in the 1979 UK General Election and which has a growing political importance in other Western European countries, campaigns on issues of energy, agriculture, employment, and general environmental concerns. Given the tendency of the British electoral system to discriminate against all minority parties the Ecology Party's 1979 poll of 40,000 votes in 52 seats was respectable if modest (and better than most other minority groups).

6. See Sanity, No. 5, Oct./Nov. 1977. Ray Buckden, General Secretary of ASLEF (one of the major Rail Unions), and the Executive of the South Wales Miners gave support to CND policy. Many other trade unions have, at various times, pledged their support for CND policies.

7. The ANC was launched as a broad-based umbrella Movement in November 1979. CND was one of the sponsoring organisations.

8. For example, ICDP, National Peace Council, etc.

9. For example, April Carter, Pat Arrowsmith.

10. See D. Elliott *et al. The Politics of Nuclear Power*, Pluto Press, 1978.

11. Henry Kissinger, quoted in R. Higgins, *The Seventh Enemy*, Hodder & Stoughton, p. 1978.

12. William Greaves, "The Power We Can't Afford to Cut Off", article in the *Daily Mail*, 9 May 1979.

13. Thirty per cent of the whole sample has not been involved in any post-Disarmament Movement activity.

14. i.e. the IMG, IS, and other quasi-Trotskyist groups. See Peter Shipley, *Revolutionaries in Modern Britain*, Bodley Head, 1977.

15. For an interesting analysis of the impact of the Anti-Vietnam War Movement on the USA see Laurie Taylor, "Roll Your Own Revolution", *The Listener*, 3 May 1979.

16. Numerous psychiatric studies on ex-Vietnam service men have shown the deleterious and continuing effects, e.g. C. R. Figley, "Symptoms of Delayed Combat Stress Amongst a College Sample of Vietnam Veterans", *Military Medicine*, Vol. 143, No. 2, pp. 107-110, 1978; R. I. H. Wang *et al.*, "Characteristics of Drug Abuse at a V. A. Hospital", *International Journal of Addiction*, Vol. 11, No. 6, pp. 1019-1030, 1976.
    See E. R. Worthington, "Post-Service Adjustment and Vietnam era Veterans", *Military Medicine*, Vol. 142, No. 11, pp. 805-866, 1977. For corroborative evidence of the damaging effects of war upon participants, see, for example, M. Melbaum, "Some Personality Characteristics of Soldiers Exposed to Extreme War Stress—a follow-up of post-hospital adjustment", *Journal of Clinical Psychology*, Vol. 33, No. 2, pp. 558-562 (Israel), 1977.

17. These were considerably more violent, aggressive and 'class oriented' than had been the CND Marches and Committee of 100 civil disobedience. Gone completely was the emphasis on 'non-violence' as both a tactic *and* a principle. The most violent demonstrations of all—on the part of both the demonstrators and the police—were those outside the US Embassy in Grosvenor Square, London, in 1967 and 1968.

18. One of the largest demonstrations ever held in London took place on 27 Oct. 1968. An estimated crowd of over 150,000 took part in a militant and impressive demonstration. But the organisers were unable to maintain the momentum and the mass movement quickly disintegrated in 1969, although the Left groups emerged far stronger than they had been previously.

19. The British Campaign for Peace in Vietnam and the Vietnam Solidarity Campaign. For a discussion of this movement see Part III.

20. Thirty-seven per cent of those in our study have been active in the Environmentalist Movement. See Part II.

21. For a random selection from the world's press in April and May 1979 see: *Der Spiegel*, "Der Alptraum Atomcraft—nach Reaktor Catastrophe vom Harrisberg", 27 April 1979; two articles by J. Fenton, on attitudes and responses to environmental issues, the *Guardian*, 26 April, and in France 11 May; report in the *Guardian* of violence in East Anglia over the issue of building of new nuclear power station, 3 May 1979; BBC TV News Report, 7 May 1979, of occupation of the proposed nuclear site in Scotland by protesters.

22. Higgins, *op. cit.*

23. Lord Rothschild, "Risk", The Richard Dimbleby Lecture, *The Listener*, p. 715, 30 Nov. 1978.

24. C. C. Pocock, "A Fast-changing World—the political challenge". Address to the World Planning Congress, 1978.

25. S. F. Cotgrove and A. Duff. Ongoing research (1980) exploring the links between values and the influence of socio-economic milieu in middle-class occupational groups; a central concern is to analyse the differences between those employed in the education/welfare complex and those in the industrial/manufacturing area.

26. For example, Professor Rotblat, in conversation with Colin Pritchard, July 1978.

27. The evidence of secrecy and frank duplicity by the authorities—see, for example, D. Boulton *et al.*, "The US Nuclear Cover-up", the *Guardian*, 21 Oct. 1978—and the series of 'near-miss' tragedies (as at Harrisberg) are undoubtedly awakening public interest and concern. See, for example, Harold Jackson, "The Great Escape", the *Guardian*, 4 May 1979; the CND Chairman, Msgr. Bruce Kent, has risked imprisonment in talking to servicemen—reported in the Diary, the *Guardian*, 15 June 1979. Similar public agitation has taken place elsewhere in the Western world and has been widely reported.

28. Of those prominent in the Disarmament Movement, George Clark is perhaps the most notable exponent—in both theory and practice—of this sort of orientation.

29. Forty-four per cent of our sample would appear to have this orientation. See Part II. There are, however, strong arguments against such a perspective—see Part III and Part IV.

30. Involving, apparently, the expenditure of £5000 million on a new missile system over the decade of the 1980s.

31. For example, D. Elliott, *op. cit.* Elliott also argues that scientists and technicians have a vested interest in such developments, thus compounding the problem of disentangling the *political* alternatives within a highly complex technological field.

32. E. F. Schumacher, *Small is Beautiful*, Sphere Books, 1974, as quoted in Higgins, *op. cit.*

33. For example, Harold Macmillan, writing as late as 1971, claimed that the first British nuclear test "cleared the atmosphere in the political sense even if it may have polluted it physically to a small degree". H. MacMillan, *Riding the Storm*, MacMillan, 1971, p. 297.

   Dr. Kissinger objected to a policy that had undoubted economic and moral merit (suspending the development of the B1 Bomber) because it gave away a potential bargaining counter to the USSR in SALT II. See Kissinger, *op. cit.*

34. See Erich Fromm, *Fear of Freedom*, Routledge & Kegan Paul, 1969.

Methodology

IN THIS book we have been able to utilise a number of methodological approaches in the gathering of evidence for our analysis. The traditional literature search is evident from the bibliography. We were able to combine empirical data obtained from a large number of people via a detailed questionnaire, and tape-recorded in-depth interviews with leading figures in the Movement. This facilitated a comparative examination of perspectives in that we were able to explore and compare statements of 'leaders' and 'rank and file', as well as considering the available documentary evidence.

On this latter point the official CND archives are deposited at the Library of the London School of Economics and Political Science, in the University of London, but these were not available for consultation as they have yet to be catalogued. We were, however, very fortunate in having access to several collections of documents from private sources (e.g. from local CND secretaries, from personal correspondence from a number of the interviewees and from numerous other activists). The range of published material in the political journals,[1] CND's own *Sanity*, the Committee of 100's *Resistance* and so on, went a considerable way in making up for the absence of access to the archives.

The empirical, attitudinal study rested upon the Interviews and the Questionnaire. With the single exception of Frank Cousins—who declined our request for an interview—all those leadership figures we approached were exceedingly helpful. All interviews were tape-recorded, though on occasion the machine was switched off as 'personal' material was discussed or 'off-the-record' matters were mentioned. Interviewees were then sent a typed transcript of the interview. Confidentiality must be maintained as must accuracy of accountability of views, and we did, of course, check with all interviewees before attributing their statements to them in print. Our observance of these standards is evidenced by the omission of disclosures of interpersonal controversy which, although perhaps of 'sensationalist' interest, would have contributed little to the overall analysis.

The second pillar to our study was the Questionnaire. Space does not permit a general discussion of the issues of the links between the information-gathering instrument and the sampling. The reader is directed to relevant specialist texts.[2] It is sufficient to state here that it is of crucial importance in any study to ensure that the sample is representative. This, and the methods by which the data is obtained, determines the level of confidence that can be placed in the subsequent statistical analysis. The questionnaire was drawn up following a careful consideration of the literature and the main exploratory hypotheses concerning the ideological perspectives within the Movement. The document was revised following a small pilot study, and a number of colleagues, and people central to CND made valuable contributions at this stage. In particular, Dr. John Cox (a former Chairman of CND), whilst disagreeing, to some extent, with the orientation of the questionnaire, made many useful comments. The questionnaire reproduced in Appendix II, was lengthy and this was a consideration in omitting a number of issues we would have liked to explore. (We were, however, strongly influenced by Oppenheim's classic text on questionnaire design and we believe we have demonstrated its efficacy and reliability.)[3]

We invited respondents to comment critically upon the actual questionnaire and three general points of criticism emerged: firstly, it was felt that we had not given sufficient opportunities for people to express views about *current* political/moral issues and respondents' allegiances; this applied to anti-racist and TU activity in particular; secondly, question 19 postulated that CND 'failed' and some respondents strongly disagreed with this statement (four respondents in fact refused to complete the questionnaire, and two further questionnaires had to be excluded from the 'effective' response rate). Thirdly, and perhaps most seriously, it was felt by some respondents that the questionnaire allowed for no description of organisational memberships and commitments in the years *intervening* between their Disarmament Movement activity and their current involvements. In effect this meant that dynamic change *through* the twenty-year period was omitted. Despite these criticisms the internal consistency of the results demonstrated the reasonable reliability of the questionnaire. Of course, this was without doubt aided by the enthusiasm and high 'political literacy' of the respondents.

Within the questionnaire were open-ended questions which required post-completion scoring. To achieve as much reliability and consistency as possible, one of the authors (CP) was responsible for all coding of the questionnaires after the establishment of categories which précised the open-ended answers. The first completed twenty questionnaires were rated independently by both authors, and an inter-rater reliability test, a Pearson correlation, was carried out. This yielded 0.89 which was highly significant; after every 100 questionnaires further inter-rater tests were carried out to maintain consistency. On all occasions the tests indicated highly significant correlations.

The obtaining of the sample was of the greatest importance. The fact that our original population was twenty years older, posed considerable difficulties: how representative could such a *post-hoc* sample be? Two features made the attempt feasible: firstly, there was considerable evidence to suggest that the Movement had been of great personal significance to many of its activists — indeed subsequently a very frequent comment was that "it had been a time I'll never forget" and the study evoked and liberated memories for an unusually highly-motivated group of people. Secondly, there was the Parkin study[4] undertaken during an Aldermaston March which provided a crucial baseline to determine just how representative our sample might be of the Movement supporters of those times.

But first we had to *reach* the Movement's supporters! To do this we wrote letters, advertisements or articles (and in some cases a combination) to national newspapers, and professional, political and religious journals, inviting people who had been active in the Movement during the 1958-65 period to write to us telling us of their experiences, retrospective assessment, and current activities, via the completion of a questionnaire (it will be remembered that during that period there had been no formal central membership, a difficulty that also faced Parkin). In addition there were interviews on National Radio (BBC Radio 4 in the 'Today' programme), on regional radio (in the West and Yorkshire regions), and on regional television (BBC TV Points West). The fact that we had to rely upon the initiative of the respondent to write to us, clearly demonstrates the special nature of the sample; yet, the sample was, as we have seen, in all likelihood representative of the core activists in the Movement. It may be remembered that 23% of the sample was currently involved in CND and that few differences were found between current and past members. In Table 1 is a list of publications which carried our appeal — the most successful response undoubtedly came from the *Observer,* with the *Guardian* and *Peace News* following a fair way behind.

TABLE 1

Publication	Letter	Advertisement	Article
Bath Evening Chronicle			×
British Medical Journal	×		
Catholic Herald	×		
Chemistry	×		
Church Times	×		
Community Care	×		
Daily Mail		×	
Daily Mirror		×	
Daily Telegraph		×	×
Guardian		×	×
Labour Monthly	×		
Methodist Recorder	×		
Morning Star		×	
New Scientist	×		
New Society	×		
New Statesman	×		
Nursing Times	×		
Observer	×		
Peace News	×		
Physics Bulletin	×		
Physics Today	×		
Red Weekly	×		
Sanity	×		
Social Work Today	×		
Socialist Challenge	×		
Socialist Worker	×		
Spectator	×		
Sunday Times	×		
The Times	×		
Tribune	×		
Workers' Press/Newsline	×		
Yorkshire Post	×		×

Just how representative our respondents were depended crucially upon a comparison with Parkin's classic study. A criticism of both his study and ours might be that neither was able to reflect the true level of 'working-class' support for the Movement,[5] and it is conceded that our method of contacting the sample was likely to underestimate working-class involvement. However, those who would assert that the proportion of working-class activists in the Movement was higher[6] have a considerable weight of empirical evidence *against* them. The onus of proof thus lies on them rather than on those—like Dr. Parkin and ourselves—who have found that the Movement was preponderantly middle-class in composition.[7] Just how successful a match on social criteria this study was with Dr. Parkin's can be seen from Table 2.[8]

TABLE 2

	Parkin	Taylor and Pritchard
Social Class N		
Non-manual	83%	90%
Manual	12%	9%
Not known	5%	1%
Christian Religious Belief	40%	41%
Education		
Ended Secondary Modern Equivalent	20%	19%
Education 18 +	44%	56%*
Under 25's in sample	55%	51%

(*The differences in 18 + levels of education can be accounted for by the increase in the provision of tertiary educational opportunities for the 18 + age group which have opened up over the past 20 years.)

Finally, on points of comparison, 33% of this study was female; unfortunately there was no record of respondents' sex in Dr. Parkin's study. Our sample might also be marginally biased towards the younger age groups, i.e. whilst 27% of our sample was aged 56 years or more, those 65- to 70-year-olds amongst the 1958/65 activists might well be under-represented in this study because of death. Nevertheless, overall, there is little doubt that there is a good match between both surveys, and there is, therefore, every reason for supposing that our sample was representative of the Movement's core activists.

In analysing the data we were conscious that it contained both 'hard' and 'soft' information; consequently the statistical analysis allowed for this by establishing semi-quantitative indicators of various trends from the semi-qualitative information.[9]

A major concern was to determine any themes or patterns that were contained, not in just one or two questions but within the whole study, and for this we turned to multivariate analysis. We used the Statistical Packages for the Social Sciences (SPSS)[10] for both parametric and non-parametric statistics; and for question 19 (on 'reasons for failure') we used Principal Component and Varimax Rotational Factor Analysis to test the hypotheses concerning different perspectives on the Movement associated with differing membership and to explore whether any other subgroup existed whose presence we had not suspected. Factor analysis results, however, can be open to various interpretations and to aid our interpretation and minimise any biases we also used Cluster

Analysis, MacQuitty's Linkage Analysis[11] in particular, which focused upon typal structures rather than composite variables. This proved to be a useful guide and adjunct in our analysis of any equivocal factors that might have emerged.

The most frequently used non-parametric statistic was the Chi Square[12] test chiefly because the data was in essence one of frequency distributions and we were seeking a goodness of fit. In all 2 × 2 tests Yates' correction was applied and only those tests of at least 5% level of confidence were noted. For ease of presentation a number of tables was given in the text on three-point scales: five-point ranges were used originally but subsequent interpretation took account of this. The computer analysis provided us with an enormous amount of information which could not possibly be reproduced here: however, the authors would be more than pleased to provide any further information to interested organisations or individuals. In the first instance, enquiries concerning the statistical material should be addressed to Colin Pritchard who holds the print-outs, whilst queries in respect of interviews and documentary evidence should be made to Richard Taylor. Appendix II reproduces the questionnaire and the raw scores on all the questions comparing the Committee of 100 supporters with the non-Committee of 100 activists. It is hoped that the availability of such information will facilitate the reader's own analysis.

References

1. The most important of these journals were: the *New Statesman*; *Tribune*; *Anarchy*; *New Reasoner*; *Universities and Left Review*; *New Left Review*. For a fuller list see Bibliography.

2. For texts examining issues of the relationship between sampling and statistical methods see, for example, H. Sellitz *et al.*, *Research in Human Relations*, Wiley, 1959.

3. See N. S. Oppenheim, *Questionnaire Design and Attitude Measurement*, Heineman, 1966.

4. F. Parkin, *Middle-Class Radicalism: The Social Bases of the British Campaign for Nuclear Disarmament*, MUP, 1968.

5. Parkin's response rate from the 'youth group' he interviewed was an impressive 81%, with a good 61% response from 'adults'. Whether it is reasonable to assume that the non-responders were 'working class' is *highly* questionable.

6. Some of our interviewees were convinced that the Movement had a high proportion of working-class supporters: e.g. Dick Nettleton, Michael Foot, Frank Allaun, all in conversation with Richard Taylor at various times in 1978.

7. Tony Lynes (1979), 'Do it yourself—a review of F. F. Piven and A. Cloward's "Poor Peoples' Movements: why they succeed, why they fail", Blackwell, 1973, in *New Society*, Vol. 48, No. 865, pp. 277-8. (This explores further 'manual' participation in radical organisations.)

8. Parkin, *op. cit.*

9. See C. Pritchard and I. R. Ward, "Family Dynamics of School Phobics", *British Journal of Social Work*, 1974, who discuss the point at some length.

10. T. Nia *et al.*, *Statistical Packages for the Social Sciences*, McGraw-Hill, 1975.

11. L. L. MacQuitty's *Elementary Linkage Analysis: Education and Psychological Measurement*, 1957, No. 17, pp. 207-29.

12. See J. P. Guildford, *Fundamental Statistics in Education and Psychology*, MacGraw-Hill, 1975; and S. Segal (ed.), *Non-parametric Statistics*, MacGraw-Hill, 1974, for expositions of the tests used, and for the methods and examples of their application.

Questionnaire on the British Disarmament Movement

THIS consists of the Questionnaire and the total scores of the sample shown as a comparison between the supporters of the Committee of 100 (C. 100) versus the Rest.

Section A   *Committee of 100 (C.100)*   *The Rest*
                         N = 206 (51%)   *N = 197 (49%)*

1. Please state your age: *Age*****   *C.100*   *The Rest*
                          35-45 years   *64%*   *35%*
                          46 years +   *36%*   *65%*

	C.100	*The Rest*
2. Male	*68%*	*62%*
Female	*32%*	*38%*

(delete as appropriate)

3. Would you please state your occupation (please be as detailed as you can):

   (a) at the time of your involvement with the disarmament movement between 1958 and 1965

Social Class	*1*	*2*	*3*	*4*	*5*	*6*	*7*	*8*
C.100	*5*	*11*	*50*	*24*	*8*	*1*	*1*	*1****
Rest	*11*	*22*	*46*	*16*	*6*	*0*	*0*	*0*

   (b) now:

	1	*2*	*3*	*4*	*5*	*6*	*7*	*8*
C.100	*24*	*27*	*26*	*7*	*5*	*1*	*1*	*8*
Rest	*22*	*29*	*24*	*6*	*3*	*0*	*0*	*16*

4. (a) at what age did you complete full-time education?

	13 +	*15 +*	*16 +*	*18 +*
C.100	*4*	*16*	*22*	*58*
Rest	*6*	*12*	*21*	*62*

(b) Please give brief details of your educational qualifications (e.g. GCE; Diplomas; Degrees):

	None	O levels	A levels	Diploma and Profession	Degree
C.100	*12*	*5*	*9*	*22*	*52*
Rest	*10*	*9*	*9*	*23*	*49*

The level of statistical significance is indicated by the following:
* = 5% level, ** = 2%, *** = 1%, **** = 0.1%

(Figures and words in italics are the subsequent results)

Section B (N.B. All the questions in this section are concerned with the 1958 to 1965 period).

5. (a) In which year did you first begin to support CND?
   (please tick as appropriate)

	C.100 %	*Rest %*		*C.100 %*	*Rest %*
1958	*47*	*55*	1962	*2*	*4*
1959	*26*	*22*	1963	*2*	*0*
1960	*13*	*6*	1964	*0*	*0*
1961	*11*	*12*	After 1964	*1*	*1*

(b) Were you a supporter of: *C.100 vs. Rest*

(i) the Direct Action Committee Against Nuclear War?	*44*	*14*	Yes/No****
(ii) the Committee of 100?	*100*	*0*	Yes/No
(iii) the Independent Nuclear Disarmament Election Committee?	*15*	*7*	Yes/No**
(iv) the British Peace Committee?	*14*	*13*	Yes/No
(v) the Peace Pledge Union?	*30*	*23*	Yes/No

6. Between 1958 and 1965 were you a member of any of the following political groups? (please tick as appropriate)

	C.100	*vs. Rest*
(a) Labour Party	*47*	*53*
(b) Young Socialists	*17*	*8***
(c) International Socialists	*3*	*2*
(d) Communist Party	*5*	*9*
(e) Young Communist League	*6*	*2*
(f) Socialist Labour League	*1*	*0*
(g) Anarchists	*14*	*1*****
(h) Liberal Party	*2*	*5*
(i) Young Liberals	*2*	*1*
(j) Conservative Party	*0*	*1*

C.100 vs. Rest

(k) Young Conservatives	0	0
(l) New Left Clubs	13	6*
(m) Solidarity	3	0*
(n) Fabian Society	4	5
(o) Any other political group (please state:		
. . . .)	9	5
(p) None Nil	29	34

7. If you were a member of any of the above organisations would you state whether membership of any of these was:

More important to you than your support for the disarmament movement?:   Yes/No

If 'Yes' please indicate which: *'Yes'*   *19%*   *17%*

. . . .

. . . .

. . . .

8. Please indicate how you voted at the General Elections of 1959 and 1964 (please tick appropriate boxes)

	C.100	*Rest*		*C.100*	*Rest*
****1959: Not eligible to vote	*43*	*18*			
Did not vote	*13*	*6*	Conservative	*1*	*2*
Labour	*41*	*68*	Liberal	*0*	*4*
Communist	*1*	*1*	Other (please state)	*2*	*1*

. . . .

. . . .

	C.100	*Rest*		*C.100*	*Rest*
****1964: Not eligible to vote	*16*	*8*			
Did not vote	*18*	*5*	Conservative	*1*	*1*
Labour	*58*	*73*	Liberal	*3*	*12*
Communist	*1*	*1*	Other (please state)	*3*	*1*

. . . .

. . . .

9. Between 1958 and 1965 were you: *C.100*   *Rest*

an absolute pacifist?   *50*   *42*   Yes/No

10. Between 1958 and 1965 were you a practising member of a religious denomination?   Yes/No

C.100	*Rest*
39%	*44%*

(a) If 'Yes' please tick the appropriate one:

	C.100	*Rest*
(i) Church of England	*41*	*29*
(ii) Methodist	*12*	*16*

	C.100	Rest
(iii) Jewish	0	1
(iv) Quaker	26	29
(v) Roman Catholic	14	8
(vi) Other (please state)	7	17

. . . .
. . . .

(b) If 'No' please tick the appropriate category

	C.100	Rest
(i) atheist	40	35
(ii) agnostic	48	56
(iii) not interested in religion	12	9

11. Was your objection to the possession of nuclear weapons by Britain based *primarily* upon:

	C.100	Rest
(a) moral/religious arguments?	34	45
(b) political arguments?	14	11
(c) equally upon both?	52	44

12. Please state briefly in your own words, your main objections to the possession of nuclear weapons by Britain at the time of your involvement with the disarmament movement between 1958 and 1965

. . . .
. . . .
. . . .

Section C. (All questions in this section are concerned with *current* attitudes and activities).

13. Are you currently a member of CND?   Yes/No

	C.100	Rest ***
	17	29

(If 'No' please state the approximate date when you ceased actively to support CND. . . . .)

14. Are you now (or have you been since 1965) a member or active supporter of any of the following? (N.B. please state the approximate dates of joining/leaving any of these organisations, e.g. *Liberal Party 1968-1972*)(please tick as appropriate)

		C.100 %	Rest %
(a) Labour Party		36	43
(b) Young Socialists		2	1
(c) National Front		0	0
(d) International Socialists/Socialist Workers' Party	**	6	1
(e) Vietnam Solidarity Campaign		13	9

	C.100 %	Rest
(f) British Campaign for Peace in Vietnam ★★★	14	25
(g) Conservative Party	2	0
(h) Young Conservatives	0	0
(i) Anarchists ★★★	6	1
(j) Socialist Labour League/WRP	1	1
(k) International Marxist Group	1	0
(l) Institute for Workers' Control ★	4	1
(m) Liberal Party	3	7
(n) Young Liberals	0	1
(o) Scottish National Party	2	1
(p) Plaid Cymru	1	0
(q) Communist Party ★	4	10
(r) Young Communist League	1	2
(s) One of the Maoist groups (please state)	0	0
(t) Fabian Society	4	5
(u) Other political groups (please state) ★	22	14
. . . .		
. . . . (Nil)	33	34

(13) Length of membership if no longer in CND (N = 173 + 140)

Years	2	4	6	8	10+
C.100	3	20	32	23	22
Rest	3	23	36	16	23

15. Are you a practising member of a religious denomination? Yes/No

(a) If 'Yes' please tick the appropriate one:

	C.100	Rest
	24	39★★★

	C.100	Rest
(i) Church of England	34	27
(ii) Methodist	8	13
(iii) Jewish	0	1
(iv) Quaker	34	33
(v) Roman Catholic	8	8
(vi) Other (please state)	16	18

. . . .

(b) If 'No' please tick the appropriate category:

	C.100	Rest
(i) athiest	42	39
(ii) agnostic	49	51
(iii) not interested in religion	10	11

16. Since your involvement in the disarmament movement have you been active at any time in any of the following:

(a) Community Politics (please specify)   Yes/No

     C.100   Rest . . . .

      48   37* . . . .

(b) Single-issue campaigns (e.g. housing, minority group rights, etc.)
    (please specify)   Yes/No

      C.100   Rest . . . .

       63   51* . . . .

(c) Women's Liberation Movement   Yes/No

      C.100   Rest . . . .

       17   9* . . . .

(d) Ecology, conservation groups (please specify)   Yes/No

      C.100   Rest . . . .

       38   36 . . . .

17. If a General Election were held now, which party would you vote for?
    (please tick as appropriate)

	C.100 %	Rest % ***
Would not vote	18	8
Liberal	7	15
Communist	6	5
Labour	58	66
Conservative	2	3
National Front	0	0
Other (please state)	8	4

. . . .

18. Please indicate your level of agreement with the following belief systems by ticking the appropriate box.

	(C.100 - Rest)				
	Strongly Agree	Agree	Neutral	Disagree	Strongly disagree
(a) Christian	** 15-25	20-26	22-22	23-15	20-12
(b) Marxist	** 13-14	40-21	22-32	17-20	9-12
(c) Social democratic	14-12	39-40	23-32	16-12	8-4

(C.100 - Rest)

		Strongly Agree	Agree	Neutral	Disagree	Strongly disagree
(d) Conservative	*	0-0	3-4	10-18	23-28	65-51
(e) Liberal humanist		11-14	35-32	35-32	13-15	7-7
(f) Apolitical		1-5	6-5	25-22	20-23	48-46
(g) Libertarian/Anarchist	****	19-2	22-11	18-22	26-21	15-43
(h) Other (please state)		. . . .

. . . .

9. Please indicate your level of agreement with the following statements (by ticking the appropriate box).

I believe that the Disarmament Movement failed in its major objectives between 1958 and 1965 because:

C.100 - Rest

		Strongly agree	Agree	Neutral	Disagree	Strongly disagree
(a) CND failed to devote sufficient attention to winning over the Labour Party to its policy		13-8	24-24	20-28	33-32	10-9
(b) The CND leadership was out of touch with the radicalism of the rank and file	****	11-4	32-11	20-31	33-41	4-12
(c) The leadership concentrated too heavily on winning the Labour Party's support	**	7-2	24-17	21-31	40-41	8-10
(d) It failed to win the support of ordinary people		23-23	46-46	14-8	15-19	4-4
(e) The movement was split by the creation of the Committee of 100 in 1960 and its subsequent activities	****	3-18	16-36	20-28	40-17	22-2

(C.100 - Rest)

	Strongly agree	Agree	Neutral	Disagree	Strongly disagree
(f) The movement was increasingly taken over by political extremists ***	6-11	14-21	20-21	39-38	21-9
(g) The single issue of unilateral nuclear disarmament could not for long unite so many conflicting groups ***	9-18	53-35	13-19	18-23	7-5
(h) The Left failed to convince the Movement that the achievement of Socialism was indissolubly linked to the specific issue of nuclear disarmament ***	14-8	32-31	21-35	25-16	8-11
(i) The movement became too political ***	2-8	9-14	17-25	50-38	22-15
(j) The movement ceased to be a centrally moral campaign	12-11	23-28	24-24	33-27	9-10
(k) CND's campaign declined naturally, as a result of changes in circumstances external to the movement (e.g. relaxation of world tension 'post-Cuba'; the Partial Test Ban Treaty; the changes in the Labour Party's defence policy)	28-33	54-52	6-7	7-6	4-1
(l) It became obvious that the policy of CND was ultimately unpatriotic	2-3	6-4	7-9	24-27	63-57
(m) Gradually, "we have learned to live with the Bomb"	10-14	55-52	16-13	14-13	5-8

C.100 - Rest

	Strongly agree	Agree	Neutral	Disagree	Strongly disagree
(n) The movement failed to develop sufficient international momen- tum	8-11	49-43	26-27	13-16	5-3
(o) All social and political movements of this kind are doomed to failure from the outset	4-5	7-10	14-15	40-44	35-26

(p) Please state any other major reason why, in your opinion, the movement failed.

. . . .

. . . .

20. Since your involvement in the Disarmament Movement, would you say:
    (please tick as appropriate)

		C.100	Rest *
(a) that your political *interest:*	has increased?	48	36
	has decreased?	11	16
	has virtually disappeared?	2	1
	has remained about the same?	39	48
(b) that your political *activity:*	has increased?	32	27 **
	has decreased?	24	28
	has virtually disappeared?	21	11
	has remained about the same?	24	34

21. Thinking back, do you consider that the Disarmament Movement has influenced your attitudes and activities?
    (please tick as appropriate)

	C.100	Rest *
very strongly	44	31 *
strongly	36	38
slightly	15	24
not at all	5	8

22. Please add any further comments you may have about the Disarmament move-ment; or about any areas which you feel have not been covered adequately by the questionnaire.

Thank you very much for completing the questionnaire. Would you please check that you have answered all the questions and return the completed questionnaire(s) to me in the s.a.e.

Thanks again.

Colin Pritchard and *Richard Taylor*

If you would like a copy of the preliminary results of the survey please tick here and give your address:

☐   Address:

NOTE: In return for the co-operation I am receiving from CND I will transmit any requests to rejoin CND. CND's current address is:

29 Great James Street,
London WC1N 3EY.

TABLE A
Objections to Nuclear Weapons

Reasons	Youth (N = 206) (%)	Adult (N = 197) (%)	Total sample (N = 403) (%)
Having Bomb exposed UK to attack hence fear of provoking attack and concern for future generations	47	53	43
Expenditure on Bomb economically wasteful	59	41	19
No proper controls, real danger of proliferation	61*	39	23
Bomb as defence was a futile strategy— not least because unworkable	43	57*	34
Repugnance and shame over example of Hiroshima and Nagasaki	49	51	25
International effect was danger of making UK dependent upon USA	72*	28	13
UK repudiation would offer moral lead to other countries (especially in 'Third World')	52	48	22
Real environmental dangers	36	64	8
General protest against unjust and corrupt society	67	33	7[a]
Weapons would be used as author- itarian means to hold the people in check	57	43	4
Effort to mobilise churches, which were condemned for pusillanimity	40	60	3

* Statistically significant.
[a] Proportionately fewer women made this objection.

TABLE B
CND Achievements

Item	Youth (%)	Adult (%)	Total sample (%)	(N = 206 and N = 197)
CND achieved a large part of its objectives	20	30*	25	
Raised public awareness of nuclear dangers	17	22	20	
Made the partial Test Ban Treaty possible	15	17	16	
United diverse groups into an effective force	14	15	14	
Engendered an almost life-long camaraderie	15	12	14	
Highlighted political potential of 'man-in-the-street'	16	12	14	
Radically politicised important sections of the population	12*	4	8	
Influenced the Anti-Vietnam War Campaigns	5	2	4	
CND became prototype for all subsequent protest movements	5	2	4	
Stopped any UK involvement in Vietnam	2	1	1	

* Statistically significant.

TABLE C
Suggested Reasons for Failure—General Response % N = 403
Women, Youth and Adult Groups Compared (N = 206 and 197)

Items mentioned	Youth (%)	Adult (%)	Total sample (%)
Apathy of general public	26	29	27
No effective political outlet to channel diverse groups' unity on the nuclear issue	18	18	18[m]
Increasingly hostile media reports	9	11	10
CND devalued by association with unpopular fringe groups, e.g. Gay Lib. and the Drug Protest	9	12	10
Overt governmental and 'establishment' disapproval discouraged and disillutioned supporters and public	11	7	9
Campaign too middle-class in approach and not enough rank-and-file trade union support	11	7	9[m]
Movement let down by the Labour Party	7	9	8[m]
Vietnam overshadowed CND and gave young an alternative and more pressing cause	12[y]	4	8
Psychologically the times were not ripe for the acceptance of the implications of UK being a second class power	5	9	7
Apparent support for 'law-breaking' lost moderate support	5	7	6
CND was sacrificed to Labour Party's electoral needs	5	5	5
Increasing sense of failure after such strong initial success concentrated feelings of impotence and certainty of failure	5	4	5

[y] 'Youth group' significantly higher frequency than 'adult group.'
[m] Male group significantly higher frequency than female group.

Brief Biographical Details of CND, DAC and Committee of 100 Leaders, and of Major Political Figures who Opposed the Movement and its Policies

EACH entry is divided into two sections:

  (i) General information,
  (ii) Disarmament Movement involvement.

Those included in this list represent the major figures, but the list is not intended to be exhaustive. For some, details are sparse: this is because they were unwilling to furnish us with the necessary information — or because we were unable to contact them.

ACLAND, Sir Richard Thomas Dyke, 15th Bt. (cr. 1644). Former Labour MP and founder of Commonwealth Party.

General

b. 26 November 1906.
Educated: Rugby, Balliol College, Oxford University.
Political career: MP Barnstaple, Devon 1935-45; MP (Labour) 1947-55 Gravesend, Kent.
From 1959 to 1974 Senior Lecturer, St. Luke's College of Education, Exeter. Publications in politics, international relations, etc.

Disarmament

   Although not involved directly in CND Acland was an important precursor; he resigned from the Labour Party over the nuclear issue in 1955. He had been a prominent Left activist with strong pacifist leanings for decades before this: during the war he was the main instigator of the Common Wealth Party which contested by-elections against the wartime coalition. His publications include *Why So Angry?* (1958) and *Waging Peace* (1958).

ALLAUN, Frank, MP (Labour), East Salford, since 1955.

General

b. 27 February 1913.
Educated: Manchester Grammar School; B.A. (Com); ACA.
Journalist: *Manchester Evening News*, *Daily Herald*; editor *Labour's Northern Voice*, 1951-67. Member NUJ; formerly of AEU and Shop Assistants' Union. PPS to the Secretary of State for the Colonies October 1964 to March 1965, resigned. Member of Labour Party National Executive 1967 to date. Chairman of the Labour Party 1978 to date.

Disarmament

   Helped to organise first Aldermaston March. Active in CND from the outset. National Chairman of Labour Action for Peace. Author of several CND, etc., pamphlets and of *Stop the H-Bomb Race* (1959); *The Wasted £30 Billions* (1975).

ALLEGRANZA, Helen, Committee of 100 Activist.

General

b. 1928 Aldershot; d. January 1963.
Career: from an Army family. Joined ATS (WRAC); member of the Conservative Party. Resigned over Suez crisis. Worked in American advertising agency in London as telephonist/receptionist. Through meeting Michael Scott's secretary began work with Oxfam and National Association for Mental Health. Not involved in ND Movement until Committee of 100.

Disarmament

Became active in Committee of 100 in 1960/1. Defendant in the Official Secrets trial following the Wethersfield *et al.* demonstrations in December 1961: sentenced to 12 months' imprisonment. Committed suicide, January 1963, shortly after her release from prison.

ARROWSMITH, Pat, prominent DAC, Committee of 100 and CND activist.

General

b. 2 March 1930.
Educated: Farringtons, Stover School; Cheltenham Ladies College; Newnham College, Cambridge (BA History); University of Ohio; University of Liverpool (Cert. in Social Science).
Numerous occupations including: Community Worker in Chicago, 1952-3; cinema usherette 1953-4; Social caseworker, Liverpool Family Service Unit, 1954; Child Care Officer 1955 and 1964; Nursing Assistant, Devon Psychiatric Hospital 1956-7; researcher for Society of Friends Race Relations Committee 1969-71; Caseworker for NCCL 1971; Assistant at Amnesty International since 1971. Publications in politics and two novels.

Disarmament

Organiser for Direct Action Committee Against Nuclear War, Committee of 100, and Campaign for Nuclear Disarmament, 1958-68 (in particular, Organising Secretary for the first Aldermaston March, planned and promoted by the DAC); heavy involvement in DAC 'fieldwork' from 1958 to 1961, especially in industrial agitation against nuclear weapons. Attempts to stimulate strike action, some partially successful, at Stevenage, Liverpool, London, Bristol, etc. Involved in 'Voters' Veto' campaign. Jailed nine times as political prisoner between 1958 and 1974. Contested Fulham at 1966 General Election as Radical Alliance candidate and again in 1970 as Hammersmith Stop the SE Asia War Committee. Contested 1979 General Election, Cardiff SE against James Callaghan as Independent Socialist (Troops out of N. Ireland) candidate.

Member of: War Resisters' International; Troops Out Movement; British Withdrawal from N. Ireland Campaign; CND; TU campaign against the Prevention of Terrorism Act.

BEVAN, Rt. Hon. Aneurin (Nye), PC 1945, MP (Labour) Ebbw Vale Division of Monmouthshire 1929-60.

General

b. November 1897 Tredegar, Monmouthshire; d. 6 July 1960.
Educated: Sirhowy Elementary School, Central Labour College.
Career: left school at 13, miner; active in South Wales Miners' Federation; elected to Local Urban District Council after return from Labour College; County Councillor, Monmouthshire, from 1928 and MP for Ebbw Vale from 1929 until his death. Minister of Health 1945-51; Minister of Labour and National Service 1951 (resigned 1951 — with Harold Wilson and John Freeman — over the issue of prescription charges in NHS); Treasurer of LP from 1956. After Gaitskell's election to the leadership following Attlee's retirement, Bevan was the major figure in the Left-wing campaign against Gaitskell's Right-wing leadership ('The Bevanites'). From 1957 onwards, however, there was a reconciliation between Gaitskell and Bevan and, had Labour won the 1959 election, Bevan would undoubtedly have achieved high office.
Publication: *In Place of Fear*, (political credo of 'democratic socialism'), 1952. See also biography of Bevan in 2 volumes by Michael Foot.

Disarmament

Bevan was associated with the Left (initially the ILP) and the *Tribune* from the outset. But, in 1957, at the Labour Party Conference, he fiercely rejected the unilateralist case thereby alienating many on the Left of the Party. The opposition of Bevan, before the Movement had properly begun, was, arguably, one of the key factors in the Movement's ultimate failure.

BOULTON, David, Granada TV producer and writer.

General

b. 3 October 1935.

Educated: Grammar School.

Career and political activities: clerk, 1952-8; RAF policeman (National Service) 1954-6; clerk 1956-7; Deputy Editor *Liberal News* 1957-9; Staff Writer *Tribune* 1959-62; 'Granada' TV Writer/Producer 1966 to date; Editor, 'World in Action' 1974-6; Editor Granada TV Drama Documentary Unit 1977 to date. Parliamentary Candidate for Labour Party, Richmond, Surrey 1966.

Publications: *Jazz in Britain*, 1958; *Objection Overruled*, 1967; (ed.) *Voices from the Crowd: Against the H-Bomb*, 1967; *The UVF*, 1973; *The Making of Tania Hearst*, 1976; *The Lockheed Papers*, 1978.

Disarmament

Founder/Chairman, Staines Group, CND 1958-62.

Editor, *Sanity*, CND publications, and CND Press Officer, 1962-6.

BROCK, Hugh Heron, Editor, *Peace News*, 1955 to 1964 (now retired).

General

b. 15 May 1914.

Educated: Westbourne Park School from age of 5 to 15; evening classes at various West London evening institutes and the London School of Printing. Also reading while in Wandsworth Prison.

Career: Printer, lorry driver, road-sweeper, coal-man, milk roundsman, gardener-handyman, assistant editor (and later editor) of *Peace News;* office-manager (and later director) of Goodwin Press.

Political activities: member of Labour Party (when not under expulsion); vice-chairman Stoke Newington Borough Council Housing Committee (1957-8).

Publications: Contributions to *Peace News* and other pacifist journals.

Disarmament

Organised small demonstrations around 1951, 1952 and 1953, aimed both at experimenting with nonviolent action and protesting against: the use of napalm bombs; the construction of a British atomic weapons plant at Aldermaston and research activities at Harwell; and the creation of an American military base at Mildenhall.

Formed the *ad hoc* Emergency Committee for Direct Action against Nuclear War in 1957 in attempt to stop the testing of British nuclear weapon at Christmas Island that year. Chaired the Committee's Aldermaston March sub-committee which organised the first big march to Aldermaston in 1958.

Joined in discussions which led to the formation of the Committee of 100 in 1960 and the winding up of the Direct Action Committee the following year. Assisted with the organisation of the European leg of the San Francisco to Moscow anti-nuclear march. Went as representative of the Direct Action Committee to the Belfast anti-H-bomb march supported by Protestants, Catholics and IRA members from both sides of the border.

BROCKWAY, Baron (cr. 1964), Archibald Fenner Brockway. Veteran Left Labour and Pacifist Activist.

General

b. 1888 (Calcutta).

Educated: School for the sons of missionaries (now Eltham College).

Political career: Secretary of No Conscription Fellowship (1917) and editor of *Labour Leader* (1912-17); imprisoned for pacifist activities (under DORA) in 1916-17; involved in Indian independence movements and in prison reform; organising secretary ILP (1922) and General Secretary ILP (1928 and 1933-9); Editor of New Leader 1926-9 and 1931-46; Labour candidate at Lancaster 1922; Chairman No More War Movement and War Resisters' International 1923-8; Labour candidate for Westminster 1924; Executive of Labour and Socialist International 1926-31; MP (Labour) East Leyton 1929-31; Chairman ILP 1931-3; Political Secretary ILP 1939-46; ILP candidate: West Ham 1934, Norwich 1935, Lancaster 1941, Cardiff East 1942. Resigned from ILP 1946 and rejoined Labour Party; MP (Labour) Eton and Slough 1950-64; Chairman Liberation (formerly Movement for Colonial Freedom) 1954-67; various organisations involving African independence, etc.

Publications: numerous political and pacifist books and pamphlets; novels.

Disarmament

Long-standing commitment to pacifist and radical politics stretching back to before World War I. Supported CND from the outset — platform speaker, etc. — but not on Executive. Member of British Council for Peace in Vietnam 1965-9; President of British Campaign for Peace in Vietnam 1970.

Publications include: *This Shrinking Explosive World* (1968); *The Next Step to Peace* (1970); and 3 volumes of Autobiography (*Inside the Left* (1942); *Outside the Right* (1963); and *Towards Tomorrow* (1977)).

CADOGAN, Peter William. General Secretary South Place Ethical Society; formerly leading activist in the Committee of 100.

General

b. 26 January 1921.
Educated: Tynemouth School, Kings College (now University of Newcastle), BA History, Dip Ed. Joseph Cowen Prizewinner 1950.
Career: Insurance 1936-40; RAF 1941-6; Student 1946-51; Teaching 1951-65; Peace Movement, Committee of 100 and Save Biafra Campaign 1965-70; South Place Ethical Society (General Secretary) 1970-9 to date.
Political activities: 1946-60 — on the Left. 1968-70 Secretary Save Biafra Committee. Co-founder of 'Turning Point' 1975. Founding Secretary of East-West Peace People 1978.
Publications: *Early Radical Newcastle* (Sagittarius Press, 1975). Papers include "The Origins of Sectarianism" (*Labour Review* 1959); "The 1959 Situation in the SLL" (The *Stamford Faction*, 1959), "The British Communist Party in the Light of 1956" (The Imre Nagy Institute for Political Research, Brussels, 1961), "The Age of Absolutism" (in *History*, MacDonald, 1962), "Harney and Engels" (*International Review of Social History*, Amsterdam, 1963), "Biafra" (Save Biafra Campaign 1969) and "From Civil Disobedience to Confrontation" (in *Direct Action and Democratic Politics*, Allen & Unwin, 1972).

Disarmament

1958: Secretary of Joint Committee, Cambridge Labour Party and Trades Council (set up to organise the demonstration at the Thor Missile Base at Mepal).
1961: Founding Secretary of the East Anglian Committee of 100. Demonstrations at V-Bomber and US bases 1961 to 1968.
1962: Secretary (and later Chairman) of the International Sub-Committee of the Committee of 100.
1962-68: On the National Council for CND (on behalf of the Committee of 100).
1965: Full-time Secretary of the National Committee of 100 — until it wound up in the autumn of 1968.

CAMERON, (Mark) James (Walter), journalist and author.

General

b. 17 June 1911.
Educated: at a variety of small schools, mainly in France.
Career: began journalism in Dundee in 1928; subsequently worked on many national newspapers — travelled widely as Foreign Correspondent. Produced TV films, travel series, etc. Numerous journalistic awards.
Publications: politics, foreign policy, travel, autobiography, plays.

Disarmament

Involved as journalist in reporting of A-Bomb and H-Bomb tests. Active in CND from the outset. One of major publicists for the Movement. Never centrally active in the organisation/politics of CND. Ceased to participate actively from *ca.* 1961 onwards, but continues to write up the 'nuclear follies' in the *Guardian* and elsewhere.

CARTER, April F., Lecturer in Politics; formerly leading activist in the DAC and CND.

General

b. 22 November 1937.
Education: left school at 16; LSE 1962-65, BSc (Econ) in Politics; School of Soviet and East European Studies, London Univ., 1972-3, MA in East European Studies.
Career: Executive Officer, Foreign Office 1956-8; Lecturer in Politics, Lancaster University 1966-9; Part-time Tutor, Open University 1971-6; Tutor in Politics, Somerville College, Oxford, 1976 to date.
Political activities: Anti-Vietnam War Movement 1966-7; Organised, with WRI, demonstration in Warsaw Pact capitals against the occupation of Czechoslovakia, 1968.
Current political attitudes: pacifist (with some qualifications); socialist (non-Marxist and not Labour Party); decentralist/ecological sympathies. Not changed significantly, since 1958-65, except rather more sympathy with Marxism, especially for East European radicals/reformers.
Publications: *Political Theory of Anarchism* (1971); *Direct Action and Liberal Democracy* (1973); *Authority and Democracy* (1979).

Disarmament

Secretary, Direct Action Committee against Nuclear War 1958-61. European organiser, Committee for Non-violent Action, San Francisco to Moscow Walk, 1961. Features and Assistant Editor, *Peace News* 1961-2. Member of CND Council 1969/70. Chairman CND 1970-71.

CHANDLER, (Terence) Terry, Committee of 100 activist.

General

b. Birmingham 1940.
Educated: Birmingham University (but left after first year after failing examinations in Mathematics and Physics).
Career: travelled in North Africa; technical officer at Fairey Aviation Ltd.; Committee of 100 activist from 1960.

Disarmament

Numerous prison sentences (including two at Foulness in 1960). Active in the DAC and the Committee of 100. Defendant in the Official Secrets trial following the Wethersfield *et al.* demonstrations in December 1961: sentenced to 18 months' imprisonment.

CLARK, George. CND, Committee of 100 activist. Community activist and Independent Councillor in West London.

General

b. 31 July 1926.
Educated: Cambridgeshire College of Technology; Goldsmiths College (External part-time) Diploma in Sociology.
Career: Market Research; Founder Director Notting Hill Housing Service; Founder Director City Poverty Committee; Director of the Association for Neighbourhood Councils; Independent Councillor for Golborne Ward, North Kensington (elected May 1978).
Publications: papers on community organising given to Annual Conferences of Social agencies; contributions to two books on Social action.
Current political attitudes: Gandhian philosophy of non-violence; seeking social and political change through non-violent means and without commitment to any particular ideology (except a firm belief that social and political change can be achieved only by an interdependence of changes in the institutional structures and changes in personal behaviour).

Disarmament

1958: Representative of *Universities and Left Review* to Council of CND.
1959: Secretary of London Region CND.
1960 and 1961: Principle organiser and recruiting agent for Aldermaston March within the London Region.
1960: Accepted an invitation to become a founding member of Committee of 100 and take charge (Chief Marshal) of demonstrations.
1961: Arrested and refused to be bound over — imprisoned for 2 months.
1962: Founded Campaign Caravan Workshops.
1962: Appointed Field Secretary of CND.
1963: Arrested during the demonstration against Queen Frederika which he attended only as observer — charged with incitement — sentenced to 18 months after being described by the Judge as "the most dangerous man in Britain". Subsequently appealed and was released after serving 11 weeks in prison.
1964: Visited America for almost 9 months, sponsored by a private donor, to see at first hand the work of the American Peace Movement, the Students for a Democratic Society and the Civil Rights Movement.
1965: Fasted for 12 days in Parliament Square to give publicity to the Vietnam issue and influence the attitude of Harold Wilson before he went to Washington to discuss the possibility of British involvement.

COLLINS, Canon Lewis John; Canon, St. Paul's Cathedral; former CND Chairman.

General

b. 23 March 1905.
Canon since 1948 and Treasurer since 1970 of St. Paul's Cathedral (Chancellor, 1948-53; Precentor, 1953-70).
Educated: Cranbrook School; Sidney Sussex College and Westcott House, Cambridge University.
Various Church of England appointments (including Priest-in-ordinary to the King; Chaplain RAFVR; and Dean of Oriel College, Oxford University).
Publications: theology; autobiography.

Politics: Christian Action, President, 1949 to date (Chairman, 1946-73); International Defence and Aid Fund, 1964 to date. Martin Luther King Foundation 1969-73.

Disarmament

Chairman of CND 1958 to 1964. Although not involved in the very first 'informal' meeting that gave birth to CND, Collins was approached immediately after this and became, from the formal inauguration of CND, a leading figure in the organisation. He controlled the divisions within the Movement with considerable diplomatic and political skill through 1958, 1959 and 1960 but, with the creation of the Committee of 100 and the personal disagreements between Russell and himself, Collins was increasingly unhappy in the organisation. His resignation in 1964 was not unexpected.

COMFORT, Alexander, medical biologist; poet and novelist.

General

b. 10 February 1920.
Educated: Highgate School; Trinity College, Cambridge University; The London Hospital. First Class Part I Nat. Sc. Tripos, 1940; Part 2 Second Class 1st Div. (Pathology) Nat. Sc. Tripos, 1941; MRCS, LRCP 1944; MB, BCh Cantab. 1944; MA Cantab. 1945; DCH London 1945; PhD London 1949; DSc. London 1963.
Career: university career at The London Hospital Medical College, London University, Stanford University (USA), Institute for Higher Studies, Santa Barbara (USA).
Publications: plays, novels, poetry, essays, social psychology, science, sex counselling, etc.

Disarmament

One of speakers at the inaugural meeting of CND. Vehemently anti-bomb from a biological and moral viewpoint. Always opposed to linkage of CND with Labour Movement and/or socialist politics. Supported DAC and Committee of 100. Quasi-anarchistic politics.

COUSINS, Rt. Hon. Frank (PC 1964), General Secretary of TGWU 1956-9.

General

b. 8 September 1904.
Educated: King Edward's School, Doncaster.
Career: TGWU. Became Assistant General Secretary TGWU 1955; General Secretary 1956-69; Seconded as Minister of Technology October 1964—July 1966; MP (Labour) Nuneaton, January 1965 to December 1966. Elected Member General Council of TUC 1956-69. Various other transport, science and political committees.
National Economic Development Council; Central Advisory Council for Science and Technology 1967 to date; Chairman, Community Relations Commission, 1968-70.

Disarmament

Spearheaded the unilateralist movement in the TUs. Opposed Gaitskell fiercely on the nuclear issue, as well as on general ideological grounds. His passionate speeches in opposition to the Bomb were couched in emotional and moral, rather than political and socialist, terms. As a powerful and charismatic TU figure he was able to play a large part in the move towards unilateralism in the TUs in the years 1959 to 1960, and was instrumental in achieving the unilateralist victory at the Labour Party conference at Scarborough in 1960. However, during 1961 he was outmanoeuvred and was unable to stem the tide of unity and pro-Gaitskell propaganda which led to the reversal of the unilateralist policy in 1961. Although such a powerful political figure in the unilateralist movement, Cousins never co-operated either personally or organisationally with CND.

COX, John. Former Chairman of CND.

General

b. 16 May 1935.
Consultant engineer.
Member of the Communist Party.

Disarmament

Joined CND 1958. Chairman Colleges and Universities CND (CUCaND) 1961. First elected to National Executive of CND in 1961. Many offices since then, including Chairman of CND from 1971 to 1978.
Publication: *Overkill, The Story of Modern Weapons,* Penguin, 1977.

DIXON, Ian. Committee of 100 activist.

General

b. April, 1936, Ilford.
Educated: Hipperholm Grammar School, Yorkshire.
Career: left school at 16; worked in Civil Service and Colonial Office. Hospital porter. CO—excused National Service. Visited India where joined Vinoba Bhave's land-gift movement. Worked in Cheshire Homes (1957).

Disarmament

Joined PPU 1953 and worked with Non-Violent Resistance group and, with Michael Randle and Chris Farley, established Pacifist Youth Action group. Joined staff of *Peace News,* 1959 and, with assent of the whole DAC in December 1959, was appointed acting secretary and organised Harrington Rocket base demonstration of January 1960. Subsequently worked for the Committee of 100. Numerous prison sentences. Defendant in the Official Secrets trial following the Wethersfield *et al.* demonstrations in December 1961: sentenced to 18 months' imprisonment.

DUFF, Peggy, General Secretary of CND 1958-67.

General

b. 8 February 1910.
Educated: Hastings High School, Bedford College, London University.
Career and political activities: administrator/organiser of several campaigns: Commonwealth; Save Europe Now; National Council for the Abolition of Capital Punishment. Also worked on the *Tribune.* Labour Councillor, St. Pancras and Camden Borough until 1967. Member of Labour Party 1945-67.
Publications: *Left, Left, Left* (political autobiography), Allison & Busby, 1971; Editor, Vietnam/South East Asia International & Peace Press.

Disarmament

Briefly, in 1957, Secretary, National Council for the Abolition of Nuclear Weapons Tests. Organising Secretary, then General Secretary, CND 1958 to 1967. Secretary, International Confederation for Disarmament and Peace, 1967 to date.

DUNCAN-SANDYS, Baron (cr. 1974, Life Peer), Duncan Edwin, PC 1944, CH 1973, Minister of Defence 1957-9, Conservative Government.

General

b. 24 January 1908.
Educated: Eton, Magdalen College, Oxford, MA.
Career: Diplomatic Service 1930-5; MP (Conservative) Norwood Division of Lambeth 1935-45; Streatham 1950-74. Army service 1939-41 (Lt. Col. disabled on active service). Financial Secretary to War Office 1941-3; Parliamentary Secretary, Ministry of Supply 1943-4; Minister of Works 1944-5; Minister of Supply 1951-4; Minister of Housing, 1954-7; Minister of Defence 1957-9; Minister of Aviation 1959-60; Secretary of State for Commonwealth Relations 1960-4; Secretary of State for the Colonies 1962-4; membership of numerous European, and commercial concerns. Chairman of Lonro Ltd. since 1972; President of European Nostra since 1969; Founder, and President since 1956, of Civic Trust. Numerous academic and political honours (UK and abroad).

Disarmament

Minister of Defence in the crucial H-Bomb years. His Defence White Papers of 1957 and 1958 brought home to 'public opinion' the full reality of nuclear warfare, and the defence and economic implications of UK involvement. Unequivocal supporter of nuclear armament as a means of deterrence, and of UK reliance on nuclear weapons for primary means of defence. Totally opposed to unilateralism and to CND.

FOOT, Rt. Hon. Michael; PC, 1974. MP (Labour) Ebbw Vale Division of Monmouthshire since 1960.

General

b. 23 July 1913.
Lord President of the Council and Leader of the House of Commons 1976 to 1979. Deputy Leader of the Labour Party since 1976.
Educated: Forres School, Swanage; Leighton Park School, Reading; Wadham College, Oxford University; President of the Oxford Union, 1933.

Political career: contested Monmouth for Labour 1935; MP (Labour) for Devonport, Plymouth, 1945-55; Secretary of State for Employment 1974-6; Member Labour Party National Executive Committee 1971 to date.

Professional career: Assistant Editor, *Tribune*, 1937-8; Acting Editor, *Evening Standard*, 1942; Managing Director, *Tribune*, 1945-74; Editor, *Tribune*, 1948-52; 1955-60; Political columnist, *Daily Herald*, 1944-64; former Book Critic, *Evening Standard*. Publications in politics and literary history. Also, 2-volume biography of Aneurin Bevan.

Disarmament

Prominent supporter of CND from the outset. Member of the Executive from 1958 to 1963. Leading figure on the Labour Left: as Editor of the *Tribune* he made the CND cause the focus of attention for the Labour Left. Despite his admiration of Bevan he disagreed fundamentally with him over the nuclear issue. After Bevan's 'defection' in 1957, Foot became the most prominent figure on the Labour Left. He did much to keep CND on the 'Labourist road', always being strongly opposed to both extra-parliamentary action (e.g. Committee of 100) and attempts to create alternative political vehicles to by-pass the Labour Party (e.g. INDEC). His enthusiasm for CND began to wane once Wilson had taken over from Gaitskell as leader and a general election was in the offing.

GAITSKELL, Rt. Hon. Hugh Todd Naylor, PC 1947, CBE 1945, MP (Labour) South Leeds 1945-63; Leader of the Labour Party 1955-63.

General

b. 9 April 1906; d. 18 January 1963.

Educated: Winchester; New College, Oxford University (PPE, 1927, First Class Honours).

Career: Rockefeller Fellow 1933/4; Head of Department of Political Economy, University College, London; Reader in Political Economy, University of London, 1938; Principal Private Secretary to Minister of Economic Warfare 1940-2; Principal Assistant Secretary to Board of Trade 1942-5; Parliamentary Secretary, Ministry of Fuel and Power, 1946-7; Minister of Fuel & Power 1947-50; Minister of State for Economic Affairs Feb. to Oct. 1950; Chancellor of the Exchequer 1950-1; 'Shadow' Chancellor of the Exchequer 1951-5; Treasurer of the Labour Party 1954-6.

Publications: politics, economics (see also, biography, ed. W. T. Rodgers, 1963; and biography by Philip Williams, published 1979).

Disarmament

Opposed to Left-wing of Party from the outset of his political career. With C. A. R. Crosland, he was the leading 'revisionist' theorist of the post-war Labour Party. His opposition to CND was principled, deeply-held, and linked to his rejection of Left-wing ideology in general. Rather than compromise Gaitskell sought, throughout the controversial years (1957-62), to confront and defeat his unilateralist opponents. The unilateralist resolutions carried at the 1960 Scarborough Labour Party Conference did not result in Gaitskell's resignation: his "fight, fight, and fight again" speech is one of the most famous of Labour Party Conference speeches. By the time of the 1961 Conference his authority had been reasserted and, from then on, unilateralism in the Labour Party was no longer an issue. When he died in 1963 the Labour Party was more united than for many years past.

GEORGE-BROWN, Baron (cr. 1970, Life Peer), George Alfred, PC 1951; Deputy Leader of the Labour Party 1960-70.

General

b. 2 September 1914.

Career: MP (Labour) Belper Division of Derbyshire, 1945-70; Parliamentary Private Secretary to Minister of Labour and National Service 1945-7 and to Chancellor of Exchequer 1947; Joint Parliamentary Secretary Ministry of Agriculture & Fisheries 1947-51; Minister of Works 1951; First Secretary of State and Secretary of State for Economic Affairs 1964-6; Secretary of State for Foreign Affairs 1966-8; stood (unsuccessfully) against Harold Wilson for election as Leader of Labour Party in 1963, following death of Hugh Gaitskell. Publication: Autobiography.

Disarmament

Passionate and emotional opponent of CND as an organisation and unilateralism as a policy. Always a significant figure on the Right of the Labour Party, he represented the working-class Trade Union opposition to CND, and was, perhaps, after Hugh Gaitskell, the most unpopular of Labour politicians in CND circles.

GIBBS, Olive Frances, National Chairman of CND 1964-8.

General

b. 17 February 1918.
Educated: Grammar School (left school at 16).
Career and political activities: qualified Librarian (children and schools) Oxford City Library, 1936-44. Lifelong Socialist activist. Joined Labour Party in 1952. Lord Mayor of Oxford; former Chairman Oxford City Labour Party; former Leader Oxford City Council; former Chairman Oxford City Education Committee; former Chairman Oxford City Parliamentary Committee; leader of opposition, Oxfordshire County Council, 1974 to date; chairman of the Governors of the Oxford College of Further Education, 1974 to date; founder member, past Chairman, President, and now Vice-President of Oxford District Society for Mentally Handicapped.
Publication: pamphlet criticising the misinformation contained in the WVS 'one in five' lectures (Coop. Women's Guild).

Disarmament

Became a pacifist immediately after the dropping of the Atomic Bomb at Hiroshima in 1945. Sponsored a visit to Oxford in 1955 of a group of survivors from Hiroshima and Nagasaki. Helped to found in 1957 the Oxford Committee for the Abolition of Nuclear Weapons Testing and was its first secretary. Joined CND in 1958 and re-formed the above Committee into the Oxford branch of CND. Co-opted in 1960 to the National Council of CND. Member of CND Executive in 1961. From 1968 to date one of three vice-chairmen of National CND.
Took part in every Aldermaston March. Active in Disarmament Politics at City and County Councils and in Labour Party.

GITTINGS, John, journalist and author.

General

b. 24 September 1938.
Educated: Grammar School; Oxford University.
Career: 1963-6 Royal Institute of International Affairs; various research fellowships and freelance work in the UK and abroad; 1971 to date, regular writer for the *Guardian*; 1976 to date, Lecturer in Chinese at Polytechnic of Central London.
Political activities: 1965-6 Anti-Vietnam War Movement; 1971-4 Indo-China Solidarity Campaign; 1978 to date, active member of Labour Party and TU branch secretary.
Publications: *The Role of the Chinese Army* (1966); *A Chinese View of China* (1973); *The World and China* (1974); (ed.) *The Lessons of Chile* (1975); *Crisis in Korea* (co-ed) (1978).

Disarmament

1960-1 Secretary CUCaND (Combined Universities Campaign for ND) also campaigned for Direct Action. 1963-4 Secretary INDEC (Independent Nuclear Disarmament Election Committee) and election agent for Michael Craft as INDEC candidate in Twickenham election Oct. 1964. January 1966 election agent for Richard Gott in Hull by-election (Anti-Vietnam war candidature). Helped plan and publish series of CND pamphlets, including *Vietnam Briefing* (1965) written jointly with Ajit Singh.
Current political attitudes: formerly a 'radical student'; now a Marxist scholar, member of the Labour Party.

GOSS, Arthur Norman. Former newspaper proprietor, now retired; activist in NCANWT and CND.

General

b. 3 April 1912.
Educated: Friends School, Saffron Walden; London College of Printing.
Career: Representative of Baines and Scarsbrook (Printers and Publishers); Director of Hampstead and Highgate Express Printing and Publishing Co. (Chairman and proprietor).
Political activities: pacifist and member of the Society of Friends (Quakers); Director of Christian Action Publications Ltd.; Trustee of The Friend Publications Ltd.; Vice-President of Christian Action; formerly member of the Fellowship of Reconciliation and Chairman of the Finchley group of FoR. During World War II given an unconditional exemption as a CO by the Fulham tribunal: spent the war years in voluntary work in Bethnal Green with Friends Relief Service.

Disarmament

Founder member of the National Council for the Abolition of Nuclear Weapons Tests (NCANWT). Chairman of NCANWT throughout its existence. Member of CND Executive from the outset in 1958 to *ca.*1963.

GOTT, Richard, journalist and author.

General

b. 28 October 1938.
Educated: Winchester College, Oxford University.
Career and political activities: Research assistant, Royal Institute of International Affairs; Leader Writer, the *Guardian*; Lecturer, University of Chile; Foreign Editor, the *Standard,* Dar Es Salaam; Features Editor, the *Guardian.* Stood for Parliament, January 1966, in North Hull supported by the Radical Alliance, campaigning on Anti-Vietnam War issue.
Current political attitudes: Far Left—particular interest in Third World revolutionary politics (supporter of Mengistu, Fidel, etc.).
Publications: *The Appeasers* (with Martin Gilbert); *Mobutu's Congo*; *Guerrilla Movements in Latin America.*

Disarmament

Treasurer, Combined Universities Campaign (CUCaND) 1959; Disarmament and Strategy Group of CND; Independent Nuclear Disarmament Election Committee (INDEC) 1964; Voters' Veto Supporter 1959; Committee of 100 supporter (arrested in 1961, Trafalgar Square demonstration).

HALL, Stuart McPhail, Director of Centre for Cultural Studies, Birmingham University. Former CND and New Left activist.

General

b. 3 February 1932.
Educated: Jamaica College, Kingston, Jamaica; Merton College, Oxford University. Career and political activities: 1956-9 Editor, *Universities and Left Review*; 1957-9 Secondary School Teacher, London; 1959-61 Editor, *New Left Review*; 1961-4 Lecturer, Film and Mass Media, Chelsea College of Science, London University; 1964-72 Assistant Director, Centre for Cultural Studies, Birmingham University; 1972 to date, Director of same. Active member of the early New Left; member of the Labour Party until 1964.
Current political attitudes: formerly, early New Left type of Marxist, now, 'Gramscian' Marxist.
Publications: *The Popular Arts,* with Paddy Whannell, Hutchinson, 1964; *Situating Marx,* ed. with Paul Walton (1972); *Resistance Through Rituals,* ed. with Tony Jefferson, Hutchinson (1976); *Policing the Crisis,* Hall *et al.,* Macmillan (1978); *Reproducing Ideologies,* MacMillan (1979).

Disarmament

Editor of *Universities and Left Review* (later, the *New Left Review*) and Chairman of the New Left Club in London. Participated in all the marches after that into the early 1960s and in the public activities of CND. Also took part in some direct action demonstrations, though not a member of the Committee of 100. Member of the CND committee, was active in the publications sub-committee, with responsibilities for pamphlets, propaganda, *Sanity,* etc. But principal involvement was as an active speaker for CND at public meetings throughout the country (including some Trafalgar Square appearances). In general, favoured the 'YCND' spirit against the 'respectables', the 'grass roots anti-nuclear movement' against the 'distinguished committee-people'. Involved in the Steps Towards Peace initiative.

HATTON, Trevor, Committee of 100 activist and Treasurer.

General

b. 1931.
Educated: Farnborough Grammar School, Roan School, Greenwich.
Career: left school at 16, qualified as Chartered Accountant. Excused National Service as CO and served with Friends Ambulance Unit. Worked for Accountants, and for St. Pancras Building Society.

Disarmament

Joined CND in 1958. Member of Lewisham group. Began work for the Committee of 100 as full-time treasurer in May 1961. Imprisoned with Bertrand Russell and others in September 1961. Defendant in the Official Secrets trial following the Wethersfield *et al.* demonstrations in December 1961: sentenced to 18 months' imprisonment.

HAWKES, Jacquetta, author and archaeologist (Mrs. J. B. Priestley).

General

b. 1910.
Educated: Perse School, Newnham College Cambridge, MA, OBE, 1952.
Career: research and excavation in Great Britain, Eire, France and Palestine, 1931-40; FSA 1940; Min. of Education: Principal and Secretary of UK National Commission for UNESCO 1943-9; retired from Civil Service to write 1949; membership of Archaeological, Film, and UNESCO committees since then; visiting Professor (University of Washington) 1971.
Publications: archaeological and literary.

Disarmament

Active from the outset of CND (J. B. Priestley, her husband, was instrumental in its creation). Moral protester *par excellence*. Active member of CND Executive and prominent on Aldermaston Marches. Organiser of women's CND. Had little interest in the politics of CND. Very opposed to Committee of 100 and became disillusioned after traumas of 1961. Also, disliked 'leftward' trend of the Movement (neutralism, etc.); always viewed Movement as a single-issue, moral campaign.

HEALEY, Rt. Hon. Denis Winston, PC 1964; MBE 1945; MP (Labour) SE Leeds, Feb. 1952-5; Leeds East since 1955; Chancellor of the Exchequer 1974-9.

General

b. 30 August 1917.
Educated: Bradford Grammar School; Balliol College, Oxford University (First Class honours, Mods.; First Class honours Lit. Hum. BA, 1940; MA, 1945).
Career: Army service 1940-5 (Major); secretary, International Department, Labour Party, 1945-52; Member Parliamentary Committee Labour Party 1959-64; Secretary of State for Defence 1964-70; membership of various bodies (European, Strategic, etc.); member of the Executive of the Fabian Society 1954-61; member of Labour Party National Executive Committee 1970-5; Parliamentary Committee of the Labour Party 1970 to date.
Although briefly a member of the Communist Party in his student days, and although on the Left of the Labour Party in the 1940s, Healey has become one of the major intellectual figures on the Right of the Labour Party since the 1950s.
Publications: politics.

Disarmament

Present (as an 'outsider') at the first informal meeting of the subsequent leadership group of CND, but highly critical from the outset. A firm opponent of CND, concentrating on the strategic and foreign policy aspects. Author of many critical journal (both 'strategic' and 'academic') and magazine articles criticising unilateralism, in the late 1950s and early 1960s. Books include: *Neutralism* (1955); *A Neutral Belt in Europe* (1958); *NATO and American Security* (1959); *The Race Against the H-Bomb* (1960).

HOME (of the Hirsel) Baron (cr. 1964), Alec Alexander Frederick, former Foreign Secretary and, later, Prime Minister, and Leader of the Conservative Party.

General

b. 2 July 1903.
(Originally 14th Earl of Home but disclaimed his peerages for life, 23 October 1963.) KT 1962; PC 1951; DL; Chancellor of the Order of the Thistle since 1973; Prime Minister and First Lord of the Treasury 1963-4. Leader of the Opposition 1964-5; MP (Unionist) Kinross and W. Perthshire 1963-74.
Educated: Eton; Christ Church, Oxford University.
Career: MP (Unionist) South Lanark 1931-45; MP (Conservative) Lanark Division of Lanarkshire 1950-1; PPS to Prime Minister 1937-40; Joint Parliamentary Under Secretary to the Foreign Office 1945; Minister of State, Scottish Office, 1951-5; Secretary of State for Commonwealth Relations 1955-60; Deputy Leader of House of Lords 1956-7; Leader of House of Lords and Lord President of the Council 1957-60; Secretary of State for Foreign Affairs 1960-3; Secretary of State for Foreign and Commonwealth Affairs 1970-4. Numerous honorary degrees. Membership of numerous bodies, trusts, etc.
Publications: Autobiography.

Disarmament

Foreign Secretary throughout the most important years of the Movement. Strongly opposed to CND; rejected completely their policies, methods and 'style'.

HUDDLESTON, Rt. Rev. Trevor, Bishop of Mauritius.

General

b. 15 June 1913.
Educated: Lancing, Christ Church, Oxford University; Wells Theological College, BA, MA, 1937. Priest 1937.
Joined Community of the Resurrection, Professed 1941. Church Appointments in South Africa 1943-55. Community of the Resurrection appointments in the UK 1955-60; Bishop of Masasi 1960-8. Suffragan Bishop of Stepney 1968-78. Vice-President of Anti-Apartheid Movement, 1969 to date; Trustee Runnymede Trust 1972 to date.
Publications: politics, theology.

Disarmament

Active in CND from beginning. Campaigned on Christian/radical politics grounds. Although not so centrally concerned with CND as with African issues, he was an influential figure of moral authority in the Movement.

HUGHES, Emrys, MP (Labour) South Ayrshire, Division of Ayrshire and Bute 1946-69, Pacifist and Left Labour Activist.

General

b. 10 July 1894; d. 18 October 1969.
Educated: Abercynon Council School; Mountain Ash Secondary School; City of Leeds Training College.
Editor of *Forward,* 1931-46.
Publications: politics, history, biography. Pacifist and socialist pamphlets, etc.

Disarmament

Lifelong pacifist and socialist in the great ILP tradition. Fiery orator: regular platform speaker for CND. Typified the old Labour Left support for CND, which he regarded as one further in the long line of socialist, quasi-pacifist, movements of the Labour Left.

JONES, Mervyn, author and journalist.

General

b. 27 February 1922.
Educated: Abbotsholme School; New York University.
Career: Assistant Editor, *Tribune,* 1955-9; *New Statesman,* 1966-8; Drama Critic, *Tribune,* 1959-67.
Publications: novels, plays, etc.

Disarmament

Central figure in the New Left. Involved in both Labour Party Left pressure for CND policies and in the New Left. His recent (1977) political novel *Today the Struggle* has a long and interesting section on the Disarmament Movement in the late 1950s and early 1960s.

KING-HALL, Baron (cr. 1966) of Headley. William Stephen Richard King-Hall, Kt. (cr. 1954). Author, journalist and publicist on Defence issues.

General

b. 21 January 1893; d. 2 June 1966.
Royal Navy, retd. 1929. Director of UK Provident Institution.
Educated: Lausanne; Osborne; Dartmouth.
Distinguished war and service record.
MP (Independent Nationalist) for Ormskirk Division of Lancashire 1939-44. Founded King-Hall newsletter service in 1936. Founded Hansard Society for Parliamentary Government 1944.
Radio and TV commentator on current events. Strategic expert.
Publications: politics, history, strategy and defence, nuclear warfare, biography, plays.

Disarmament

Unique figure in Movement. Solid establishment background. Respected strategic thinker with superlative service and war record; staunch anti-communist, knowledgeable and experienced in politics. Rejected whole basis of traditional strategy in the nuclear context and advocated transition to a peace-oriented society; detailed arguments *against* deterrence and *for* nuclear pacifism. Very influential on general public opinion (via broadcasting media and books).

Publications include: *Defence in the Nuclear Age* (1958); *Common Sense in Defence* (1960); *Power Politics in the Nuclear Age* (1962). Influenced not only CND, but the DAC too: the non-violent society he portrayed was not altogether different from the radical pacifist society envisaged by DAC activists — though, of course, he rejected strongly any notion of a necessary link between radical politics (whether socialist or libertarian) and his schema for non-violence.

LASKI, Marganhita (Mrs. J. E. Howard), novelist, critic, journalist.

General

b. 24 October 1915.
Educated: Ladybarn House School, Manchester; Somerville College, Oxford University, MA.
Career: various commissions, etc., writing. Frequent broadcaster.
Publications: plays, novels, religious studies, history, etc.

Disarmament

Involved, as were many others of the mildly radical, humanitarian establishment, on a *moral* basis in CND. Active campaigner against nuclear tests and their effects: opposed both to the links with socialist politics and the illegal direct action of the DAC and the Committee of 100. Became disillusioned with the Movement *ca.* 1960-1.

LESSING, Mrs. Doris May, author.

General

b. 22 October 1919.
Lived in Southern Rhodesia 1924-49.
Publications: numerous novels; one play.

Disarmament

One of many creative artists to join the Movement. Supported both CND and Committee of 100: platform speaker and active demonstrator.

LOVELL, Alan, freelance lecturer and journalist; former New Left and DAC activist.

General

b. 9 June 1935.
Educated: Grammar School; Oxford University.
Career and political activities: journalist with *Peace News*; British Film Institute; active in opposition to Immigration Acts and racialism generally: member of the group that preceded CARD; active in 'Arts' politics around the British Film Institute; recently involved with Anti-Apartheid Movement. Current political attitudes: pacifist/anarchist or Libertarian Socialist.
Publications: *Anarchist Cinema*; *Don Siegal—American Cinema*; Studies in documentary.

Disarmament

Journalist with *Peace News* 1958-63; member of the Direct Action Committee (*ca.* 1958-60); member of the Committee of 100 (*ca.* 1961-3); Editorial Board of *Universities and Left Review*, then *New Left Review* (*ca.* 1959-62).

MACMILLAN, Rt. Hon. (Maurice) Harold, PC 1942, OM 1976, FRS 1962. Prime Minister and First Lord of the Treasury 1957-63. MP (Conservative) Bromley 1945-64.

General

b. 10 February 1894.
Educated: Eton; Balliol College, Oxford University (First Class Honours, Moderations 1919).
Career: 1914-18 war service in Special Reserve Grenadier Guards (wounded 3 times); ADC to Governor General of Canada 1919-20; MP (Conservative) Stockton-on-Tees 1924-9, 1931-45; Parliamentary Secretary to Ministry of Supply 1940-2; Parliamentary Under Secretary of State, Colonies, 1942; Minister Resident Allied HQ N. West Africa 1942-5; Secretary for Air 1945; Minister of Housing and Local Government 1951-4; Minister of Defence 1954-5; Secretary of State for Foreign Affairs 1955; Chancellor of Exchequer 1955-7. Chancellor of University of Oxford since 1960; President, Macmillan Ltd. since 1974 (Chairman 1963-74). Membership of numerous associations and trusts, etc. Numerous honorary degrees, etc.
Publications: politics, economics, 6 volumes of memoirs.

Disarmament

Prime Minister all through the most important years of the Movement. Consistently opposed to unilateralism: effective propagandist and shrewd tactician. Instrumental in bringing about the Partial Test Ban Treaty of 1963.

MARQUAND, David Ian; Chief Adviser, Secretariat-General, Commission of the European Communities, 1977/8; Professor of History, 1978 to date.

General

b. 20 September 1934.
Educated: Emmanuel School; Magdalen College, Oxford University; St. Antony's College, Oxford University (First Class Honours, Modern History, 1957).
Career: University of California (Teaching Assistant 1958-9); Leader Writer, the *Guardian*, 1959/62; University posts (Oxford, Sussex (1962-6)); contested Barry (Labour) 1964; MP (Labour) Ashfield 1966-77; PPS to Minister of Overseas Development, 1967-9; Junior Opposition Front-bench spokesman on economic affairs 1971-2; member of various select Committees, etc.; Professor of Contemporary History and Politics at Salford University since 1978.
Publications: journalism and political articles in journals and magazines; biography of Ramsay MacDonald (1977).

Disarmament

Early and perceptive critic of CND as a Movement. Wide influence in 'serious' press of both the UK and the USA; many articles appeared in such journals as *Encounter* and *Commentary*.

MARTIN (Basil) Kingsley, Editor of the *New Statesman* and *Nation* 1930-60.

General

b. 28 July 1897. d. 16 February 1969.
Educated: Mill Hill School; Magdalene College, Cambridge University, MA. University Lectureships in Politics in the UK and the USA, 1921-7; *Manchester Guardian* 1927-31.
Publications: politics, history, current affairs, etc.

Disarmament

It was his initiative, following Priestley's *New Statesman* article, that created CND. The first meeting to discuss the establishment of the new organisation took place at his flat. He was the archetypal Labour Left figure, presiding over the *New Statesman* (which he had moulded and built into the influential journal of the Labour Left through 1930s, 1940s and 1950s). He was convinced from the outset that CND had to work through the Labour Party if it were to achieve its objectives. His influence in the early months of the Campaign was very great indeed — with Collins and Russell he was the most important of the early leaders — but, as the Campaign began to turn from a pressure group into a mass movement, and as it began to turn away from the 'conventional' politics of the Labour Left, he became less of a key figure. Following his retirement from the Editorship of the *New Statesman* in 1960 he continued to campaign, personally, for the CND's policies, but, to his great sadness, the *New Statesman* itself became somewhat more tentative in its commitment.

MATTHEWS, George Lloyd, head of Press and Publicity Department, Communist Party of Great Britain, since 1974.

General

b. 24 January 1917.
Educated: Bedford Modern School; Reading University; President of Reading University Students' Union 1938-9; Vice-President, National Union of Students 1939-40; Vice-President University Labour Federation 1938-9; County Chairman, National Union of Agricultural Workers 1945-9. Member of the Executive Committee of the Communist Party 1943 to date; Assistant General Secretary of the Communist Party 1949-57; Assistant Editor, 1957-9, and Editor, 1959-74, of the *Daily Worker*, later the *Morning Star*.

Disarmament

Presided over the *Daily Worker* in the years of the Movement's greatest activity. Wrote a number of influential articles during the 1950s and 1960s on general international relations/defence issues and on specific questions of British unilateral disarmament and CP/CND relations. Key figure in the gradual change of CP attitudes to CND through 1959 and 1960.

MAYHEW, Christopher Paget, formerly Labour, now Liberal, politician.

General

b. 12 June 1915.
Educated: Haileybury College; Christ Church College, Oxford University, MA (President of the Union, 1937).
Career: Army Service 1939-44 (Major); MP (Labour) South Norfolk 1945-50; MP (Labour) Woolwich East,

later Greenwich, Woolwich East, 1951-74; PPS to Lord President of the Council 1945-6; Parliamentary Under Secretary of State for Foreign Affairs 1946-50; Minister of Defence (RN) 1964, resigned 1966; transferred allegiance to Liberal Party: MP (Liberal) Greenwich, Woolwich East July-September 1974; Liberal Party Spokesman on Defence 1974; contested Bath (Liberal) October 1974; Parliamentary candidate (Liberal) 1974, 1979.

Chairman: Middle East International (Publishers) Ltd.; ANAF Foundation; MIND, etc.

Active in Middle Eastern Affairs, from a generally 'pro-Arab' viewpoint.

Publications: politics.

Disarmament

Consistent and active opponent of CND from the outset. Attacked both the specific strategic/foreign policy aims and arguments of the Movement, and its general, politically 'left', orientation and associations. Published widely in the late 1950s and early 1960s in this area.

MIKARDO, Ian, MP (Labour) Tower Hamlets, Bethnal Green and Bow since 1974 (Poplar from 1964-74).

General

b. 9 July 1908.

Educated: Portsmouth.

Political career: MP (Labour) Reading 1945-50; South Division of Reading 1950-5; Reading 1955-9. Member National Executive Committee of Labour Party 1950-9 and 1960-78 (Chairman 1970-1); International Committee of Labour Party (Chairman 1973-8). Chairman of Parliamentary Labour Party, March to November 1974. Chairman Select Committee on Nationalised Industries 1966-70. President ASTMS 1968-73.

Publications: politics.

Disarmament

Active in CND from the outset. Gave practical help, as MP for Reading, on the early Aldermaston Marches. Author of numerous articles in the *Tribune* and elsewhere advocating the CND case. A stalwart of the Bevanite Left, he was and is committed totally to the cause of the Left in the PLP and Labour Movement. He thus lost full commitment to, and enthusiasm for, the Disarmament Movement once the battle inside the Labour Party had been lost (i.e. after the 1961 Conference).

NETTLETON, (Richard) Dick. General Secretary CND 1967-73.

General

b. 29 January 1922.

Educated: Central School.

Career and political activities: apprentice, fitter, Age Concern Organiser; TU Branch Secretary, Town Councillor. Activist on Labour Left for many years.

Publications: CND pamphlets on 'Polaris'.

Disarmament

Joined Bolton CND 1958, founded Walkden Branch CND 1960; North West Organiser CND 1963-7; CND Member since membership introduced, to date; Secretary British Council for Peace in Vietnam (*ca.* 1970).

OSBORNE, John (James). Dramatist and actor.

General

b. 12 December 1929.

Educated: Belmont College, Devon.

Career: stage and TV acting (including English Stage Co. at Royal Court, Rep., etc.). First play produced 1949; numerous successful stage, TV and film productions thereafter.

Publications: numerous plays (including *Look Back in Anger, The Entertainer, Inadmissible Evidence, The World of Paul Slickey*, etc.).

Disarmament

The most famous of the 'Angry Young Men' generation. *Look Back in Anger* was the watershed for a new wave of artistic and intellectual disenchantment — this found its political expression in large part through CND and the Committee of 100. Osborne's 'Damn You England!' letter to *The Times* epitomised the mood of bitter rejection of conventional politics and morality which characterised many young dramatists and artists. When the Committee of 100 began to lose its momentum, following Wethersfield and the Official Secrets Trial in 1962, Osborne and many of the other original 'big name' supporters began to lose interest in the Committee.

PAPWORTH, Andrew John, Committee of 100 activist.

General

b. 9 May 1944.
Educated: State education; left school 1961; 1969-70: Fircroft Residential College, Birmingham; 1970-4: University of Sussex — BA Sociology; 1975-6: CQSW and MA Applied Social Studies — Warwick University. Career: political organising secretary (London Committee of 100) 1965-6; printer 1966-9; social worker 1972 to date.
No significant political activity apart from nuclear disarmament.

Disarmament

   1960: Became active in CND and joined Committee of Hampstead CND. Active helper of Committee of 100 — took part in major demonstrations; 1961 (September): became member of newly founded London Committee of 100; 1963: formed (with others — including Jane Buxton) Hampstead group of Committee of 100, which attracted national press publicity by publishing "Mail Interception and Telephone Tapping in Britain" and leaflet addressed to Soldiers, Sailors, and Airmen; 1965-6: Secretary of London Committee of 100; 1966: arrested with others on picket at Downing Street, led to High Court appeal and revision of police commissioner's ruling about demonstrations near Parliament (Coventry *vs.* Papworth); 1966: London organiser of sit-down demonstration at launching of one of Britain's first polaris subs. at Barrow-in-Furness; 1967: took part in non-violent occupation of Greek Embassy (April) in protest against coup by colonels; member of Non-violent Action Group which organised non-violent 'siege' of Elliott Automation Ltd., London, to demonstrate British involvement in supply equipment for US Forces in Vietnam; 1968: deported from Moscow for distributing leaflets in WRI 'Support Czechoslovakia' action. Active supporter of *Peace News* since 1960 and in recent years a company member and trustee.

POTTLE, Pat, Committee of 100 activist.

General

b. August 1938.
Educated: Regent's Park Secondary Central School, Paddington.
Career: compositor, club manager, RAF national service, full-time worker in Committee of 100.

Disarmament

Stimulated by the DAC into activity; took part in 1958 Aldermaston March. Helped found Paddington CND. Defendant in Official Secrets Trial, following the Wethersfield *et al.* demonstrations of December 1961: sentenced to 18 months' imprisonment.

PRIESTLEY, John Boynton. Author.

General

b. Bradford, 1894.
OM 1977; MA, Litt.D.; LLD; D.Litt.
Educated: Bradford; Trinity Hall, Cambridge University.
Served in World War I with Duke of Wellington's and Devon Regiments; UK delegate to UNESCO Conferences 1946-7; Chairman of various national and international theatre bodies; Freedom of City of Bradford, 1973. Frequent broadcaster and contributor to Radio and TV.
Publications: Plays, novels, essays, film scripts, travel writing, history, biography, etc.

Disarmament

   Involved from the outset in CND. His *New Statesman* article "Britain and the Nuclear Bombs" (2 Nov. 1957) provided the immediate cause of CND's coming into being. Vice-President of CND in the early years, but became disenchanted with the tactics (and some of the objectives) of the Movement. Was always opposed to the Aldermaston March and other extra-Parliamentary/demonstration-oriented activities. Also opposed to increasingly Left-wing direction of the Movement.

RANDLE, Michael. Chairman of the DAC, Secretary of the Committee of 100.

General

b. 21 December 1933.
Educated: Donai School 1945/50; University College, London University, 1963-6 (BA in English).
Career and political activities: 1950-7 — farming; 1957-8 working for *Peace News*; 1958-60 — working for Direct Action Committee Against Nuclear War (included a spell of one year working in Ghana with the Sahara Protest Team and the Bureau of African Affairs); 1960-1 Secretary, Committee of 100; 1963-6

University; 1966-7 — part-time teaching and writing in London; October 1967 to May 1968, prison. 1968-9 part-time teaching and writing. 1969-74 — Lecturer in Complementary Studies, Bradford University; 1974-5 Research Assistant in School of Peace Studies, Bradford University. Last five months of 1976 — working with UNESCO on research regarding training for non-violent action; 1977 to date — part-time lecturing (School of Peace Studies, Bradford University), printing, farming and writing.

Publications: mainly articles in *Peace News, War Resistance,* and some reviews for the *New Society* and the *New Humanist. Towards Liberation*: an extended essay on non-violent/radical politics published by War Resisters' International, 1975. *Bibliography on Training for Non-Violent Action,* published January 1978 by the International Seminar for Training in Non-Violent Action (USA). (Research assistant from UNESCO.) "Militarism in Developed and Developing Countries" — paper produced for UNESCO consultation, April 1978, and to be included in a UNESCO publication. Pamphlet (approx. 27,000 words) published by the International Seminar on Training for Non-Violent Action and War Resister's International: *Militarism and Repression.*

Disarmament

Council and Executive of War Resisters' International since 1960; Chairman from 1966-72. Worked closely with Marian Glean and Alan Lovell in mid-sixties, and with them helped to set up the Campaign Against Racial Discrimination (CARD). Two long prison sentences: 1962 (Feb.) to 1963 (Feb.) for work with the Committee of 100 helping to organise a civil disobedience demonstration at the USAF base in Wethersfield, Essex; Oct. 1967-May 1968 for taking part in occupation of Greek Embassy. Member of British Withdrawal from Northern Ireland Campaign. Operation Gandhi and Non-Violent Resistance Group in early and mid-fifties. Founder member of Direct Action Committee against Nuclear War. Member of the Aldermaston March Committee 1957-8. Went to Ghana Oct. 1959 to help organise Sahara Protest Team, and stayed on in Ghana after the event, working in the Bureau of African Affairs in Accra to help with the Pan African Conference which took place there in June 1960. Returned to Britain 1960 (October). Active in Committee of 100.

Current political attitudes: non-violent libertarian socialist.

REDGRAVE, Vanessa, CBE 1967, Actress.

General

b. 30 January 1937.
Educated: Queensgate School; Central School of Speech and Drama.
Career: Extensive stage and film.

Disarmament

Unlike most others who came into the Movement from the 'Arts', Vanessa Redgrave was a very active, dedicated and *political* supporter. She was one of the central figures in the Committee of 100. Following the demise of the Movement she became further involved in socialist politics in the Socialist Labour League (now Workers' Revolutionary Party) for which she has stood as Parliamentary candidate on a number of occasions. She was also very active in the Movements against the American War in Vietnam, etc.

RITCHIE-CALDER, Baron (cr. 1966) of Balmashannar, Peter Ritchie Calder, CBE 1945, MA (Edinburgh) 1961, author and journalist.

General

b. 1 July 1906.
Educated: Forfar Academy.
Career: journalism (local and national, various) 1922-56; Montague Burton Professor of International Relations, Edinburgh University 1961-7; various visiting chairs, visiting lectureships, etc.; member of numerous UN missions, enquiries, etc.; Senior Fellow, Center for the Study of Democratic Institutions, Santa Barbara, California 1972-5; involved, as Chairman, President, or member of: the Association of British Science writers, Mental Health Film Council, British Sub-Aqua Club, Workers' Educational Association, Open University, etc.
Publications: politics, international relations, science, United Nations, etc.
Various awards (national and international) for political, international and journalistic work. Several honorary degrees.

Disarmament

Through involvement in international relations and the work of the UN, became active in CND. Was a Vice-President of CND. Contributor of science-based (as well as UN-oriented) articles, pamphlets, etc., in the Movement's press. Regular platform speaker, marcher at Aldermaston, etc. President of National Peace Council.

RODGERS, Rt. Hon. William Thomas; PC 1975, MP (Labour) Teesside, Stockton, since 1974 (Stockton-on-Tees 1962-74), Secretary of State for Transport 1976-9.

General

b. 28 October 1928.
Educated: Sudley Road Co. School; Quay Bank High School, Liverpool; Magdalen College, Oxford University.
Career: General Secretary, Fabian Society 1953-60; Parliamentary Under Secretary of State, Department of Economic Affairs 1964-7; Foreign Office 1967-8; Leader UK delegation to Council of Europe and Assembly of WEU 1967-8; Minister of State, Board of Trade, 1968-9; Treasury 1969-70; MoD 1974-6; Chairman, Expenditure Committee on Trade and Industry 1971-4; Borough Councillor, St. Marylebone, 1958-62.
Publications: Editor of a biography of Hugh Gaitskell, political pamphlets, etc.

Disarmament

   Important organiser of the Gaitskellite campaign in the Labour Party in late 1950s and early 1960s. Polemics against unilateralism, neutralism, etc. Secretary and organiser of Campaign for Democratic Socialism.

ROTBLAT (Professor), Joseph, scientist and founder member of 'Pugwash'.

General

b. 4 November 1908.
MA, DSc (Warsaw); PhD Liverpool; DSc (London); F Inst P; Professor of Physics in the University of London, at St. Bartholomew's Hospital Medical College 1950-76 (now Emeritus); Physicist to St. Bartholomew's Hospital 1950-76. University career at Warsaw, Liverpool, Los Alamos (New Mexico), London.
Member, Polish Academy of Sciences 1966; Hon. Foreign Mem. American Academy of Arts and Sciences 1972; Hon. DSc Bradford 1973.
Publications: nuclear physics, medical physics, and radioactivity, etc.

Disarmam nt

   Involved with Russell and others in the establishment of the Pugwash Movement following the Russell-Einstein Manifesto of 1955. Became General Secretary of 'Pugwash'. Active in CND from the outset: particularly concerned with the scientific consequences of nuclear warfare. Author of numerous books and pamphlets in this area: e.g. *Pugwash, the First Ten Years* (1967); *Scientists in the Quest for Peace* (1972).

RUSSELL, Bertrand Arthur William Russell, 3rd Earl (cr. 1861), philosopher, political radical, President of CND and later President of the Committee of 100.

General

b. 18 May 1872; d. 2 February 1970.
OM 1949, FRS 1908; MA; Nobel Prize for Literature 1950; Fellow of Trinity College, Cambridge. Second son of Viscount Amberley and Katherine.
Educated: Trinity College, Cambridge; First Class in Mathematics and Moral Sciences Part II.
Numerous publications in philosophy, mathematics, logic, politics, history, social and political theory, novels, sciences, etc.; 3-volume autobiography.

Disarmament

   Long history of radical and pacifist activity—from World War I and the No Conscription Fellowship onwards. From 1940s onwards Russell totally committed to the nuclear issue: through Pugwash, CND and the Committee of 100. President of CND from 1958 to 1960; President of the Committee of 100 from 1960 to January 1963. (Full details in Russell's Autobiography Vol. 3; and R. W. Clark's *Life of Bertrand Russell*.)

RUSTIN, Bayard, American Civil Rights activist.

General

b. 17 March 1910, Westchester, Pennysylvania, USA.
Education: Wilberforce, Ohio University, 1930-1; Chezney (Pa) State Teachers College 1931-3; Coll. City, NY, 1933-5; LLD, New School for Social Research 1968; Brown University 1972; LittD, Montclair State College, 1968; hon. degree, Michigan State University.
Political career: Race Relations director Fellowship of Reconciliation 1941-53; Field Secretary of Congress for Racial Equality 1941; Executive Secretary of War Resisters' League 1953-5; special assistant to Dr. Martin Luther King, Jr., 1955-60; organiser of March on Washington for Jobs and Freedom 1963; Chairman of Social Democrats USA; Chairman Executive Committee Leadership Conference on Civil Rights, etc. Membership of various social democratic, Labour, Civil Rights and educational organisations in the USA.

Various awards: e.g. John Dewey award United Federation of Teachers (1968); Family of Man award, National Council of Churches (1969); John F. Kennedy award, National Council of Jewish Women (1971); Lyndon Baines Johnson award Urban Coalition (1974).
Member of the Society of Friends (Quakers).
Publications: *Down the Line* (1971); *Strategies for Freedom* (1976).

Disarmament

The Civil Rights Movement in the USA had a mutually influential relationship with the Disarmament Movement in the UK. The DAC in particular was greatly influenced by US Civil Rights ideas and strategies — and the US Marches, etc., in the 1960s owed much to the example of CND and Committee of 100 mass demonstrations.

Bayard Rustin was a frequent participant in Disarmament Movement demonstrations and was a speaker at several of the Aldermaston rallies in the 1960s.

SCHOENMAN, Ralph Benedek, Committee of 100 activist.

General

b. 1936 USA.
Educated: Princeton University, AB in Philosophy; came to the LSE, London University, to undertake post-graduate research in Politics. (Because of his involvement in the Movement this research was not completed.) Career and political activities: currently Director of Studies in the Third World, Pennington, New Jersey, USA. Recently active in Iran during the revolutionary upheaval.

Disarmament

Joined CND in 1958. Although always 'militant', never involved closely with the DAC. The Committee of 100 was Schoenman's idea and it was he who persuaded Russell to give it his backing. From July 1960 to July 1969 Schoenman was Russell's private secretary and a major influence on Russell's thinking and activities. Through the whole Committee of 100 experience (and, subsequently, through Russell's involvement in the Anti-Vietnam War Movement and numerous other international campaigns) Schoenman was the central figure. Russell's reasons for breaking finally and completely with Schoenman, in 1969, are given in Russell's "Private Memorandum concerning Ralph Schoenman" (reprinted in Ronald Clark's *Life of Bertrand Russell* as an Appendix).

SCOTT, Rev. (Guthrie) Michael, Anglican Priest, Diocese of Chichester since 1950. Radical activist in African politics and one of the founders of the Committee of 100.

General

b. 30 July 1907.
Educated: King's College, Taunton; St. Paul's College, Grahamstown, S. Africa; Chichester Theological College.
Ordained 1930; various appointments in UK, India, South Africa. Particularly active in campaign over South-West African mandated territory, and in the struggle, through the international courts, against Apartheid.
Publications: politics, African Affairs, autobiography.

Disarmament

Pacifist. Active in CND from the outset — and in the DAC. Always opposed 'working through the Labour Party'; had no interest in the links between the Movement and socialist politics. Co-founder, with Bertrand Russell, of the Committee of 100. Active in Direct Action protests; imprisoned several times.

SOPER, Baron (cr. 1965); Rev. Donald Oliver Soper, Methodist Minister; President of the Methodist Conference 1953; Superintendent West London Mission, Kingsway Hall, 1936-78.

General

b. 31 January 1903.
Educated: Aske's School, Hatcham; St. Catharine's College, Cambridge University; Wesley House, Cambridge University, MA; LSE, London University, PhD. Minister, South London Mission 1926-9; Central London Mission 1929-36. Chairman, Shelter 1974 to date; President, League Against Cruel Sports.
Publications in the area of Christianity and society.

Disarmament

Lifelong pacifist. Active in PPU and other pacifist organisations. Keen supporter of CND but not closely involved in the established hierarchy. Some contact with the DAC in the early days but increasingly identified himself with the *Tribune* Left's attitudes towards the Movement and its strategy. Dynamic and charismatic speaker and columnist. He always emphasised the integration and interdependence of his Christianity, socialism and pacifism.

TAYLOR, Alan John Percival, Historian and journalist; Hon. Fellow of Magdalen College, Oxford, 1976.

General

b. 25 March 1906.
Educated: Bootham School, York; Oriel College, Oxford University. University career at Manchester, Magdalen College, Oxford and Bristol. Wide journalistic writing, principally in Beaverbrook Newspapers. Publications in history, international relations, biography, etc.

Disarmament

   Active in CND from 1958 to 1962. Member of CND Executive Committee from 1958 to 1962. One of the major public speakers for CND. Based his support for CND's case on "a mixture of reason and emotion", and regarded his political involvement in the Movement as "*extremely* enjoyable. It was the best political time I have ever had. The only time when I had a cause in which I believed 100%. . . . I had no reservations about CND: it was right." (Source: A. J. P. Taylor, in conversation with Richard Taylor, April 1978.)

THOMPSON, Edward, P., historian; New Left activist; political polemicist.

General

b. 1924.
Educated: Cambridge University.
Career: war service in Italy. From 1948 to 1965 lecturer in history in the Department of Adult Education and Extramural Studies, Leeds University. From 1965 to *ca.* 1970 Reader in the Centre for the Study of Social History, Warwick University. Since then, full-time research and writing.
Publications include: *The Making of the English Working Class* (1963); *William Morris, Romantic to Revolutionary* (1955); (ed.) *Out of Apathy* (1960); *Whigs and Hunters* (1978).

Disarmament

   Co-editor, with John Saville, of the *New Reasoner* (which developed from *The Reasoner*, following the Hungarian crisis of 1956). Resigned from the Communist Party in 1957 and became the most accomplished and formidable of the New Left activists of the late 1950s and early 1960s. Prominent in the attempt to create a fusion of CND and New Left forces.
   After the decline of the Disarmament Movement, and the change of emphasis of the *New Left Review,* Thompson and others continued the politics of the early New Left in various contexts. Contributor to *May Day Manifesto* (1968) and to various editions of the *Socialist Register.*

WEISZ, (Victor) 'Vicky', political cartoonist.

General

b. 25 April 1913 (E. Berlin; Hungarian citizen); d. 23 February 1966.
Educated: Berlin Art School.
Political cartoonist from 1929. Emigrated to the UK 1935: worked on the *News Chronicle, Daily Mirror; Evening Standard* (1958-66) and *New Statesman* (1954-66).
Publications: various political cartoon collections.

Disarmament

   Always a committed Bevanite, Labour Left supporter. His cartoons consistently ridiculed the theory of deterrence in general, and the Labour Party leadership's stance on defence in particular. Vicky's own emotional, idealistic, and romantic view of Socialism gelled with and complemented the dominant mood of CND itself. His influence was important, though he never involved himself in organisational politics.

WESKER, Arnold, playwright.

General

b. 24 May 1932.
Educated: Upton House School, Hackney.
Founder Director of Centre 42, 1961 (dissolved 1970). Various occupations including: furniture maker's apprentice, carpenter's mate, RAF, bookseller's assistant, plumber's mate, kitchen porter, pastry cook.
Publications: plays for stage, film, TV.

Disarmament

Socialist/Communist background. Involvement in British Peace Committee, etc. Supported CND, active in Committee of 100 in 1961 — imprisoned for 1 month. Ceased activity, though still gave support, from 1962 onwards. (One of many young, radical/socialist, activists from the arts who came together in the Movement. Others included: John Osborne (q.v.); Vanessa Redgrave (q.v.); John Arden, Alan Sillitoe, John Braine, Lindsay Anderson, Doris Lessing (q.v.), Robert Bolt and Kenneth Tynan.)

WILSON, Rt. Hon. Sir (James) Harold; KG 1976, PC 1947, OBE 1945; FRS 1969; MP (Labour) Huyton Division of Lancashire, since 1950 (Ormskirk Division, 1945-50). Leader of Labour Party 1963-76. Prime Minister and First Lord of the Treasury 1964-70; 1974-76.

General

b. 11 March 1916.
Educated: Milnsbridge Council School, Royds Hall School, Huddersfield; Wirral Grammar School, Bebington, Cheshire; Jesus College, Oxford University (Gladstone Memorial Prize, Webb Medley Economics Scholarship, First Class Honours PPE).
Career: Lecturer in Economics, New College, Oxford University 1937; Fellow of University College, Oxford University, 1938; Praelector in Economics and Domestic Bursar 1945; Director of Economics & Statistics, Ministry of Fuel & Power, 1943-4; Parliamentary Secretary to Ministry of Works 1945-7; Secretary for Overseas Trade, 1947; President of Board of Trade 1947-51; Chairman Labour Party Executive Committee 1961-2; Public Accounts Committee, 1961-3; Numerous Honorary Degrees, etc.
Chairman, Committee to Review the Functioning of Financial Institutions, since 1976; Chancellor of Bradford University since 1966.
Publications: politics, political economy, political memoirs.

Disarmament

Wilson was identified with the Left and the Bevanites in his early political career (he resigned with Bevan from the Labour Government in 1951). He was never involved with the Disarmament Movement — though he has expressed sympathy with its aims. Following the 1960 Conference he stood against Gaitskell for the Party Leadership but made it clear that this was in the interests of 'Party unity', not because he supported a unilateralist policy. With the consummate political skill typical of his whole career he adroitly defused the unilateralist issue inside the Labour Party without conceding any of CND's major demands. (He was, however, less successful in containing the criticism from the Left over Britain's support for American policy in Vietnam through the mid to late 1960s.)

Bibliography

THERE is a voluminous amount of material on the general question of nuclear weapons, in book, article and pamphlet form. There is also a very large number of articles, etc., on British foreign policy since the war and the related defence and strategic issues. We have included here only those *books* which we consider to be of central relevance to the Nuclear Disarmament Movement *per se*. Therefore not all referenced authors are presented here.

There has also been, over the years, a very large number of political articles in newspapers, journals and periodicals which are relevant to the issues discussed in this book. Rather than list these all individually we have noted here only the main journal titles: references to specific articles are made frequently in the text and these are accredited in detailed form in the References for each Part.

Finally, as previously noted, the CND Archive, containing the collected papers and correspondence from the CND office, is deposited at the Library of the London School of Economics and Political Science in the University of London, although at the time of writing it was not available for consultation.

Section I

Primary Sources

The questionnaire (see Appendix II), and the interviews with leading Movement figures (see Preface), form the basis of Parts II and III of this study.

Private collections of papers were made available as follows: Direct Action Committee (Hugh Brock and April Carter); National Council against Nuclear Weapons Tests (Arthur Goss).

Section II

Unpublished Theses

David Van Deusen Edwards, "The Movement for Unilateral Nuclear Disarmament in Britain", BA Thesis, Swarthmore College, USA, 1962.

R. A. Exley, "The CND: Its Organisation, Personnel and Methods in its First Year", MA (Econ.) Thesis, University of Manchester, 1959.

David R. Holden, "The First New Left in Britain 1956-62", PhD Thesis, University of Wisconsin-Madison, 1976.

F. E. Myers, "British Peace Politics: The Campaign for Nuclear Disarmament and the Committee of 100, 1957-1962", B Phil Thesis, Columbia University, 1965.

Frank Parkin, "A Study of the CND: the Social Bases of a Political Mass Movement", PhD Thesis, University of London, 1966.

Andrew Rigby, "The British Peace Movement and its Members", MA dissertation, University of Essex, 1968.

Section III

Main journals/newspapers/periodicals, etc., containing articles relevant to the Nuclear Disarmament Movement:

Anarchy, Bulletin of the Atomic Scientist, CND Bulletin, Commentary, Crossbow, Direct Action, Encounter, Freedom, the *Guardian, Inside Story, International Socialism, Labour Monthly,* the *Listener, Midwest Journal of Political Science, New Left Review, New Reasoner, Newsletter, New Statesman,* the *Observer, Peace News, Political Quarterly,* the *Reporter, Resistance, Sanity, Solidarity, Socialist Commentary, Socialist Review,* the *Statist, Survival, The Times, Tribune, War and Peace,* the *War Resister, War Resistance, Western Political Quarterly, Vanguard.*

Other material in this category consulted included:

CND, DAC, and Committee of 100 papers (minutes of meetings, reports, etc.) and pamphlets.
Labour Party and TUC Annual Conference Reports 1957 to 1965.
Hansard
Defence White Papers

Section IV

Books: this section is divided into (a) those books which are centrally concerned with the Movement and (b) those which have a more secondary concern with the Movement and the issues and problems raised directly by its activities between 1958 and 1965.

(a)
Boulton, D. (ed.), *Voices from the Crowd: against the H-Bomb,* Peter Owen, 1964.

Clark, G., "Remember Your Humanity and Forget the Rest" (in Benewick, R. and Smith T. (eds.), *Direct Action and Democratic Politics,* Allen & Unwin, 1972).

Collins, Canon L. John, *Faith Under Fire,* Leslie Frewin, 1966.

Driver, C., *The Disarmers: a Study in Protest,* Hodder & Stoughton, 1964.

Duff, Peggy, *Left, Left, Left,* Allison & Busby, 1971.

Greer, H., *Mud Pie: the CND story,* Max Parrish, 1964.

Groom, A. J. R., *British Thinking About Nuclear Weapons,* Frances Pinter, 1974.

Parkin, F., *Middle Class Radicalism: the Social Bases of the British Campaign for Nuclear Disarmament,* Manchester University Press, 1968.

(b)
Acland, Sir Richard, *Why So Angry?,* Gollancz, 1958.

Allsop, K., *The Angry Decade,* Peter Owen, 1958.

Anderson, P. and Blackburn, R. (eds.), *Towards Socialism,* Fontana & New Left Books, 1965.

Apter, D. and Joll, J. (eds.), *Anarchism Today,* Macmillan, 1971.

Arnold, G. L., "Britain: The New Reasoners" (in Labedz, L. (ed.), *Revisionism,* New York, Praeger, 1962).

Atomic Challenge—a symposium (BBC Talks, n.d.).

Barker, R., *Political Ideas in Modern Britain,* Methuen, 1979.

Bealey, F. (ed.), *Social and Political Thought of the Labour Party,* Weidenfeld & Nicolson, 1970.

Beer, S. H., *Modern British Politics,* Allen & Unwin, 1959.

Bennett, J. C. (ed.), *Nuclear Weapons and the Conflict of Conscience,* Lutterworth Press, 1962.

Benewick, R. and Smith, T. (eds.), *Direct Action and Democratic Politics,* Allen & Unwin, 1972.

Bevan, A., *In Place of Fear,* Heinemann, 1952.

Blackett, P. M. S., *Atomic Weapons and East/West Relations*, Cambridge University Press, 1956.

Blackett, P. M. S., *Military and Political Consequences of Atomic Energy*, Turnstile Press, 1948.

Blackett, P. M. S., *Studies of War*, Oliver & Boyd, 1962.

Birnbaum, N., "The CND" (in Theobald, R. (ed.), *Britain in the 1960s*, New York, H. W. Wilson, 1961).

Birnbaum, N., "Great Britain: The Reactive Revolt" (in Kaplan, M. A. (ed.), *The Revolution in World Politics*, New York, Wiley, 1962).

Booth, A. R., *Christians and Power Politics*, SCM Press, 1961.

Brockway, F., *Outside the Right*, Allen & Unwin, 1963.

Bunyan, T., *History and Practice of the Political Police in Britain*, Julian Friedmann, 1976.

Butler, D. E., *The British General Elections of 1955, 1959 and 1964* (three separate studies each published after the relevant General Election, and co-authored, in 1959, with R. Rose, and, in 1964, with A. King), Macmillan.

Buxton, Jane and Turner, Margaret, *Gate Fever*, Cresset Press, 1962.

Buxton, Jane and Turner, Margaret, *Inside Story*, Prison Reform Council, 1963.

Carter, April, *Direct Action and Liberal Democracy*, Routledge & Kegan Paul, 1973.

Carter, April, *The Political Theory of Anarchism*, Routledge & Kegan Paul, 1971.

Carter, April, "The Sahara Protest Team" (in Hare, P. A., and Blumberg, H. H. (eds.), *Liberation without Violence*, Rex Collings, 1977).

Clark, R. W., *The Life of Bertrand Russell*, Jonathan Cape & Weidenfeld & Nicolson, 1975.

Coates, D., *The Labour Party and the Struggle for Socialism*, Cambridge University Press, 1974.

Cockburn, A. and Blackburn, R. (eds.), *Student Power*, Penguin Special, 1969.

Cox, J., *Overkill: the Story of Modern Weapons*, Penguin, 1977.

Cranston, M., *The New Left*, Bodley Head, 1970.

Crick, B. and Robson, W. A., *Protest and Discontent*, Pelican, 1970.

Crouch, C., *The Student Revolt*, Bodley Head, 1970.

Dowse, R. E. and Hughes, J., *Political Sociology*, Wiley, 1972.

Dunn, T. (ed.), *Alternatives to War and Violence*, James Clarke, 1963.

Edwards, D. L., *Withdrawing from the Brink*, SCM Press, 1963.

Elliott, D., Coyne, P., George, M. and Lewis, R., *The Politics of Nuclear Power*, Pluto Press, 1978.

Fletcher, R., *£60 a Second on Defence*, MacGibbon & Kee, 1963.

Foot, M., *Aneurin Bevan: a biography* (2 volumes: vol. 1: 1897-1945; vol. 2: 1945-1960), MacGibbon & Kee, 1962 and 1973.

Gilpin, R., *American Scientists and Nuclear Weapons Policy*, Princeton University Press, 1962.

Gordon, M. R., *Conflict and Consensus in Labour's Foreign Policy*, Stanford University Press, 1969.

Greig, I., *Today's Revolutionaries*, Foreign Affairs Publishing Company, 1970.

Hall, R. T., *The Morality of Civil Disobedience*, USA: Harper & Row, 1971.

Halloran, J. D., *Demonstrations and Communication: a Case Study*, Penguin, 1970.

Harris, N. and Palmer, J. (eds.), *World Crisis: Essays in Revolutionary Socialism*, Hutchinson, 1971.

Haseler, S., *The Gaitskellites: Revisionism in the British Labour Party 1951-64*, Macmillan, 1969.

Harrison, M., *Trade Unions and the Labour Party since 1945*, Allen & Unwin, 1960.

Healey, D., "Britain and NATO" (in Knorr, K. (ed.), *NATO & American Security*, Princeton University Press, 1959).

Hersey, J., *Hiroshima*, Penguin Special, 1946.

Higgins, R., *The Seventh Enemy—The Human Factor in the Global Crisis*, Hodder & Stoughton, 1978.

Home, Alec Douglas (Lord Home), *The Way the Wind Blows*, Time Books, 1977.

Horowitz, D., *From Yalta to Vietnam*, MacGibbon & Kee, 1965.

Hunter, L. *The Road to Brighton Pier*, Barker, 1959.

Hyams, E., *The New Statesman: the History of the First Fifty Years, 1913/1963*, Longmans, 1963.

Jones, M., *Today the Struggle*, Quartet Books, 1978.

Jungk, R., *Brighter than a Thousand Suns*, Gollancz, 1958.

Jungk, R., *The Nuclear State*, John Calder, 1979.

de Kadt, E., *British Defence Policy and Nuclear War*, Frank Cass, 1964.

Kahn, H., *On Thermonuclear War*, Oxford University Press, 1960.

Kaplan, M. A., *Dissent and the State in Peace and War*, USA: Dunnellen Publishing Company, 1970.

Kaplan, M. A. (ed.), *The Revolution in World Politics*, New York: Wiley, 1962.

Kaufman, G. (ed.), *The Left*, Blond, 1966.

Kennan, G., *Russia, The Atom and the West*, Oxford University Press, 1958.

Kidron, M., *Western Capitalism Since the War*, Penguin, 1970.

Kilroy-Silk, R., *Socialism Since Marx*, Allen Lane, Penguin Press, 1972.

King-Hall, Sir Stephen, *Defence in the Nuclear Age*, Gollancz, 1958.

King-Hall, Sir Stephen, *Power Politics in the Nuclear Age*, Gollancz, 1962.

Kornhauser, R. F., *The Politics of Mass Society*, Routledge, 1960.

Krug, M., *Aneurin Bevan: Cautious Rebel*, New York: Yosseloff, 1961.

Labedz, L. (ed.), *Revisionism*, New York: Praeger, 1962.

McKenzie, R. T., *British Political Parties*, Mercury Books, 1959.

MacKinnon, D. M. *et al.*, *God, Sex, and War*, Fontana, 1963.

Macmillan, H., *Riding the Storm*, Macmillan, 1971.

Mander, J., *Great Britain or Little England?*, Penguin, 1963.

Meehan, E. J., *The British Left Wing and Foreign Policy*, USA: Rutgers University Press, 1960.

Middleton, D., "The Deeper Meaning of British Neutralism" (in Theobald, R. (ed.), *Britain in the 1960s*, New York, H. W. Wilson, 1961).

Miliband, R., "Moving On" (in Miliband and Saville (eds.), *Socialist Register* 1976, Merlin Press, 1976).

Miliband, R., *Parliamentary Socialism*, 2nd edn., Merlin Press, 1973.

Miliband, R., *The State in Capitalist Society*, Weidenfeld & Nicolson, 1969.

Minkin, L., *The Labour Party Conference*, Allen Lane, 1978.

Moss, N., *Men Who Play God: The Story of the Hydrogen Bomb*, Gollancz, 1968.

Mulley, F. W., *The Politics of Western Defence*, Thames & Hudson, 1962.

Mumford, L. *et al.*, *Breakthrough to Peace*, USA: New Directions, Norfolk, Connecticut, 1962.

Nairn, T., "The Nature of the Labour Party" (in Anderson and Blackburn (eds.), *Towards Socialism*, Fontana and New Left Books, 1965).

Nakhnikian, G. (ed.), *Bertrand Russell's Philosophy*, Duckworth, 1974.

Neustadt, R., *Alliance Politics*, Columbia University Press, 1970.

Noel-Baker, P., *The Arms Race*, Calder, 1960.

Nuttall, J., *Bomb Culture*, MacGibbon & Kee, 1968.

Pierson, S., *Marxism and the Origins of British Socialism: the Struggle for a New Consciousness*, Cornell University Press, 1973.

Paloczi-Howarth, G., *Youth Up in Arms*, Weidenfeld & Nicolson, 1971.

Pritchard, C. and Taylor, R., *Social Work: Reform or Revolution?*, Routledge & Kegan Paul, 1978.

Pierre, A. J., *Nuclear Politics*, Oxford University Press, 1972.

Pirie, Antoinette (ed.), *Fall-Out*, MacGibbon & Kee, 1958.

Ramsey, P., *War and the Christian Conscience*, Cambridge University Press, 1961.

Reid, Betty, *Ultra-Leftism in Britain*, Communist Party Publication, 1969.

Rigby, A., *Alternative Realities*, Routledge & Kegan Paul, 1974.

Roberts, A., *The Strategy of Civilian Defence*, Faber & Faber, 1967.

Roberts, G. K., *Political Parties and Pressure Groups in Britain*, Weidenfeld & Nicolson, 1970.

Russell, Bertrand (Earl Russell), *Autobiography*, 3 volumes, *1967, 1968* and *1969*, Allen & Unwin.

Russell, Bertrand, *Common Sense and Nuclear Warfare*, Allen & Unwin, 1959.

Russell, Bertrand, *Has Man a Future?*, Penguin Special, 1961.

Russell, Bertrand, *Unarmed Victory*, Penguin, 1963.

Schoenman, R. (ed.), *Bertrand Russell: Philosopher of the Century*, Boston: Little & Brown, 1967.

Schoenman, R., "Bertrand Russell and the Peace Movement" (in Nakhnikian, G. (ed.), *Bertrand Russell's Philosophy*, Duckworth, 1974).

Scott, Rev. M., *Pacifism is Not Enough*, Twentieth Century Books, 1964.

Sharp, G., *The Politics of Non-Violent Action*, USA: Porter Sargent, 1975.

Shipley, P., *Revolutionaries in Modern Britain*, Bodley Head, 1976.

Snyder, W. P., *The Politics of British Defence Policy 1945/62*, Ohio State University Press, 1964.

Stedman Jones, G., "The Meaning of Student Revolt" (in Cockburn and Blackburn (eds.), *Student Power*, Penguin Special, 1969).

Stein, W. (ed.), *Nuclear Weapons and the Christian Conscience*, Merlin Press, 1961.

Stewart, M., *Protest at Power*, Allen & Unwin, 1974.

Stonier, T., *Nuclear Disaster*, Penguin, 1964.

Strachey, J., *On the Prevention of War*, Macmillan, 1962.

Thayer, G., *The British Political Fringe*, Blond, 1965.

Theobald, R. (ed.), *Britain in the 1960s*, New York: H. W. Wilson, 1961.

Thompson, C. (ed.), *Morals & Missiles*, James Clark, 1959.

Thompson, E. P. (ed.), *Out of Apathy*, Steven & Sons, 1960.

Toynbee, P. (ed.), *The Fearful Choice*, Gollancz, 1958.

Urquhart, C. (ed.), *A Matter of Life*, Cope, 1963.

Urry, J. and Wakeford, J. (eds.), *Power in Britain*, Heinemann, 1973.

Vincent, J. J., *Christ in a Nuclear World*, Crux Press, 1962.

Vincent, J. J., *Christian Nuclear Perspective*, Epworth, 1964.

Westergaard, J. and Resler, H., *Class in a Capitalist Society*, Penguin, 1978.

Widgery, D., *The Left in Britain 1956-1968*, Penguin, 1976.

Williams, R. (ed.), *The May Day Manifesto*, Penguin, 1969.

Wilson, B., *The Youth Culture and the Universities*, Faber & Faber, 1970.

Windlesham, Lord, *Communication and Political Power*, Cape, 1966.

Winter, J. M., *Socialism and the Challenge of War*, Routledge & Kegan Paul, 1974.

Wood, N., *Communism and British Intellectuals*, Gollancz, 1959.

Wright, M., *Disarm and Verify*, Chatto & Windus, 1964.

Young, N., *An Infantile Disorder? The Crisis and Decline of the New Left*, Routledge & Kegan Paul, 1977.

Young, W., *Strategy for Survival*, Penguin, 1959.

Zuckerman, Sir Zolly, *Scientists and War: the Impact of Science on Military and Civil Affairs*, Hamish Hamilton, 1966.

Index

This index includes all those individuals cited in the text (though not in the Preface, References, Appendices and Bibliography). It does not include the organisations, groups and concepts which recur throughout the text, except where there is a need to specify a particular and readily identifiable aspect.

The following are not therefore included under their general heading in the index: Anarchism, 'Apolitical', CND, Committee of 100, DAC, 'Extra-Parliamentary groups', Labour Party, Labourism, 'Liberal Left', Marxism, 'Moral Protesters', New Left, Nuclear weapons, 'Political protesters', Pacifism, Socialism, Unilateralism.